Communications in Computer and Information Science 626

Commenced Publication in 2007
Founding and Former Series Editors:
Alfredo Cuzzocrea, Dominik Ślęzak, and Xiaokang Yang

More information about this series at http://www.springer.com/series/7899

Junjie Wu · Lian Li (Eds.)

Advanced Computer Architecture

11th Conference, ACA 2016
Weihai, China, August 22–23, 2016
Proceedings

Editors
Junjie Wu
State Key Laboratory of High Performance
  Computing
National University of Defense Technology
Changsha
China

Lian Li
State Key Laboratory of Computer
  Architecture
Chinese Academy of Sciences
Beijing
China

ISSN 1865-0929   ISSN 1865-0937   (electronic)
Communications in Computer and Information Science
ISBN 978-981-10-2208-1   ISBN 978-981-10-2209-8   (eBook)
DOI 10.1007/978-981-10-2209-8

Library of Congress Control Number: 2016947183

Printed on acid-free paper

This Springer imprint is published by Springer Nature
The registered company is Springer Science+Business Media Singapore Pte Ltd.

Preface

Welcome to the proceedings of ACA 2016, the 11th Conference on Advanced Computer Architecture, which was held in Weihai. As one of the most important conferences in the field of computer architecture in China, the ACA conference is 21 years old. The conferences are held once every two years, and ACA 2016 was held in Weihai during August 22–23 with a lot of exciting activities. We believe this event provided an excellent platform for the presentation of important research and the exchange of views.

We would like to express our gratitude to all the authors who submitted papers to ACA 2016 and our congratulations to those whose papers were accepted. There were 89 submissions in this year. Each submission was reviewed by at least three Program Committee (PC) members. Only the papers with an average score of $\geq$ 1.0 were considered for final inclusion, and almost all accepted papers had positive reviews or at least one review with a score of 2 (accept) or higher. Finally, the PC decided to accept 38 submissions, including 17 papers in English and 21 in Chinese.

We would like to express our great appreciation to our PC members. Each member reviewed at least nine papers, and they gave constructive reviews in time. We also would like to thank our general chairs, Prof. Ninghui Sun and Prof. Xiangke Liao, our steering committee chair, Prof. Yong Dou, organization chairs, Prof. Chenggang Wu and Prof. Zhenzhou Ji, and all other members of the conference committees. Our thanks also go to the China Computer Federation (CCF), Technical Committee on Computer Architecture of CCF, Institute of Computing Technology of Chinese Academy of Sciences, Harbin Institute of Technology (Weihai), Springer, and all other institutes that offered help.

August 2016

Junjie Wu
Lian Li

Organization

ACA 2016 was organized by the China Computer Federation.

General Chairs

Ninghui Sun	ICT, Chinese Academy of Sciences, China
Xiangke Liao	National University of Defense Technology, China

Steering Committee Chair

Yong Dou	National University of Defense Technology, China

Steering Committee

Zhenzhou Ji	Harbin Institute of Technology, China
Dongsheng Wang	Tsinghua University, China
Xingwei Wang	Northeastern University, China
Gongxuan Zhang	Nanjing University of Science and Technology, China
Chenggang Wu	ICT, Chinese Academy of Sciences, China
Junjie Wu	National University of Defense Technology, China

Local Chair

Zhenzhou Ji	Harbin Institute of Technology, China

Organization Chairs

Chenggang Wu	ICT, Chinese Academy of Sciences, China
Zhenzhou Ji	Harbin Institute of Technology, China

Organization Committee

Yong Dou	National University of Defense Technology, China
Yun Liang	Peking University, China
Xiaofei Liao	Huazhong University of Science and Technology, China
Dongsheng Wang	Tsinghua University, China
Xingwei Wang	Northeastern University, China
Chuliang Weng	Huawei Techonologies Co., Ltd, China
Chunfeng Yuan	Nanjing University, China
Kuanjiu Zhou	Dalian University of Technology, China

Web Chair

Gongxuan Zhang   Nanjing University of Science and Technology, China

Program Chairs

Junjie Wu   National University of Defense Technology, China
Lian Li   ICT, Chinese Academy of Sciences, China

Program Committee

Yungang Bao   ICT, Chinese Academy of Sciences, China
Qiong Cai   Hewlett Packard Labs, USA
Yangjie Cao   Zhengzhou University, China
Zhilei Chai   Jiangnan University, China
Jicheng Chen   INSPUR Co., Ltd, China
Tianhan Gao   Northeastern University, China
Wen Hu   University of New South Wales, Australia
Yu Hua   Huazhong University of Science and Technology, China
Chuanhe Huang   Wuhan University, China
Weixing Ji   Beijing Institute of Technology, China
Lei Ju   Shandong University, China
Chao Li   Shanghai Jiao Tong University, China
Dongsheng Li   National University of Defense Technology, China
Jingmei Li   Harbin Engineering University, China
Tao Li   Nankai University, China
Xiaoyao Liang   Shanghai Jiao Tong University, China
Xiaoyi Lu   Ohio State University, USA
Yi Lu   Oracle Labs, Australia
Songwen Pei   University of Shanghai for Science and Technology, China
Feng Qin   Ohio State University, USA
Zhenghao Shi   Xi'an University of Technology, China
Tian Song   Beijing Institute of Technology, China
Yulei Sui   University of New South Wales, Australia
Guangyu Sun   Peking University, China
Jin Sun   Nanjing University of Science and Technology, China
Biao Wang   National High-Performance IC Design Center (Shanghai),
                          China
Haixia Wang   Tsinghua University, China
Tao Wang   Peking University, China
Wei Wang   Hefei University of Technology, China
Wei Wang   Tongji University, China
Xiaoyin Wang   University of Texas, San Antonio, USA
Yu Wang   Tsinghua University, China

Contents

An OS-level Data Distribution Method in DRAM-PCM Hybrid Memory

Hongbin Zhang[1,2], Jie Fan[1,2], and Jiwu Shu[1,2(✉)]

[1] Department of Computer Science and Technology,
Tsinghua University, Beijing 100084, China
{zhanghb10,fanjie11}@mails.tsinghua.eud.cn, shujw@tsinghua.edu.cn
[2] Tsinghua National Laboratory for Information Science and Technology,
Beijing 100084, China

Abstract. Hybrid memory composed of DRAM and PCM has gained substantial research recently. Compared to each other, DRAM has lower read/write latency and higher endurance, and Phase Change Memory (PCM) has higher density and consumes less energy. Hybrid memory has been proposed to exploit the benefits of both these technologies, while at the same time mitigating their disadvantages. The data distribution methods of state of art approaches were managed by either hardware or compiler, which had some shortcomings. The disadvantage of hardware based approaches is that it need large storage, and the required data swapping degrades overall performance, which is not suitable for certain program which has poor locality. While the compiler based technique requires dynamic program analysis, thus increasing run time overhead and also requires programmer's help, thus making it a cumbersome approach. We present an OS-level Data Distribution (OSDD) method, in which data sections that have respective read/write features in virtual address space were assigned to different memory medium by memory management module of operating system. Since our approach needs no input from programmer, thus making it transparent. The OSDD based hybrid memory put appropriate data to corresponding memory medium at system level in page granularity and gained better performance and energy saving than former methods, with less overhead. The experiment showed that on average our method get 52 % energy saving at 6 % performance overhead than uniform DRAM memory.

Keywords: Phase change memory · Hybrid memory · Data distribution

1 Introduction

As the number of CPU cores increases, so does the number of concurrent applications and threads. The capacity of main memory also keeps increasing in order to keep their data in main memory. However, the density, capacity and energy cost of main memory made by DRAM are approaching physical limit and becoming a critical bottleneck of computer systems.

© Springer Science+Business Media Singapore 2016
J. Wu and L. Li (Eds.): ACA 2016, CCIS 626, pp. 1–14, 2016.
DOI: 10.1007/978-981-10-2209-8_1

For these reasons, many architectures are searching out for new alternative of DRAM. As a potential substitute, Phase Change Memory (PCM) has caught much attention for its larger density than DRAM. It has little idle energy because it needs no refresh. Furthermore, its property of non-volatile and byte address-able makes system IO optimization possible. However, PCM also has disadvantages such as higher read/write latency and higher write energy than DRAM, and it has limited endurance and lifetime [7,8,12,20,23,24]. In order to achieve the advantages while hiding the disadvantages of PCM, many researchers are trying out to design hybrid main memory architecture which contains both DRAM and PCM. Their aim is to benefit from large capacity and low energy cost offered by PCM and the low latency, high endurance offered by DRAM at the same time [5,13–16,18,19,25].

There are many potential challenges for designing DRAM-PCM hybrid memory systems. The most important question is which component of the system should be in charge of the data allocation, and how to distribute them to DRAM and PCM to best exploit the strength of each technology while avoiding their weaknesses as much as possible [22]. Many data distribution methods based on memory controller were proposed in previous work [13–15,18,19]. Most of them record the access pattern of memory data in granularity of pages or blocks and rank them by their read/write features. And then the controller swap them to appropriate memory medium at runtime in order to balance the performance, energy cost and lifetime. All these work exploit the benefits of hybrid memory to some extent. However, these methods has some shortages. First, they require certain storage to record the page access hotness and mapping relation. Second, the data swapping degrade system efficiency.

There are also application-level data distribution methods proposed [5,16,25]. These approaches try to complete the data distribution in compiler or user application through user annotation or analysis program. In contrast with controller based methods, these approaches have more flexibility. But these approaches have shortages too. First, they require extra user annotation to help memory allocating, which is not friendly to user. Second, they need dynamic code analysis before program execution, which degrades the overall performance of application. Thirdly, the analysis program itself does not benefit from the allocation regulation it itself prefer.

In this paper, we propose a new DRAM-PCM hybrid memory system using OS-level Data Distribution (OSDD) method in which the data distribution is conducted by memory management module of operating system. OSDD is based on following observations. The linear logic address space of a process includes code section, static data section and dynamic data section etc. And different sections has various read/write characteristic, such as read/write frequency, proportion, locality, average access frequency etc. We find out that sections with specific read/write features are suitable for each memory medium's characteristics respectively. The OSDD recognizes which section the page belong to and maps it to specific memory medium dynamically. Then the page will not be swapped to another medium until the process end. From doing so, OSDD puts appropriate data with certain access features to DRAM or PCM respectively.

This approach extracts the merits of DRAM and PCM with no extra storage cost and data swapping overhead, and it is transparent to user program. In some way, OSDD delivers program's semantic information to memory management module of OS, and brings certain intelligence to data allocation module. The evaluation showed that it exhibits more energy saving at lower performance overhead than the methods based on controller or application.

Overall, the primary contributions of our work are:

(1) We outline and testify the read/write feature of different data sections in logic memory spaces of a process.
(2) We propose and evaluate a new data assignment approach of DRAM-PCM hybrid memory, which is conducted at operating system level.
(3) We present evaluation and analysis of the system's benefits, overhead and limitation based on OSDD.

The rest of the paper is organized as follows. Section 2 provides background and related work. Section 3 explains our observation and motivation. Section 4 introduces the design of OSDD based hybrid memory. Section 5 presents evaluation and result analysis. In Sect. 6, we discuss about some limitations of OSDD. And the conclusion will be given in Sect. 7.

2 Background and Related Work

2.1 DRAM and PCM

DRAM has been used to compose main memory in modern computers for a long time. Though strides in DRAM technology have enabled it to scale to smaller size and thus higher densities, it is predicted that DRAM density scaling will become costly as feature size continues to reduce [6,21]. Satisfying increasingly higher memory demands with DRAM exclusively will become expensive in terms of both cost and energy.

PCM is an emerging non-volatile random access memory technology that offers a competitive alternative to DRAM. The difference in resistance between its two states, amorphous and crystalline, can be used to represent binary states [12,21]. PCM has larger density and less static energy consumption than DRAM because it need no dynamic refresh. The read latency of PCM is a little slower than but close to DRAM, which is better than FLASH to be an alternative of memory. Besides, the non-volatile and byte addressable property are also helpful for system to reduce the IO cost. However, PCM has also disadvantages that prevent its adoption as a direct DRAM replacement. PCM exhibits higher write latencies and higher dynamic energy consumption than DRAM. And it has finite write endurance (limited write times) [12,21].

2.2 Related Work

There are many hybrid memory systems proposed which aim to benefit from the large capacity and low energy offered by PCM, while achieving the low latency and high endurance of DRAM. The data distribution of these works are based on either memory controller or application. The quality of distribution mechanism will directly affect the performance of hybrid memory.

PDRAM [13] is trying to detect hot data and cold data dynamically and move the hot data to DRAM and cold data to PCM. The first shortcoming of PDRAM is the storage cost for recording access count of each page. It will cost 4 MB to record 4 GB memory for each 4K page, if each record costs 4 bytes (2 for page number and 2 for access count). The other shortcoming is the frequent data swapping which disturb normal memory accessing and affect overall performance. Their evaluation showed that PDRAM achieves 30 % energy saving with 6 % performance overhead. Page placement [19] use the similar method with PDRAM and rank the pages by critical feature at the same time, which also has the disadvantage of PDRAM. The Row Buffer Locality (RBL) [14,15] based data assignment method distribute data in smaller granularity. They observe the row buffers have the same latency and bandwidth in both DRAM and PCM, and only row buffer miss will cause much more latency and bandwidth in PCM than in DRAM. So they put the data with higher RBL to PCM and the lower one to DRAM at runtime. This approach received better performance for workloads with good locality, but exhibited poor behavior for certain workloads with poor locality. Furthermore, the data swapping cost certain performance too.

HaVOC [5] is a hybrid memory model which allow programmer or compiler to partition the application's address space, and generate data and instruction layouts. HaVOC map instruction blocks onto NVM since their volatility is quite low and code blocks to SRAM since their volatility is high. The disadvantage of this method is it needs programmer's annotations, which is not friendly with user. Power-aware variable partition [25] is an approach which partition variables into different banks to reduce power consumption and the number of writes on PCM. Based on the graph models, the variables with higher write rations are put in DRAM bank and that with lower write rations are put in PCM bank. This method reduce 53 % power consumption on average. However, this method is based on static analysis which increase 2–18 % execution time. Data allocation optimization for hybrid SPM [16] proposed a dynamic algorithm which generate optimal data allocations for each program region. Before the execution of each program region, the data management code is executed first to generate data allocation which will move most written data into SRAM and the most read data into NVM. The dynamic analysis degrade tlhe performance of application.

These approaches exploit the merits of hybrid memory to certain extent. However, they are accompanied with apparently extra storage cost or swapping cost or dynamic analysis, which degrade overall system performance.

2.3   Data Sections in Logical Address Space

The operating system allocate each process a linear address space whose size is usually 4 GB in 32bit machine. In virtual memory space, the compiler organize the instruction and data in different address sections in order to make it easy to run and manage. Different operating system has various logical address space in detail, but in general, the logical memory space includes system code section, system data section, user code section and user data section [11]. According to their respective mission, different sections have different read/write feature, such as access frequency and locality and access variance etc. In this work, we focus our design and experiment on user code section and user data section to prove its effectiveness.

3   Observation and Motivation

3.1   Observation

In order to find out the memory access feature of each section in logical address space, we analyzed memory access trace of 20 benchmarks from Splash2 [4,9] and Parsec3 [3,9] using Pin tools [2,10], which was used to collect memory trace of running program. The benchmark program domain includes financial analysis, computer vision, physical modeling, future media, content-based search, etc., which represents main aspect of computer application at present. We analyzed memory trace of each bench in detail and got a series of statistics from multi point of view. The analytical index includes independent address number, total read/write counts, average access counts of independent address, and variance of memory access frequency. Among all these index, we mainly inspect two of them. The first one is independent address numbers of code section and data section for each bench as Fig. 1 shows, another one is average access frequency of independent address of code section and data section as Fig. 2 shows. Since there are both read and write access in data section, we seperate them apart in order to distinguish them respectively.

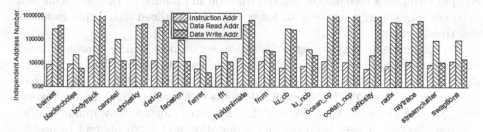

Fig. 1. Footprint(Independent Address Numbers): data section has far more independent address than code section.

From the observation, we find out several regular pattern of memory accessing: (1) Code section has far more small size and data section has relatively larger one. Because independent address numbers in data section is 10–500 times that of instruction section as Fig. 1 shows; (2) The average access frequency of code section is far more great than that in data section. Because this index in code section is 10–1000 times greater than that in data section as Fig. 2 shows; (3) Code section is read all the time, and data section has more read than write.

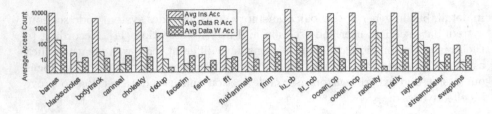

Fig. 2. Hotness(Average Access Counts): code section has far more access than data section.

3.2 Motivation

We consider that to exploit the maximum potential of hybrid memory system, both hardware and software innovations are needed. Besides memory controller and user program, operating system can also implement data distribution. Under the von neumann machine architecture [17], the program is organized in constant pattern by compiler in order to make it easy to run. One of the pattern is the distribution of instruction and data in logical address space, which is saved in page descriptor and can be recognized by operating system at runtime. That means operating system has the ability to place the data anywhere in memory as needed, except reserved space. Since instructions and data of program has their own access feature, which cater to the features of DRAM and PCM respectively, the operating system is able to assign them to different memory medium logically and transparently, making appropriate memory distribution for each data sections.

Our motivation is to find a better way out at operating system level to complete the data recognition and distribution in granularity of pages. Our aim is to get more energy saving with lower cost and overhead than other methods described before.

To implement and demonstrate this idea, we propose OSDD approach based on the analysis above. The OSDD allocates and distributes data sections to different memory medium at system level, without intervening in controller or user program. The OSDD will exhibit benefits of hybrid system and has several advantage at the same time. First, it has no extra storage or swapping cost at runtime. Second, it need no program's annotation and is transparent to user.

4 Hybrid Main Memory Design

4.1 Overview of Architecture

Based on our observation and research, we design a new data distribution model OSDD in DRAM-PCM hybrid memory system, in which the data allocation and distribution is done by memory management module of operating system.

Under traditional memory management, logical memory space is split into sections by compiler such as code section, static data section and dynamic data section etc. And then the sections are split into pages whose size is 4K or 4M, depending on different architecture. The physical memory space is split into frames correspondingly and the memory mapping is done by unit of page.

In one process, each data page belongs to one section, whose type are depicted in LDT (Local Description Table) or GDT (Global Description Table) [11] in virtual memory descriptor. The LDT structure is displayed as Fig. 3 shows, in which the tag 'S' shows whether the section belong to system or application, and the tag 'Type' shows the section type, code section or data section. When OS receives the memory request from CPU, it first recognize the section type from LDT or GDT. Then the OS allocate memory page frames of specified memory medium and complete the page mapping. In order to minimize the performance cost, the page mapping and data distribution will not be changed until the process end. The mapping relationship between logical address and memory medium is depicted as Fig. 4 shows.

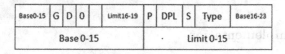

Fig. 3. LDT structure of A process.

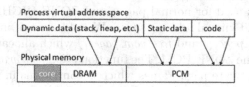

Fig. 4. Distribution of data sections of A process.

4.2 Mapping and Allocation Regulation

According to [6,12,24], the read and write latency and energy cost parameters are described in Table 1. We observe that although the read latency of PCM is higher than DRAM (around 2 times), their difference in term of write latency is more noticeable which is an order of magnitude. At the same time, the write power of PCM is about 4 times than DRAM, which constitute the main power consumption of PCM. So the number of writes to PCM will be conclusive to overall latency and energy cost. From this point of view, together with the analysis we made in second section, we map code sections and static data sections to PCM to reduce the write operation to minimum (code section is read only). That will keep minimum writing power consumption of PCM and zero refresh power consumption. At the same time, the lifetime of PCM will also benefit from less writing action. Dynamic data sections are mapped to DRAM to benefit its

Table 1. DRAM and PCM features

Parameter	DRAM	PCM
Row read power	210 mW	78 mW
Row write power	195 mW	773 mW
Row Act power	75 mW	25 mW
Standby power	90 mW	45 mW
Refresh power	4 mW	0 mW
Row read latency	50 ns	75 ns
Row write latency	50 ns	750 ns

read and write efficiency. What should be point out is, we did not use wear leveling algorithms of underlying PCM in our current work. In future work, we plan to include this as part of allocation process.

4.3   System Implementation

We implement the experiments in X86-64 platform. In our experiment, we add a new memory zone into the kernel, ZONE_PCM. In Linux, physical memory is allocated from a memory zone, which is composed of page frames. There are three memory zones in original Linux: ZONE_DMA is use for DMA pages, ZONE_NORMAL is used for normal pages, and ZONE_HIGHMEM is used for those address beyond virtual address space. We add a set of memory allocation functions, *alloc_pcm_pages()* and *free_pcm_pages()* which allocate and deallocate memory from the zone ZONE_PCM. The function *alloc_pcm_pages()* derives from *alloc_pages()*, and allocate page frames which is contiguous in physical memory space. The function *free_pcm_pages()* derives from *free_pages()*, which free the memory which has no use. The function *alloc_pcm_pages()* has two parameters: gfp_mask indicates where the system should allocate the page, which is read from LDT or GDT, and order of 2 is how many pages should be allocated.

According to OSDD's idea, if the required pages belong to code section or static data section, then they are mapped to PCM bank. And if the required pages belong to dynamic data section, then they are mapped to DRAM bank. Since each page in a section has LDT or GDT which has a tag indicating its section type, the system has chance to recognize their type from the memory request. If the tag is code section or static data section then gfp_mask is ZONE_PCM.

We simulate three memory architectures respectively using Gem5. With Gem5, many new style memory can be simulated by modifying its parameter. We simulate uniform DRAM, uniform PCM and hybrid memory, in which DRAM and PCM are addressed in one linear space. PCM is simulated by modifying the read and write latency and power consumption parameters described in Table 1. The DRAM parameters are based on 78 nm technology [1] and PCM parameters are obtained from [6,12,24]. Gem5 outputs parameters in detail in output file, such as read and write counts of instruction and data, and extract number of LLC miss rate and execution time etc., we calculate the energy saving and performance overhead using these parameters.

In order to compare OSDD with other controller based or application based approach, we also implement PDRAM method with Gem5 as the paper describe, using the same experiment setup. We test the two methods using the same PCM parameters as Table 1 describes and benchmarks introduced above.

5 Evaluation

5.1 Methodology and Metrics

In this section, we describe our simulation and design methodology. For our experiment, we assume a baseline system with 4 GB DRAM. We evaluate it against two experimental systems: (1) Uniform PCM system, which comprises of 4 GB of PCM. (2) OSDD based hybrid system, which comprises of 2 GB DRAM and 2 GB PCM. (3) PDRAM based hybrid system, which also comprises of 2 GB DRAM and 2 GB PCM. The motivation of the comparison is to show how heterogeneity in memory organization can result in better overall performance and energy efficiency.

For workload, we use 7 benchmarks from Splash2 and Parsec3, which represent different style applications. We execute the benchmarks on Gem5 using a ALPHA processor running at 2.66 GHz. The simulated processor has two levels of caches: 64 KB of data and instruction L1 caches, and 4 MB of L2 cache, which is the same with PDRAM's experiment environment.

We mainly evaluate the performance of hybrid memory in two dimension, normalized energy consumption and normalized performance overhead. Using the same suite of benchmarks, we measure the energy cost and performance overhead under the circumstance of uniform DRAM, uniform PCM, PDRAM hybrid and OSDD hybrid memory respectively. Unless otherwise indicating, the uniform DRAM system is used as the baseline for all comparisons, and the results are normalized to the baseline.

5.2 Results and Comparison

Figure 5 shows the results of normalized energy consumption, baselined against the DRAM-only system for 7 benchmarks. We see that the uniform PCM system has less energy consumption than hybrid memory (PDRAM and OSDD), because uniform PCM need no refresh while hybrid memory contains DRAM access. What is important is, on average, the OSDD has 48 % energy consumption, which is less than controller based method PDRAM (64 %). Specially, for OSDD, the bench *fft, cholesky* consumed relatively more energy because they are computation intensive program and most data accessing is done in DRAM.

Figure 6 shows the result of normalized performance overhead in terms of execution time, baselined against the DRAM-only system for 7 benchmarks. In this figure, the normalized DRAM performance is consider as one. We see that

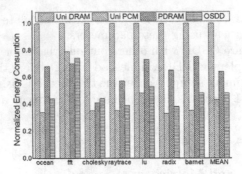

Fig. 5. Comparison of normalized energy consumption.

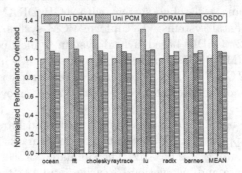

Fig. 6. Comparison of normalized performance overhead.

hybrid memory has less performance overhead than uniform PCM as a whole. And on average, OSDD get 6 % performance overhead and PDRAM get 7.2 %, which are close to each other. What should be pointed out is, for some benches like *ocean, fft, cholesky, raytrace*, OSDD get less performance overhead than PDRAM. But for other benches like *lu, radix and barnet*, situation is on the contrary, the reason and analysis will be given in Sect. 5.3 in detail.

From the evaluation, we can see that OSDD use less energy consumption than PDRAM, under the similar performance overhead. And, as we quote in Sect. 2.2, the power-aware variable partition [25] method, which based on static analysis, mentioned in their paper that it reduce 53 % power consumption on average and increase 2–18 % execution time. This testified that OSDD has better appropriate data distribution mechanism than controller based and application based methods.

5.3 Sensitivity Analysis

From the evaluation we can see that, (1) Overall, hybrid memory gain much less energy consumption than uniform DRAM memory, with small performance overhead. (2) On average OSDD gain more energy saving than PDRAM, at the similar performance overhead. (3) Just as Sect. 5.2 point out, OSDD is suitable for some benches and not suitable for others. In order to find out the reason of this phenomenon, we evaluate the "variance of memory access frequency", which measures how far a set of memory access count is spread out. A small variance indicates that the access count tend to be very close to the mean and hence to each other, while a high variance indicates that the memory access are very spread out around the mean and from each other. For example, a lower variance means all the address has almost similar access count, and a higher variance means maybe 10 % of address occupied 80 % access of the whole program trace. There are some factor which affect the result of the experiment. The reasonable analysis are:

(1) Benchmarks have different variance of memory access frequency, which affect the effectiveness of OSDD. Figure 7 describe the access variance of the seven benches. Some program has higher access variance (like *lu, radix, barnet*), and others has lower variance (like *ocean, fft, cholesky and raytrace*).

(2) As Fig. 6 shows, for those program which have higher variance such as *lu, radix, barnet*, PDRAM has lower performance overhead because it swap the hot data to DRAM with limited swapping, but OSDD keep frequent access data in PCM until program end. On the other hand, for those program which have lower variance such as *ocean, fft, cholesky and raytrace*, OSDD has lower performance overhead because PDRAM need frequent swapping but OSDD need not.

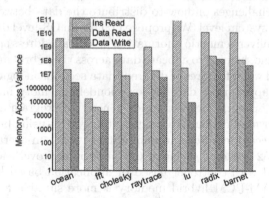

Fig. 7. Variance of memory access frequency.

6   Discussion and Future Work

In this research work, we have implemented a DRAM-PCM hybrid memory system and showed some advantages compared to existing approach. However, this hybrid memory has some disadvantages and limits, and we will consider them in future work.

According to the Fig. 1, data section is usually larger than code section in one or two order of magnitudes. In our current experiment, the size of DRAM is 2 GB, which can contain the dynamic data section of each benchmark. But for large applications, the DRAM will be not enough to contain all the dynamic data sections. If we expand the size of hybrid memory with the same ratio, the DRAM still has possibility of space shortage and PCM will perhaps be large enough to have rest space. And that will decease the effectiveness of the whole hybrid system. In future work, we plan to swap inactive dynamic data sections from DRAM to PCM to relieve the space pressure of DRAM, which will be also implemented at OS level.

From the analysis, we can see that OSDD is more suitable for program whose memory access is even (with lower variance of memory access frequency). This is its limitation, our future work will focus on how to refine the mechanism to make it more universal.

What should be pointed out is, we did not use any wear leveling algorithms of underlying PCM in our current work. In future work, we plan to include this as part of allocation process.

7   Conclusion

In this paper, we reveal the question that which part of the system should in charge of the data allocation in DRAM-PCM hybrid memory, and highlight the methods and challenges on how to distribute the data between DRAM and PCM at operating system level. We propose OSDD, an OS-level data distribution approach, which deliver semantic information of logical address space to memory management module, helping to allocate data across the hybrid memory. According to the read and write features of different data sections in logic address space, OSDD distribute appropriate data to corespondent memory medium, with no extra storage cost or swapping cost. Since it need no program annotation, it is transparent to user application. We evaluate the system using benchmarks with varying memory access features and demonstrate that, on average, the system can achieve up to 52 % energy saving at 6 % performance overhead than uniform DRAM. Compared with controller based or application based hybrid memory, OSDD based DRAM-PCM hybrid memory is more suitable for common program to get more energy saving at lower performance overhead. And, OSDD based hybrid memory is more suitable for program or application which has lower variance of memory access frequency.

Acknowledgements. This work is supported by the Beijing Municipal Science and Technology Commission of China (Grant No. D151100000815003).

References

1. Drem DDR3 technology. http://www.micron.com/products/dram/ddr3-sdram/. Accessed 1 Jul 2015
2. Pin - a dynamic binary instrumentation tool. https://software.intel.com/en-us/articles/pin-a-dynamic-binary-instrumentation-tool. Accessed 1 Jul 2015
3. The parsec benchmark suite. http://parsec.cs.princeton.edu/index.htm. Accessed 10 Jan 2016
4. Splash-2 benchmarks suite. http://www.capsl.udel.edu/splash. Accessed 10 Jan 2016
5. Bathen, L.A., et al.: HaVOC: a hybrid memory-aware virtualization layer for on-chip distributed ScratchPad and Non-Volatile Memories. ACM (2012)
6. Lee, B.C., et al.: Architecting phase change memory as a scalable dram alternative. ACM SIGARCH Comput. Archit. News **37**, 2–13 (2009)
7. Lee, B.C., et al.: Phase change memory architecture and the quest for scalability. Commun. ACM **53**, 99–106 (2010)
8. Lee, B.C., et al.: phase-change technology and the future of main memory. IEEE Micro **30**(1), 143 (2010)
9. Bienia, C., et al.: PARSEC vs. SPLASH-2: a quantitative comparison of two multithreaded benchmark suites on chip-multiprocessors. In: 4th International Symposium on Workload Characterization (2008)
10. Luk, C.K., et al.: Pin: building customized program analysis tools with dynamic instrumentation. ACM SIGPLAN Not. **40**, 190–200 (2005)
11. Bovet, D.P., et al.: Understanding the Linux Kernel. O'Reilly Media, Sebastopol (2005)
12. Bedeschi, F., et al.: An 8Mb demonstrator for high-density 1.8V Phase-Change Memories. In: Proceedings of IEEE Symp on VLSI Circuits (2004)
13. Dhiman, G., et al.: PDRAM: a hybrid PRAM and DRAM main memory system. In: Proceedings of 47th ACM Design Automation International Conference (DAC) (2009)
14. Yoon, H.B., et al.: Row buffer locality-aware data placement in hybrid memories. SAFARI Technical report (2011)
15. Yoon, H.B., et al.: Row buffer locality aware caching policies for hybrid memories. In: IEEE ICCD (2012)
16. Hu, J., et al.: Data allocation optimization for hybrid scratch pad memory with SRAM and nonvolatile memory. Proc. IEEE Trans. VLSI **21**, 1094–1102 (2012)
17. von Neumann, J.: The general and logical theory of automata. Cerebral mechanisms in behavior (1951)
18. Meza, J., et al.: Enabling efficient and scalable hybrid memories using fine-granularity DRAM cache management. Comput. Archit. Lett. **11**, 61–64 (2012)
19. Ramos, L.E., et al.: Page placement in hybrid memory systems. In: ACM ICS (2011)
20. Qureshi, M.K., et al.: Scalable high performance main memory system using phase-change memory technology. ACM SIGARCH Comput. Archit. News **37**, 24–33 (2009)
21. Qureshi, M.K., et al.: Phase Change Memory: From Devices to Systems. Synthesis Lectures on Computer Architecture (2011)
22. Mutlu, O., et al.: Memory scaling: a systems architecture perspective. In: Memory Workshop (IMW) (2013)

23. Zhou, P., et al.: A durable and energy efficient main memory using phase change memory technology. ACM SIGARCH Comput. Archit. News **37**, 14–23 (2009)
24. Bheda, R.A., et al.: Energy efficient phase change memory based main memory for future high performance systems. In: Proceedings of IEEE on International Green Computing Conference and Workshops (2011)
25. T, L., et al.: Power-aware variable partitioning for DSPS with hybrid PRAM and DRAM main memory. In: Design Automation Conference (DAC) (2011)

Coarse Granularity Data Migration Based Power Management Mechanism for 3D DRAM Cache

Litiao Qiu[✉], Lei Wang, Hongguang Zhang, Zhenyu Zhao, and Qiang Dou

School of Computer, National University of Defense Technology,
Changsha 410073, Hunan, China
{qiulitiao,hongg_z}@163.com, {leiwang,zyzhao}@nudt.edu.cn,
douq@vip.sina.com

Abstract. 3D-stacked technology is a promising solution to improve the performance of on-chip memory system. In our work, a 3D DRAM Cache with high density and wide bandwidth is utilized as the Last Level Cache (LLC). With the same Cache area, a 3D DRAM Cache shows superior capacity, bandwidth, cost performance ratio to a SRAM Cache. However, 3D DRAM storage has a problem of high power consumption. The power consumption of die-stacked DRAM is 5x compared to plane DRAM. In order to solve this problem, we proposed a power management mechanism for 3D DRAM Cache in this paper. The core idea of our mechanism is closing the infrequent accessed banks for saving power consumption. We design and implement a trace-driven 3D DRAM Cache simulator based on DRAMSim2. Experiment result of SPEC CPU2006 shown that for most applications, some banks have little access during execution. We proposed a coarse granularity data migration based power management mechanism. Compared with the system without power management mechanism, the static power consumption of some application decreased to 0.75x, a portion of application reach to 0.375x.

Keywords: 3D-stacked · DRAM cache · Memory system · Power management · LLC

1 Introduction

3D stacking technology applies through-silicon-vias (TSV) to connect different dies. Thus, in the same area, 3D DRAM has a bigger capacity and wider bandwidth compares to a 2D DRAM. However, 3D DRAM has the problem of high power consumption. In Fig. 2, power consumption of 3D DRAM is 5x larger than 2D DRAM.

Based on the comparison results between 2D DRAM and 3D DRAM, although 3D DRAM cache has a smaller area and bigger capacity, we cannot ignore the huge power consumption caused by 3D DRAM.

This work was supported by the National Nature Science Foundation of China (61402501, 61272139).

© Springer Science+Business Media Singapore 2016
J. Wu and L. Li (Eds.): ACA 2016, CCIS 626, pp. 15–27, 2016.
DOI: 10.1007/978-981-10-2209-8_2

In recent works, many researchers proposed various way to manage the power of on-chip memory. They focus their attention on the different cause of power consumption, dynamic power and leakage power. Some studies dealt with the hit rate of Cache, the higher the hit rate, the more power can be saved. Other researchers [4] tried to redesign the framework of Cache, they separate the data array of the Cache into sub-banks. Only activate the bank when the corresponding data is needed. In addition to that, in order to save the dynamic power, activate less tag bits and data in an access is a method adopted by [5]. They access the tag array in the first phase. In the second phase, only the corresponding tag bits are accessed, can the data referenced. However, in a big capacity LLC, leakage power accounts a big portion in whole power consumption. Coarse granularity execution is practical enough to figure out the power consumption problem of 3D DRAM Cache.

In this paper, we proposed a Coarse Granularity Data Migration power management mechanism. Based on the access pattern of the application, we choose the unlikely accessed banks to be powered-off. Thus, we design and implement a simulation platform which has a core, 3-level Cache (LLC is a 3D DRAM Cache) and 2D main memory. Experiment result with SPEC CPU2006 shown that in most applications, some banks have little access during execution. Thus, the static power consumption of some application decreased to 0.75x, a portion of application reach to 0.375x.

The organization of the rest of the paper is as follows: In Sect. 2, we demonstrate the background and motivation of our work. The main idea of power management in 3D DRAM Cache is shown in Sect. 3. Section 4 gives a detail analysis on experimental setup and results of our mechanism. Section 5 presents a brief review of power management and 3D-stacked system. Section 6 is the conclusion of the paper.

2 Background and Motivation

Recent works proposed many DRAM-cache prototypes to address the memory bandwidth and latency wall in Last Level cache. Hit ratio, hit latency and tag overhead determine the challenges of implementing a DRAM Cache.

In order to reduce the miss rate, a cached DRAM [1] integrates SRAM cache in the DRAM memory to exploit its locality in memory accesses and storage efficiency. In such DRAM caches, SRAM tags are placed in the stacked DRAM along with the data blocks [1, 2]. However, this can potentially require two DRAM accesses per cache lookup (one for the tag look up and one for data). Thus, in the worst case, it costs double access latency.

A state-of-art DRAM cache method, Alloy Cache [2], organizes as a direct-mapped Cache, which is optimized for latency. Although reduce the hit rate, improving the cache access latency greatly. The DRAM cache model used in our work is inspired by Alloy Cache, which bursts tag and data in a single stream to wipe out the tag serialization delay.

Compare to other DRAM caches, Alloy cache has no SRAM tag overhead, low hit latency and scalability. For a die-stacked DRAM Cache, we can get high effective capacity and high hit rate as well. Thus, we exploit a die-stacked DRAM cache as our experimental model.

In our work, Alloy Cache is used as DRAM cache prototype. Our L3 DRAM cache saves two kinds of information, tag and data. Alloy Cache is an effective latency-optimized Cache architecture. It alloys or combines the tag and data into one basic unit (Tag and Data, TAD), instead of separating cache constructions into two parts (tag store and data store). For Alloy cache streams tag and data in one burst, it can get rid of the delay because of tag serialization. It helps handle cache misses faster without wasting time to detect cache miss in the same situation.

In Fig. 1, each TAD represents one set of the direct-mapped Alloy Cache. In our DRAM cache, every data line has a tag. The address is compared with the tags in DRAM cache. If it is the same, then hit. Or vice versa. In our paper, for a physical address space of 64 bits, 41 tag bits are needed. The minimum size of a TAD is thus 72 bytes (64 bytes for data line and 8 bytes for tag). There are 28 lines in a row of an Alloy Cache.

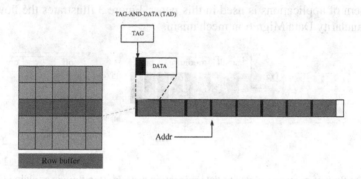

Fig. 1. Structure of alloy cache

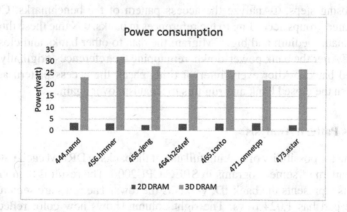

Fig. 2. Power consumption in baseline and 3D DRAM cache system with no power management

We conduct some experiments on power consumption of die-stacked DRAM. We run 200 billion instructions for each application. Then, using the trace from Gem5 feed to DRAMSim2. Comparing to a 2D DRAM, it demonstrates big leakage power consumption in 3D DRAM. The result is shown in Fig. 2.

3D-stacked framework shows great merits in capacity and bandwidth. However, as is shown in Fig. 2, power consumption is a big problem in improving processor performance. For 3D DRAM, the power consumption is 5x larger than a 2D DRAM in average. Thus, the main purpose of our research is to maintain the big capacity of the L3 die-stacked DRAM Cache, while reduce power consumption as well.

3   Main Idea

The main idea of Coarse Granularity Data Migration based power management mechanism is closing the infrequent accessed banks of 3D DRAM Cache to save power consumption. How to find the bank that should be closed and how to migrate the data in these banks are the challenges that we must solve. An offline method to figure out the access pattern of applications is used in this paper. Figure 3 illustrates the flow of our Coarse Granularity Data Migration mechanism.

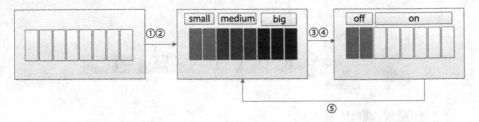

Fig. 3. The flow of coarse granularity data migration method. (the flow is explained below)

Bank closing steps. ①Analyze the access pattern of the benchmarks. Cluster the banks into three groups according to the references in banks. ②Name these three groups as Cluster small, medium and big. ③Migrate the data to other banks and close the last two banks. ④After the bank power-down, remapping the references originally mapping to the closed bank. ⑤After every interval time, check the access pattern again. If it changes, open the closed bank and run this mechanism over again.

3.1   Access Pattern Analysis

For exploring the possibility of making full use of the banks in DRAM cache, we analyze the access pattern of some programs in SPEC CPU2006. The result is demonstrated in Fig. 4, x-axis represents the bank ID, y-axis is the rows. The rows are separated into 8 parts, every part has 1,024 rows. The right column shows how color reflects access number. In these hot spot figures, deeper the color, more references in that area.

In Fig. 4, except 437, we can see obvious cluster in each application. For example, references concentrate in bank 0 and bank1 in 456.hmmer. While in 444.namd, there is no access in bank 5, 6 and 7. It means some of the banks in an application are not fully utilized. These infrequent used banks can be closed during its runtime.

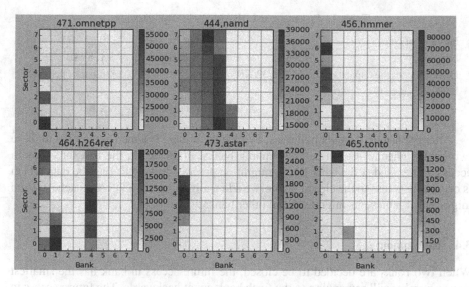

Fig. 4. Access pattern of different applications

3.2 Cluster Banks Using K-Means

In order to reduce power consumption, we can power down those unusually used banks. Thus, we exploit K-means to find out those banks have little references. Banks are separated into three clusters.

First of all, pick three access number of banks as centroids randomly. Then, it calculates the distance from other access number to the centroid. The banks have the closing access number with one centroid will be allocated to the same cluster. The next step is calculating the average value of each cluster, regard it as the new centroid. Thus, we have three new centroids. Calculating the distance between the access number in all banks and the update centroids. We get three new clusters. Then iterating the process continuously. Until we get the final three clusters of banks.

In our work, we have 8 banks. With the purpose of closing the unlikely accessed banks. We divide these 8 banks into three groups. In Cluster big, banks get the most of the access. So we leave it alone. Our focus is in Cluster small, which has the least number of the reference.

3.3 Data Migration

Once the banks are decided to shut down, dirty bit of each access in closed banks will be checked. If data in closed banks is dirty, that is to say, the data in DRAM cache is different from the data stored in main memory, the data in DRAM cache would write back to main memory. If data in closed banks is clean, drop it. Table 1 shows the bank configuration in DRAM cache.

Table 1. Processor and DRAM Cache configuration

Number of cores	1	L3 bus frequency	0.67 MHz
Frequency	2 GHz	L3 capacity	128 MB
L1 dcache/icache capacity	64 KB/32 KB	Bank	8 banks per rank
l2 Cache capacity	2 MB	Die	4
–	–	Row buffer size	2 KB

After we handle the data in the last two banks, if there is a memory access to these two banks, migrate it to the corresponding banks. In our work, the first three bits in access address index the bank ID. In migration process, for identifying the data which is originally access to the closed banks, we add a migration bit in DRAM cache. 0 is no migration, 1 represents migrated from other banks.

3.4 Remapping

When two banks are decided to be closed, the future access in bank has the smallest access number will remapping to the forth bank count backwards. The future access in bank has the last but one reference number will remapping to the third bank count backwards. What is more, before remapping begins, we set a migration bit in order to know whether the data is migrated or not. Upon an access comes, it maps to a bank. If this bank is open, migration bit stay the same. All the access behavior does not change as well. But when the access mapped to a closed bank. The migration bit switch to 1. In the meantime, tag bits stay still, only bank bits change.

3.5 Reopen

At every 10,000 ticks, we check the access pattern again. In the new 5000 ticks, if the distribution of clusters changes, that is, the Small cluster is no more the same, we will reopen the closed banks and do our power management mechanism over again.

3.6 Example

In application 464.h264ref. Its access pattern shows bank 2, 5, 6 and 7 are in Small cluster. Bank 1 and 3 are in Medium cluster. The rest bank 0 and bank 4 in Big cluster. Then we calculate and get that the reference number in Small cluster occupies 0.073 of Medium cluster. Thus, migrate the data in bank 7 (has least access number) to bank 2 (the forth bank count backwards according to reference number), bank 6 (the last but one) to bank 5(the third bank count backwards). Meanwhile, set the migration bit of those migrated data bit to 1. At last, data migration finished.

3.7 Hardware Implementation

Figure 5 shows the possible hardware implementation of our Coarse Granularity Data Migration power management mechanism. Every bank has a gating signal to control the state of the bank (open or close). In each rank, there are four banks. A memory controller is used to manipulate which rank is activated. *Rank_Sel* chooses the determined rank. In order to select the desired bank, rank number and bank number are both needed to be confirmed. In other words, we use *Rankx_Bankx* to choose the bank we want.

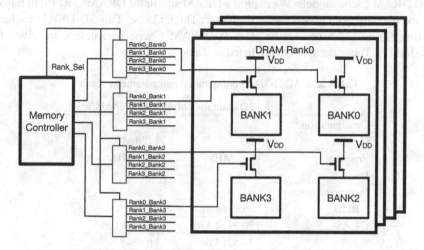

Fig. 5. Hardware implementation of power management

4 Experimental Evaluation

4.1 Experiment Setup

In our experiments, we use GEM5 simulator with a detailed memory model. The instruction set used is ARM V7 ISA. Table 1 gives the configuration used in our work. The 3D DRAM Cache used in the experiments is 128 MB.

Experiment Platform. The experiment platform is shown in Fig. 6. It contains 5 major parts: The processor simulator (Gem5), 3D DRAM Cache model (3D DRAM Cache),

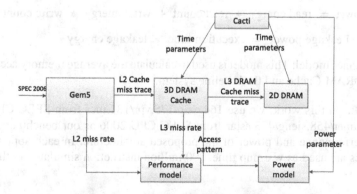

Fig. 6. Infrastructure of the whole experimental platform

main memory model (2D DRAM), power model (Power model), performance model (Performance model). Cacti offers timing and power parameter for our 5 parts except Gem5. Gem5 is configured to generate complete DRAM access traces (after L2 cache).

3D DRAM cache models: We exploit a DRAM simulator DRAMSim2 [6] to implement the trace-driven DRAM cache simulator: Thick Cache. This 3D-DRAM cache is an Alloy Cache [2] based Cache. The 3D DRAM Cache parameters are given by Cacti-3dd [7]. These parameters are listed in Table 2.

Table 2. CACTI-3DD configuration and parameter result

	2D main memory	3D DRAM Cache
Configuration		
Capacity	2G	128 MB
Frequency	677 MHz	677 MHz
Die	1	4
Parameter(latency)		
t_RCD	5.9164 ns	4.37031 ns
t_RAS	20.3714 ns	5.44791 ns
t_RC	34.5217 ns	6.68482
t_CAS	9.85235 ns	6.54791 ns
t_RP	14.1503 ns	1.7791 ns
Parameter(energy)		
Activate energy	0.489495 nJ	0.076035 nJ
Read/write energy	0.543979 nJ	0.367355 nJ
Prefetch energy	0.405572 nJ	0.065765 nJ

Main Memory model: The 2D main memory model is simulated by DRAMSim2 [6]. The configuration and timing parameters for DRAMSim2 are generated by Cacti [7].

Power model: The number of access of the 3D DRAM Cache during simulation is counted in the Thick Cache simulator. Then the following equation is used to calculate the power consumption:

$$\text{Dynamic power } = \text{ read energy } * \text{ read count } + \text{ write energy } * \text{ write counts} \qquad (1)$$

$$\text{Leakage power } = \text{ execution time } * \text{ leakage energy} \qquad (2)$$

Performance model: This model is used to calculate the average memory access time of the 3D DRAM Cache and the baseline system.

Benchmark. In this work, we use 164.gzip/175.vpr/181.mcf from SPEC CPU 2000 and 456.hmmer/458.sjeng/473.astar from SPEC CPU 2006 as our benchmark to estimate the performance and power of the proposed architecture. In each application, 2 million ticks are used as warmup time. 200 million instruction simulated in the whole process.

We get the L2 miss trace generated by Gem5. Then the traces are fed into our Thick Cache simulator to do the performance and power estimation.

4.2 Baseline System

The baseline system in this work is a processor core with L1 Cache and L2 Cache, without L3 Cache and a plane main memory based on DRAMSim2. The common parts of these two architectures share the same parameter of each hierarchy, except L3 Cache. The parameters of processor core and memory system are listed in Tables 1 and 2.

4.3 Implementation

For the one and only difference between baseline system and 3D-stacked system is a L3 3D DRAM Cache, a Cache simulator Dinero [8] is used to verify the accuracy of the DRAM Cache. We use the same configuration and traces to DRAM Cache and Dinero, miss rates are compared to see if our DRAM Cache is right. As is depicted in Fig. 7, we can see our Thick Cache simulator is basically accurate.

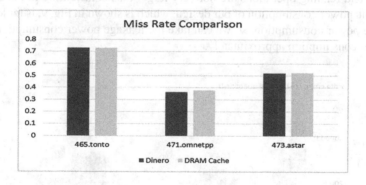

Fig. 7. Miss ratio comparison between Dinero and Thick Cache

4.4 Experimental Result

Performance Comparison. For our proposed 3D-DRAM LLC system, we got the LLC average access time and use it as the metric of performance. The results are shown in Fig. 8.

As it is depicted in Fig. 8, the performance behavior in these two systems are almost the same. In some cases, such as 437.lesli3d and 471.omnetpp, 3D DRAM Cache system shows shorter access time. And in a 3D DRAM Cache system, it has bigger capacity and no high area consumption, which makes our optimizing system a proper way to upgrade memory system.

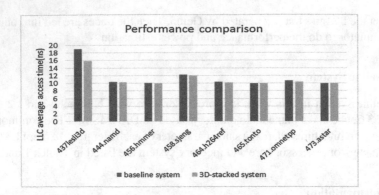

Fig. 8. Performance comparison between baseline and 3D DRAM Cache system

Power Comparison. In this section, we analysis the power consumption of the proposed design, including dynamic power and leakage power. Dynamic power results from writing and reading operations, which is determined by the total amount of the two kinds of operation. Leakage power comes from the leakage current of DRAM cells.

From the results of SPEC2006, it can be seen that for last level cache, the number of writing and reading operations are not very large, thus contributing to the fact that the dynamic power consumption of our design, which is shown in Fig. 9, is far less than its leakage power consumption, so we can take the leakage power consumption as the total power consumption approximately.

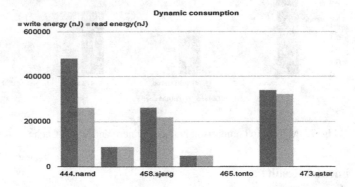

Fig. 9. Dynamic power consumption

In order to reduce its leakage power, we adopted bank migration and partial power down. The power results after optimization shown in Fig. 10 are much less. We can see that the leakage power consumption has decreased obviously, which prove that our solution is effective.

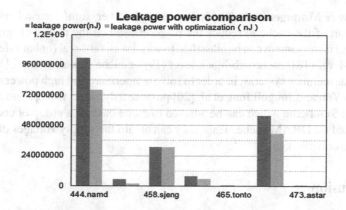

Fig. 10. Comparison between leakage power before power management and after

5 Related Work

5.1 DRAM Cache

In previous research, many studies have been explored the model of DRAM cache. In order to reduce the miss rate, Cached DRAM [22] integrates SRAM cache in the DRAM memory to exploit its locality in memory accesses and storage efficiency. In such DRAM caches, SRAM tags are placed in the stacked DRAM along with the data blocks [21–23]. However, this can potentially require two DRAM accesses per cache lookup (one for the tag look up and one for data). Thus, a state-of-art DRAM cache method, Alloy Cache [2] proposed to reduce latency. It organizes as a direct-mapped organization. Although reduce the hit rate, improving the cache access latency greatly. Our DRAM cache model is inspired by a latency-optimized cache architecture, named Alloy cache [2] which bursts tag and data in a single stream to wipe out the tag serialization delay.

5.2 Power Optimization of DRAM Cache

DRAM power management approaches basically developed into two parts: those aim to solve dynamic power such as memory traffic reshaping and increase the locality of memory reference [9], and those try to figure out leakage power by using decrease memory access or memory footprint [12]. Recently, there have been a large number of researches using adaptive power saving ability offered by several-banked DRAM [9–11].

Dynamic Power Management. For saving dynamic power, some techniques reduce the number of access to the specific memory level by using additional storage structures [13]. Some techniques utilize frequent accessed data with lower energy mode to reduce dynamic power per access [14]. Some other techniques perform tag bits match in several-step manner, while other techniques cut down the required bits for comparison [15]. Also, the techniques mentioned above can be extended to utilize in multiprocessor systems. In 3D multicore systems, Meng et al. [16] proposed a runtime optimization technique to maintain performance and power consumption in the same time.

Leakage Power Management. For saving leakage power, some researchers adaptive selecting a part of the cache to reduce the power. Based on the power-off granularity, leakage power management can be classified to way-level, set-level (or bank-level) [17], cache block-level [18], cache sub-block level [19] or cache sub-array level [12] etc. In 3D integration memory systems, in order to solve temperature and high power consumption, Woojin Yun and Jongpil Jung et al. [20] propose a dynamic voltage and frequency scaling (DVFS) scheme which can be adapted to cache bank or a group of cache banks for 3D-stacked L2 DRAM cache. Thus, they can obtain the supply voltages of different cache zones (or banks).

6   Conclusion

A key design methodology for improving the performance of processor core lies in breaking the Memory Wall. In our work, a L3 3D DRAM Cache is used in the new memory hierarchy to obtain higher capacity and wider bandwidth. However, for each 3D system, power consumption is a critical issue for a better performance. As for a big capacity LLC, leakage energy consists a big portion of the whole energy consumption. Thus, a bank closing mechanism is adopted to decrease leakage energy in our design. First of all, we analyze the access pattern offline of some applications from SPEC CPU 2006, determines which banks are not likely used in execution. Then, we shut them down. At last, static power consumption of some application decreased to 0.75x, a portion of application reach to 0.375x. In the future, in order to decrease the dynamic power in LLC, the migration of data in the process of closing banks can be put in to a further study.

References

1. Loh, G.H., Hill, M.D.: Efficiently enabling conventional block sizes for very large die-stacked dram caches. In: Proceedings of Annual International Symposium Microarchitecture, pp. 454–464 (2011)
2. Qureshi, M.K., Loh, G.H.: Fundamendal latency trade-off in architecture dram caches: out performing impractical sram-tags with a simple and practical design. In: 2012 45th Annual IEEE/ACM International Symposium on Microarchitecture, pp. 235–246 (2012)
3. Jevdjic, D., Loh, G.H., kaynak, C., Falsa, B.: Unison cache: a scalable and effective die-stacked dram cache. In: 2014 47th Annual IEEE/ACM International Symposium on Microarchitecture (MICRO), pp. 25–37 (2015)
4. Su, C., Despain, A.: Cache design tradeoffs for power and performance optimization: a case study. In: Proceedings of International Symposium on Low Power Design, pp. 63–68 (1997)
5. Hasegawa, A., Kawasaki, I., Yamada, K., Yoshioka, S., Kawasaki, S., Biswas, P.: Sh3: high code density, low power. IEEE Micro 15(6), 11–19 (1995)
6. Rosenfeld, P., Cooper-Balis, E., Jacob, B.: DRAMSim2: a cycle accurate memory system simulator. IEEE Comput. Archit. Lett. 10(1), 16–19 (2011)
7. Chen, K., Li, S., Muralimanohar, N., et al.: CACTI-3DD: architecture-level modeling for 3D die-stacked DRAM main memory. In: Proceedings of the Conference on Design, Automation and Test in Europe, pp. 33–38. EDA Consortium (2012)
8. http://self.gutenberg.org/articles/dinero_(cache_simulator)

9. Amin, A., Chishti, Z.: Rank-aware cache replacement and write buffering to improve DRAM energy efficiency. In: Proceedings of the 16th ACM/IEEE International Symposium on Low Power Electronics and Design, pp. 383–388. ACM (2010)

10. Ware, M., Rajamani, K., Floyd, M., Brock, B., Rubio, J., Rawson, F., Carter, J.: Architecting for power management: the IBMR POWER7 approach. In: HPCA, pp. 1–11. IEEE (2010)

11. Chandrasekar, K., Akesson, B., Goossens, K.: Runtime power-down strategies for real-time SDRAM memory controllers. In: Proceedings of the 49th Annual DAC, pp. 988–993. ACM (2012)

12. Yang, L., Dick, R.P., Lekatsas, H., Chakradhar, S.: Online memory compression for embedded systems. ACM Trans. Embed. Comput. Syst. 9, 1–30 (2010)

13. Kin, J., Gupta, M., Mangione-Smith, W.: The filter cache: an energy efficient memory structure. In: 30th International symposium on Microarchitecture (MICRO), pp. 184–193 (1997)

14. Udipi, A., Muralimanohar, N., Balasubramonian, R.: Non-uniform power access in large caches with low-swing wires. In: International Conference on High Performance Computing (HiPC). IEEE, pp. 59–68 (2009)

15. Kwak, J., Jeon, Y.: Compressed tag architecture for low-power embedded cache systems. J. Syst. Archit. 56(9), 419–428 (2010)

16. Meng, J., Kawakami, K., Coskun, A.K.: Optimizing energy efficiency of 3-D multicore systems with stacked DRAM under power and thermal constraints. In: Design Automation Conference, pp. 648–655. ACM (2012)

17. Ku, J., Ozdemir, S., Memik, G., Ismail, Y.: Thermal management of on-chip caches through power density minimization. In: International Symposium on Microarchitecture (MICRO), pp. 283–293 (2005)

18. Kaxiras, S., Hu, Z., Martonosi, M.: Cache decay: exploiting generational behavior to reduce cache leakage power. In: 28th International Symposium on Computer Architecture (ISCA), pp. 240–251 (2001)

19. Alves, M.A.Z., et al.: Energy savings via dead sub-block prediction. In: International Symposium on Computer Architecture and High Performance Computing (SBAC-PAD) (2012)

20. Yun, W., Jung, J., Kang, K., et al.: Temperature-aware energy minimization of 3D-stacked L2 DRAM cache through DVFS. In: Soc Design Conference, pp. 475–478 (2012)

21. Loh, G.H.: Extending the effectiveness of 3d-stacked dram caches with an adaptive multi-queue policy. In: Proceedings of the 42nd International Symposium on Microarchitecture, December 2009

22. Loh, G.H., Hill, M.D.: Efficiently enabling conventional block sizes for very large die-stacked dram caches. In: Proceedings of the 44th International Symposium on Microarchitecture, December 2011

23. Qureshi, M., Loh, G.H.: Fundamental latency trade-offs in architecting DRAM caches. In: Proceedings of the 45th International Symposium on Microarchitecture, December 2012

A Novel Hybrid Last Level Cache Based on Multi-retention STT-RAM Cells

Hongguang Zhang[1(✉)], Minxuan Zhang[1,2], Zhenyu Zhao[1],
and Shuo Tian[1]

[1] College of Computer, National University of Defense Technology,
Changsha 410073, People's Republic of China
{zhanghongguang14,mxzhang,zyzhao,
tianshuo14}@nudt.edu.cn
[2] National Key Laboratory of Parallel and Distributed Processing,
National University of Defense Technology,
Changsha 410073, People's Republic of China

Abstract. Spin-transfer torque random access memory (STT-RAM) is one of the most promising substitutes for universal main memory and cache due to its excellent scalability, high storage density and low leakage power. A much larger cache capacity in the same die footprint can be implemented with STT-RAM because its area is only 1/9 to 1/3 that of SRAM. However, the non-volatile STT-RAM also has some drawbacks, such as long write latency and high write energy, which limit its application in cache design. To solve the two problems, we relax the retention time of STT-RAM to optimize its write performance and energy, and propose a novel multi-retention STT-RAM hybrid last level cache (LLC) architecture, which is realized with three different kinds of cells. In addition, we design the data migration scheme to manage its block allocation, thus improving overall system performance further. The experiment results show that our multi-retention hybrid LLC reduces the total power consumption by as much as 96.6 % compared with SRAM LLC, while having almost the same (at 99.4 %) instruction per cycle (IPC).

Keywords: STT-RAM · Last level cache · Multi-retention · Data migration

1 Introduction

Power has been the dominator of the increasing of CPU's frequency since one decade ago. This has generated a considerable volume of research in multi-core processor to provide sustainable performance enhancement of computer system. However, the gap of access speed between main memory and processor is becoming larger and has been the bottleneck of overall system performance. Cache is developed to alleviate this mismatch problem.

SRAM has been the mainstream of caches for many years because it owns high access speed, low dynamic power and other good characters. However, with more and more cores are embedded on chip, caches need larger size. However, increasing capacity of SRAM caches lead to high leakage power, which takes up the dominator of

© Springer Science+Business Media Singapore 2016
J. Wu and L. Li (Eds.): ACA 2016, CCIS 626, pp. 28–39, 2016.
DOI: 10.1007/978-981-10-2209-8_3

the microprocessor's overall power consumption, therefore, researchers are focusing on alternative substitutes for SRAM.

Spin-transfer torque random access memory (STT-RAM) is regarded as the most promising replacement for SRAM because it has almost all desired characters of the universal memory and cache, such as high storage density, fast read access speed and non-volatility. However, we are faced with two drawbacks of STT-RAM, namely, long write latency and high write energy, which result in the reduction of system performance and the enhancement of dynamic power consumption.

Hybrid cache scheme is proposed to address the write access speed and energy of STT-RAM. For example, the SRAM/STT-RAM hybrid cache in [7, 8] moves write intensive data blocks into SRAM region to reduce the average write latency. However, even a small SRAM partition can bring in very high leakage power. Researchers discover that relaxing the data retention time could significantly optimize its write performance, which can even exceed that of SRAM. That makes the multi-retention hybrid cache architecture possible. In [2], a new cache hierarchy is proposed to improve the overall system performance with multi-retention STT-RAM cell, and the outcome is good.

In this paper, we relax the retention time of STT-RAM and propose a novel multi-retention STT-RAM hybrid last level cache with three kinds of STT-RAM cells, which is different with the design in [2, 11], to obtain an improvement of overall performance. We simulate the proposed cache design on architecture simulator, and collect the test results of benchmarks to analysis the overall system performance and power consumption.

2 STT-RAM Features

2.1 MTJ Features

The magnetic tunnel junction (MTJ) shown in Fig. 1 is the basic storage device of STT-RAM. The MTJ has two layers, namely, free layer and reference layer. The magnetic direction of reference layer is fixed, however, that of free layer can be switched by current. If the magnetic directions of two magnetic layers are parallel, the MTJ is in low-resistance state; otherwise it is in high-resistance state.

The most widely used STT-RAM storage cell is one transistor one MTJ (1T1J) at present. In memory array, the STT-RAM cell is connected to word line (WL), bit line (BL) and source line (SL). The WL is used to select the specific row, and the voltage gap between SL and BL is used to complete write and read operation. When executing a read operation, we add a negative voltage between SL and BL and use a sense amplifier to get the current flowing throw the MTJ, thus knowing the current resistance of MTJ. When writing "0" into STT-RAM cell, there is a positive voltage between SL and BL. However, when writing "1" into STT-RAM, a negative voltage is applied. The current used to switch the MTJ's state is called switching current, and its value is mainly determined by the write pulse width, which is represented by T_w in this paper.

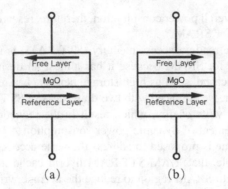

Fig. 1. The MTJ design (1T1J). (a) MTJ in high-resistance state. (b) MTJ in low-resistance state.

2.2 MTJ Non-volatility

The MTJ's non-volatility can be analyzed quantitatively with the retention time of MTJ. We use τ to represent its retention time. τ is related to the thermal stability factor Δ and can be calculated with Eq. (1) [1].

$$\tau \approx \tau_0 \, exp(\Delta) \tag{1}$$

τ_0: The attempt time and set as 1 ns.
Δ is derived from Eq. (2).

$$\Delta = \frac{E_F}{k_B T} = \frac{M_s V H_K}{2 k_B T} \tag{2}$$

M_s: The saturation magnetization.
H_k: The effective anisotropy field.
T: The working temperature.
K_B: The Boltzmann constant.
V: The volume for the STT-RAM write current.

From Eqs. (1) and (2), we can know that the data retention time of a MTJ decreases exponentially when its working temperature T increases.

According to the different T_w, MTJ has three regions, namely, the thermal activation, dynamic reverse and processional switching. Their distribution is shown as Fig. 2.

The switching current in each working region can be calculated approximately by Eqs. (3)–(5) [2].

$$J_C^{Therm} T_w = J_{C0} \left(1 - \frac{1}{\Delta} ln \left(\frac{T_w}{\tau_0} \right) \right) \quad (T_w > 20 \text{ ns}) \tag{3}$$

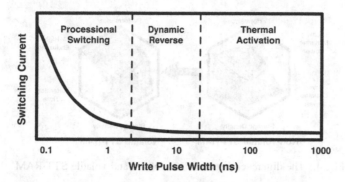

Fig. 2. The three working region of MTJ

$$J_c^{Dyn}T_w = \frac{J_c^{Therm}T_w + J_c^{Prec}T_w e^{(-A(T_w - T_{PIV}))}}{1 + e^{(-A(T_w - T_{PIV}))}} \qquad (20 \text{ ns} > T_w > 3 \text{ ns}) \qquad (4)$$

$$J_C^{Prec}T_w = J_{C0} + \frac{C \ln\left(\frac{\pi}{2\theta}\right)}{T_w} \qquad (T_w < 3 \text{ ns}) \qquad (5)$$

$$J_{C0} = \left(\frac{2e}{\hbar}\right)\left(\frac{\alpha}{\eta}\right)(t_F M_S)(H_k \pm H_{ext} + 2\pi M_S) \qquad (6)$$

Where $J_C T_w$ is required switching current, A, C, and T_{PIV} are fitting parameters, J_{CO} is the threshold of switching current density, e is the electron charge, $\hbar$ is the reduced Planck constant, α is the damping constant, H_{ext} is the external field, η is the spin transfer efficiency, t_F is the free layer thickness.

Based on the above analysis, we can adjust the value of J_C and Δ by changing several related parameters, such as M_S, t_F, H_k and V.

We get three $I_C - T_w$ curves shown in Fig. 3. for STT-RAM cells whose retention time are 2.5 years ($\Delta = 38.9$), 3 s ($\Delta = 21.8$) and 30 μs ($\Delta = 10.3$). In this paper they are called HRS, MRS and LRS respectively.

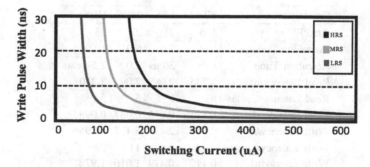

Fig. 3. The $I_c - T_w$ for HRS, MRS and LRS MTJ cells

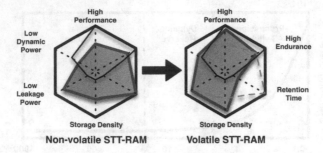

Fig. 4. The difference between non-volatile and volatile STT-RAM

It is clear that the higher the retention time, the lower the $I_c - T_w$ curve. With the same switching current, LRS's write pulse width is the shortest one and HR is the longest. If their write pulse widths are the same, the switching current required by LRS is the lowest. The performance difference between non-volatile and volatile STT-RAM is shown in Fig. 4 [3]. The dotted border is optimal and black line is SRAM. The blue region is STT-RAM.

3   STT-RAM LLC Design

3.1   Cache Parameters

Although the long retention time of STT-RAM can offer low leakage power consumption, it leads to long write latency and high write energy. To reduce the write latency and energy, we relax the retention time of STT-RAM to improve its write performance.

In Sect. 2, we find that the STT-RAM cells whose retention time are relaxed to μs and ms level can satisfy the access speed of all level caches. So we simulate the proposed HRS, MRS and LRS cells on NVSim [6] to get their parameters in 1 MB last level cache design. The results are shown in Table 1 .

Table 1. The parameters for multi-retention STT-RAM cells.

Parameters	SRAM	LRS	MRS	HRS
Area/F^2	125	21	22	23
Switching Time/ns	/	2.0	5.0	10.0
Retention Time	/	30 μs	3.0 s	2.5 years
Read Latency/ns	2.735	2.085	2.097	2.210
Read Latency/Cycles	6	5	5	5
Read Energy/nJ	0.181	0.083	0.087	0.099
Write Latency/ns	2.301	2.431	5.427	10.936
Write Latency/Cycles	5	5	11	22
Write Energy/nJ	0.112	0.479	1.016	1.978
Leakage Power/mW	1261.7	26.9	31.1	36.2

From Table 1, it can be seen that the performance varies with different retention time. LRS's access speed is even better than SRAM, while HRS's write latency is longer than 10 ns.

3.2 Hybrid LLC Architecture

In previous section, we get their overall performance of LRS, MRS and HRS cells. We find that LRS owns the fastest access speed, so if we adopt LRS to design LLC, the LLC's performance can be enhanced significantly. However, it should be noticed that the data stored in LRS or MRS blocks will be invalid after its short retention time, so we must use refresh scheme to improve the reliability. For LLC with large capacity (1 MB or larger), it can be foreseen that the refresh energy and the hardware overhead are unbearable in this situation. Typically, the hardware overhead is 0.80 %. So it is not suitable to design LLC with LRS or MRS purely. Considering the existed SRAM/STT-RAM hybrid cache architecture [13], which fully utilize both the fast write speed of SRAM and the excellent features of STT-RAM, and other designs in [4, 5], the hybrid LLC based on volatile STT-RAM is possible. A multi-retention hybrid cache design is proposed in [2], however, the large capacity of LLC offers more choices, so we propose to design an optimized novel multi-retention hybrid cache architecture.

We find that if we add a MRS-Region in LRS/HRS hybrid LLC, its performance can be promoted further and power consumption can be reduced although the hardware overhead is a bit higher than the original design. The reason why we do not expand LRS-Region is that the block-refresh and counter-reset happen frequently in LLC in case that the size of LRS-Region is too large, thus leading to a very high power consumption. In addition, the large amount of counter requires larger on-chip area and hardware overhead. These factors make it unsuitable to expand LRS-Region further. The LRS/MRS hybrid LLC is also one choice, however, the retention time of MRS can not make sure all data are reliable though the retention time of MRS is longer than LRS. We still need the refresh scheme, thus contributing to serious refresh power consumption problem.

Based on the above analysis, the LRS/MRS/HRS multi-retention hybrid LLC is one of the best choices that we can find at present. we separate the 1 MB LLC into 16 ways, way0 is LRS-Region and realized by LRS cells, way1–3 is MRS-Region and made by MRS cells, way4–15 is HRS-Region and consist of HRS cells only.

To improve the reliability of LRS-Region and MRS-Region, we add a refresh-counter and an access-counter for every LRS or MRS block. The refresh-counter is used to monitor the duration that the data has been stored in that block while the access-counter is utilized to record its read access number during the retention time. The refresh counters are controlled by a global clock whose period is T_{gc}. The value of refresh-counter is N_{ref}, and that of access-counter is N_{ac}. At the end of each T_{gc}, all refresh-counters will be increased by 1. If there is a read access to one block, its access-counter is increased by 1. However, if there is a write access to the block, both its refresh-counter and access-counter are initialized to 0. The maximum value of refresh-counter N_{max} depends on their different retention time. When a LRS or MRS block's N_{ref} reaches N_{max}, we do not conduct a refresh operation but check its

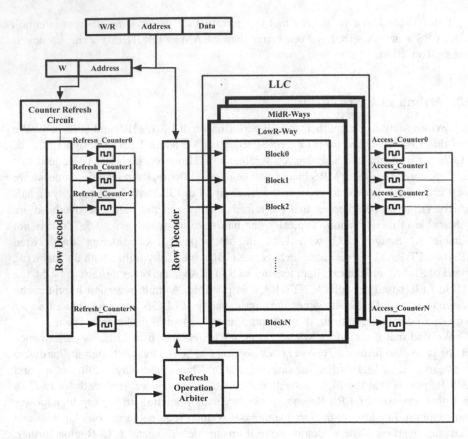

Fig. 5. The counter-based writeback refresh scheme

N_{ac}. We write it back to HR-Region in case of $N_{ac} > 5$, otherwise write it back to main memory. The whole scheme shown in Fig. 5 is called Counter-based Writeback Refresh Scheme (CWRS).

The design of counter is shown as Fig. 6. The hardware overhead of CWRS is (4 bits × 2 × 4)/(64 bytes × 16) = 0.39 %, the overall area needed is $(4 × 125F^2 × 2 × 4)/(64 × 8 × 40F^2 × 16) = 1.22$ %. Based on simulation results, these counters' power consumption takes up only less than 1 % of the total power consumption, which has little influence on the overall performance.

To improve overall system performance, we create a write intensive block prediction table (WIBPT) to predict and monitor write intensive blocks. WIBPT has 64 entries, and each entry consists of an address and a counter. We divide all write intensive blocks (WIB) into three levels, namely, WIB1, WIB2 and WIB3, to support the migration scheme in our hybrid LLC.

When a request comes to LLC, firstly we detect what kind of operation it is and if it is a hit. If it is a miss, we allocate a LRS block for it. If the request is a write hit, we detect if its address is already in WIBPT. If so, its access counter is increased by 1, otherwise we add its address to WIBPT and reset the counter to 0. If WIBPT is full, we

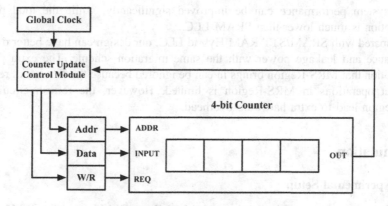

Fig. 6. The counter design

kick the LRU entry and add this new address. Then we detect the value of its counter, if the counter is less than 4, we define it as WIB1 and do nothing; if it is larger than 4 and less than 8, we define it as WIB2 and swap it with blocks in MRS-Region; if the counter is larger than 8 [12], we name it as WIB3 and migrate it to LRS-Region. A migration operation needs read the data from original cache block firstly, and then write it to the target. It consumes two read and write operations. This dynamic power is added into the final results.

The proposed data migration policy is demonstrated by Fig. 7. In this way, we obtain a better tradeoff between performance and power consumption. To illustrate, the

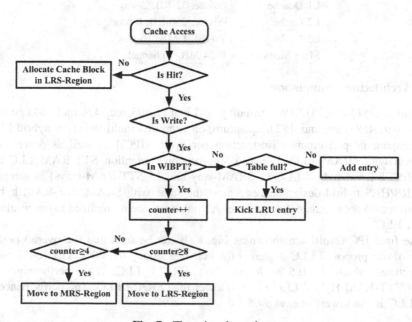

Fig. 7. The migration scheme

overall system performance can be improved significantly, while the total power consumption is much lower than SRAM LLC.

Compared with SRAM/STT-RAM Hybrid LLC, our design can have better overall performance and leakage power with the same migration scheme. The extra power consumption that MRS-Region brings in can be ignored because the number of refresh and reset operations in MRS-Region is limited. However, the refresh circuits of MRS-Region lead to extra hardware overhead.

4 Simulation

4.1 Experimental Setup

We evaluate proposed multi-retention hybrid LLC on GEM5 [9, 10]. GEM5 is an universal architecture simulator. It has a highly configurable simulation framework, including support for various universal ISAs and multiple cache coherence protocols (MESI, MOESI, etc.).

The configuration for GEM5 is shown as Table 2. The private L1 cache is 32 KB, the private L2 cache is 256 KB, and the shared L3 cache is 1 MB. The ISA we use is X86 instruction set.

Table 2. GEM5 configuration

Computer system	Configuration
CPU	X86, O3, 2 GHz
L1 Icache	Private, 32 KB, 2-way
L1 Dcache	Private, 32 KB, 2-way
L2 Cache	Private, 256 KB, 8-way
L3 Cache	Shared, 1 MB, 16-way
Main Memory	1024 MB, 1-channel

4.2 Architectural Simulation

We simulate SPEC CPU2006, including 401.bzip2, 403.gcc, 429.mcf, 445.gobmk, 456.hmmer, 458.sjeng and 462.libquantum, on proposed multi-retention hybrid LLC, and compare its performance [instruction per cycle, (IPC)] as well as power consumption with SRAM LLC. We also simulate high-retention STT-RAM LLC and SRAM/STT-RAM hybrid LLC (1 SRAM-way and 15 STT-RAM-ways) as samples. The LRS/HRS hybrid design shares almost the same with SRAM/STT-RAM hybrid LLC, so we do not simulate it again here. All outcomes are normalized to the results of SRAM LLC.

The final IPC results are shown as Fig. 8. It can be seen that the overall performance of our proposed LLC design is the best one among the three STT-RAM cache architecture, which is 0.6 % lower than SRAM LLC. The performance of SRAM/STT-RAM Hybrid LLC is 2.8 %lower than SRAM LLC. The performance of HRS LLC is the lowest one, at 94.8 %.

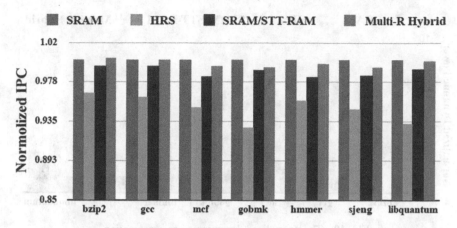

Fig. 8. The normalized IPC results

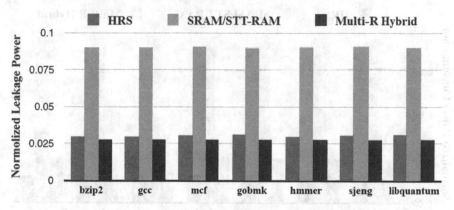

Fig. 9. The normalized leakage power consumption

The leakage power consumption results are shown as Fig. 9. The SRAM/STT-RAM Hybrid LLC has the highest leakage power consumption, at 9.0 %, while that of Multi-R Hybrid LLC is only 2.7 %.

The dynamic power consumption results are shown in Fig. 10. We can find that the average dynamic power consumptions of the three STT-RAM-based LLC designs are all much higher than SRAM. The HRS LLC shares the highest one, at 582 %. The Multi-R Hybrid LLC (at 401 %) is a bit higher than SRAM/STT-RAM Hybrid LLC (at 382 %).

The overall power consumption shown in Fig. 11 is the sum of leakage and dynamic power consumption. The overall power consumption of Multi-R Hybrid LLC is only 3.2 % that of SRAM, which is 52.3 % lower than SRAM/STT-RAM Hybrid LLC (at 9.1 %).

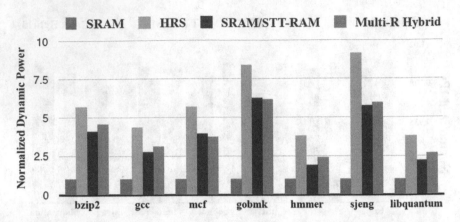

Fig. 10. The normalized dynamic power consumption

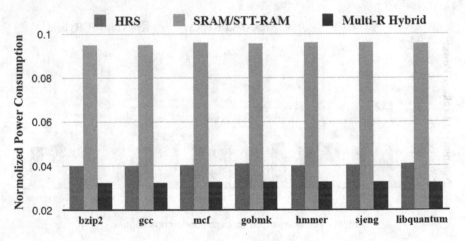

Fig. 11. The normalized overall power consumption

5 Conclusion

In this paper, we propose a novel hybrid last level cache architecture based on three different kinds of STT-RAM cells. Each kind of cells has totally different write performance.

Our simulation results show that the proposed Multi-R Hybrid design has almost the same overall performance with SRAM LLC (at 99.4 %), while having only 3.2 % power consumption. In addition, the total on-chip area of Multi-R Hybrid LLC can be saved by 81.6 % ideally. Compared with SRAM/STT-RAM Hybrid LLC, the Multi-R Hybrid LLC's IPC is increased by 2.2 % while its power consumption is reduced by 70 %.

Acknowledgements. The project is sponsored by National Science and Technology Major Project, "The Processor Design for Super Computer" (2015ZX01028) in China and the Excellent Postgraduate Student Innovation Program (4345133214) of National University of Defense Technology.

References

1. Jog, A., Mishra, A.K., et al.: Cache revive: architecting volatile STT-RAM caches for enhanced performance in CMPs. In: IEEE Design Automation Conference, pp. 243–253 (2012)
2. Sun, Z., Bi, X., et al.: STT-RAM cache hierarchy with multiretention MTJ design. IEEE Trans. Very Large Scale Integr. Syst. **22**(6), 1281–1294 (2014)
3. Smullen, C., Mohan, V., et al.: Relaxing non-volatility for fast and energy-efficient STT-RAM caches. In: IEEE Symposium on High-Performance Computer Architecture, pp. 50–61 (2011)
4. Li, J., Shi, L., et al.: Low-energy volatile STT-RAM cache design using cache-coherence-enabled adaptive refresh. ACM Trans. Des. Autom. Electron. Syst. **19** (1), 1–23 (2013)
5. Zhao, J., Xie, Y.: Optimizing band width and power of graphics memory with hybrid memory technologies and adaptive data migration. In: Proceedings of the International Conference Computer-Aided Design, pp. 81–87 (2012)
6. NVSim. http://www.rioshering.com/nvsimwiki/index.php
7. Li, Q., Li, J., et al.: Compiler-assisted STT-RAM-based hybrid cache for energy efficient embedded systems. IEEE Trans. Very Large Scale Integr. Syst. **22**(8), 1829–1840 (2014)
8. Raychowdhury, A., et al.: Design space and scalability exploration of 1T-1STT MTJ memory arrays in the presence of variability and disturbances. In: IEEE International Electron Devices Meeting, pp. 1–4 (2009)
9. Binkert, N., Beckmann, B., et al.: The gem5 simulator. ACM SIGARCH Comput. Archit. News **39**(2), 1–7 (2011)
10. Gem5. http://gem5.org
11. Sun, Z., Bi, X., Li, H.: Multi retention level STT-RAM cache designs with a dynamic refresh scheme. In: 44th Annual IEEE/ACM International Symposium on Microarchitecture, pp. 329–338 (2011)
12. Ahn, J., Yoo, S., et al.: Write intensity prediction for energy-efficient non-volatile caches. In: IEEE International Symposium on Low Power Electronics and Design, pp. 223–228 (2013)
13. Wang, Z., Jimenez, D., et al.: Adaptive placement and migration policy for an STT-RAM-based hybrid cache. In: 20th IEEE International Symposium on High Performance Computer Architecture, pp. 13–24 (2014)

Overcoming and Analyzing the Bottleneck of Interposer Network in 2.5D NoC Architecture

Chen Li, Zicong Wang, Lu Wang, Sheng Ma, and Yang Guo$^{(\boxtimes)}$

College of Computer, National University of Defense Technology,
Changsha 410073, China
{lichen, wangzicong, luwang, masheng,
guoyang}@nudt.edu.cn

Abstract. As there are still a lot of challenges on 3D stacking technology, 2.5D stacking technology seems to have better application prospects. With the silicon interposer, the 2.5D stacking can improve the bandwidth and capacity of memory. Moreover, the interposer can be explored to make use of unused routing resources and generates an additional network for communication. In this paper, we conclude that using concentrated Mesh as the topology of the interposer network faces the bottleneck of edge portion, while using Double-Butterfly can overcome this bottleneck. We analyze the reasons that pose the bottleneck, compare impacts of different topologies on bottlenecks and propose design goals for the interposer network.

Keywords: 2.5D stacking technology · Topology · Interposer network · Performance bottleneck

1 Introduction

Recently, process scaling becomes increasingly difficult to maintain Moore's law. Some technologies emerge to continuously develop the semiconductor integrated circuit, such as multi-core, multi-threading and virtualization technologies. However, these technologies face the challenges of the Memory Wall [1]. Therefore, the three-dimensional (3D) stacking technology has emerged to deal with these problems, as it offers interconnect length reductions, memory bandwidth improvements, heterogeneous integration and smaller chip sizes.

Although 3D stacking technology has many benefits to the conventional 2D layout, there are several challenges that could potentially hinder its adoption, such as the thermal issue, the absence of EDA tools and testing issues [2]. In comparison, silicon interposer-based stacking, known as "2.5D stacking" [3], is gaining more traction [4]. As shown in Fig. 1, with 2.5D stacking technology multiple silicon dies can be stacked side-by-side on a silicon interposer carrier. The 3D-stacked approach is a revolutionary approach that it needs new co-design and methods for design flow and testing, while the 2.5D-stacked approach is evolutionary [5]. It side-steps many challenges in 3D stacking and has been supported by current design tools.

© Springer Science+Business Media Singapore 2016
J. Wu and L. Li (Eds.): ACA 2016, CCIS 626, pp. 40–47, 2016.
DOI: 10.1007/978-981-10-2209-8_4

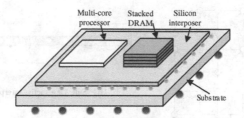

Fig. 1. 2.5D stacking technology

Recent years, some commercial 2.5D-stacked products have already emerged [6, 7]. The most widely application of 2.5D stacking technology is the integration of memory (DRAM) with a multi-core processor. Larger capacities and higher bandwidth for in-package memory can be offered by the silicon interposer, as it has enough areas for much memory to be integrated and many thousands of connections available across the interposer. The interposer memory stacking also requires large bandwidth for processor-to-memory traffic. In order to continuously increase the bandwidth, previous work [8, 9] shows that significant routing resources inside the silicon interposer can be exploited to implement an additional network. We call it interposer network in this paper.

The topology determines the physical layout and connections between nodes and channels in the network. Moreover, the number and locations of TSVs depend on the topology. It is thus clear that the effect of a topology on overall network cost-performance is profound. There are many topologies can be implemented in the interposer network. Owing to the simplicity and scalability, the Mesh has been widely used in CMPs [10, 11]. In order to reduce the μbump area overhead, the concentrated method is used that four nodes in CPU multi-core layer connects one node in the interposer network.

In this paper, we conclude that using the concentrated Mesh as the topology of the interposer network faces the bottleneck of edge portion network, while using Double-Butterfly can overcome this bottleneck. We analyze the reasons that pose the bottleneck, compare impacts of different topologies on bottlenecks and propose design goals for the interposer network.

2 Target System and Evaluation Methodology

In our 2.5D interposer-based system, a 64-core CPU and 4 stacked DRAMs are stacked on a silicon interposer [8]. In order to reduce the cost of NoC in the interposer (TSV/μbump) [12], the topology of our 2.5D NoC architecture is Mesh on the CPU die and Concentrated Mesh or Double-Butterfly on the interposer die shown in Fig. 2. The concentrated method means that each of the 16 interposer nodes connects four nodes on the CPU die. There are totally 8 nodes of memory controllers on left and right sides of the interposer network. Each one connects a nearby interposer node. Figure 2 also shows two types of interposer implementations. In the near term, passive type without active devices in the interposer is a practical way, while active interposer is more likely to be a 3D integrated way. That is to say all logic/gates are placed on the CPU die and

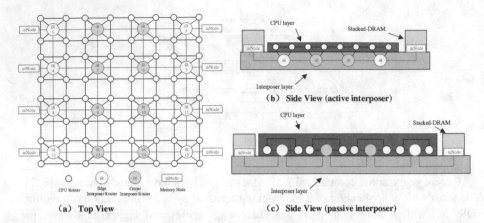

(a) Top View

(b) Side View (active interposer)

(c) Side View (passive interposer)

Fig. 2. Target system (Color figure online)

only metal routing on the passive interposer. Besides, there are two types of traffic, including the core-to-core coherence traffic transferred on the CPU die and the core-to-memory traffic transferred on the interposer die.

We use a cycle accurate interconnection network simulator (Booksim) [13] for the evaluation. We modify Booksim to implement our 2.5D NoC architecture. As the comparison will be focused on the interposer layer topologies, all configurations use an 8 × 8 Mesh for the multi-core die. We evaluated the CMesh, CMesh2 and DB (Double-Butterfly) topologies on interposer layer as shown in Fig. 3. Our NoC designs utilize 4

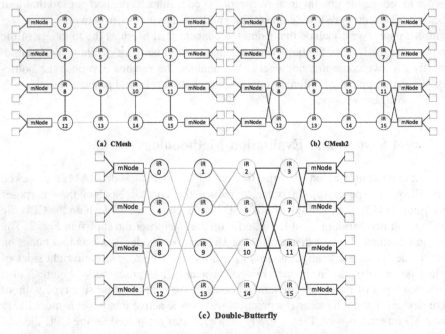

(a) CMesh

(b) CMesh2

(c) Double-Butterfly

Fig. 3. Topologies

cycles router and 2 cycles link for the interposer layer. There are totally four DRAM stacks on the interposer. Each DRAM stack provides four memory channels, for a system-wide total of 16 channels. Each two channels share a memory node. The interposer layer network dimensions include 8 memory nodes that interface with the DRAM stacks memory channels.

3 Bottleneck Description and Analysis

3.1 Bottleneck Description

As the 2.5D NoC architecture leverages Mesh on the CPU die, CMesh on the interposer die and memory nodes are located in two sides, the topology of the whole 2.5D NoC is asymmetric. There are 3 possible performance bottlenecks of the 2.5D NoC architecture, including the upper layer network (Black nodes), the center portion of the lower layer (Yellow nodes) and the edge portion of the lower layer (Red nodes), as shown in Fig. 2(a). Any one of these parts may lead the 2.5D NoC to be saturated, while other partial networks are still working in unsaturated state.

We evaluate average latencies of messages passing through network nodes in these 3 parts. We leverage the baseline design with XY-Z routing, and results are shown in Fig. 4. We find that CPU nodes on the upper layer lead the whole network saturation when memory traffic accounts for 25 % of total traffic. The bisection bandwidth of the upper layer is two times of the bisection bandwidth of the lower layer. Thus, when memory traffic occupancy rate is more than 30 %, the lower layer becomes the bottleneck. Figure 4 shows that edge nodes on the lower layer lead the whole network saturation when the percentage of memory traffic is larger than 30 %. However, when edge interposer nodes are saturated, latencies of messages passing through center interposer nodes are still low. Even when the memory traffic account for larger than 50 % of total traffic, the edge network of the lower layer is still the performance bottleneck.

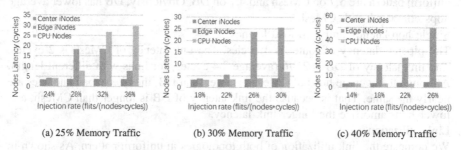

(a) 25% Memory Traffic   (b) 30% Memory Traffic   (c) 40% Memory Traffic

Fig. 4. Performance bottlenecks of CMesh

First, we suppose that the bottleneck of edge portion comes from the small bandwidth of edge portion. We evaluate the CMesh2 with more bandwidth in the edge portion as shown in Fig. 3(b). Compared with CMesh, we add 4 links on each side of edge portion network. However, the evaluation result shows that the edge portions are

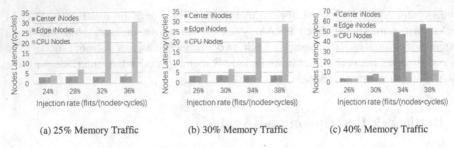

(a) 25% Memory Traffic   (b) 30% Memory Traffic   (c) 40% Memory Traffic

Fig. 5. Performance bottlenecks of double-butterfly

still the performance bottleneck of the whole network. Then, we find that DB overcomes the bottleneck of edge portion. Workloads in interposer network are balanced and uniform as shown in Fig. 5(c). In next subsection, we will compare these two topologies in the interposer network, and then analyze reasons that pose the bottleneck. Based on the analysis, we will propose design goals of the interposer network in 2.5D interposer-based system.

3.2 Impacts of Topologies on Bottlenecks

We compare these two topologies and analyze their features in following points: hops of memory traffic, link utilization, path diversity, bisection bandwidth and Latency-Injection rate. We can find out impacts of topologies on bottlenecks.

1. Hops of memory traffic
   The interposer network mainly used for transferring memory traffic. Those messages are injected from nodes in multi-core layer to memory nodes on edge sides of interposer layer. Thus, the average hops of memory traffic are 6 on CMesh and 4.75 on DB according to our computing. The experimental result of average hops in uniform pattern are 5.7 on CMesh and 4.7 on DB. Obviously, DB has lower average hops compared with CMesh.

2. Single hop latency and zero load latency
   The pipeline latency of router is 4 cycles. The link latency of CMesh is 2 cycles. The link latency of DB is 2/4/6 (average 3.4 cycles) for links with different length. Although the average hops of CMesh is larger than DB, their zero load latencies are nearly the same. That is because the link latency of DB is longer than CMesh, and lower hops amortize the longer link latency.

3. Link utilization
   We compare the link utilization of both topologies in uniform pattern. As shown in Fig. 3(a), considering different portions of links for CMesh, the utilization ratio of blue links is 25 %, while the yellow links is 37.5 % and the green links is 50 %. The other side is symmetrical with this side.
   The link utilization of DB is similar to CMesh. For DB, the utilization ratio of blue links and green links are the same with CMesh. The utilization of yellow links is 43.75 %. The 6.25 % more utilization comes from the case that message from IR0

or IR4 need to be transferred to the lower half of the memory channels on the left side. In this case, routes must divert to the previous stage. We can find that the link utilization of both topologies are similar and it has little impact on the bottleneck.

4. Path diversity

The XY-Z routing is leveraged in CMesh. As the deterministic routing is leveraged, there is no path diversity in CMesh. The path diversity of DB is a little complex. The path diversity of memory traffic which need to be transferred through blue links are 2, while the path diversity is 1 in other situation.

In some traffic patterns, such as hotspot, no path diversity may make some links fall into high traffic pressure. If packets are from yellow nodes to the left memory nodes in DB as shown in Fig. 3(c), it can choose a path with low workload to the destination node. Thus congestion can be alleviated.

5. Bisection bandwidth

For CMesh, the ratio of bisection bandwidth between the upper layer and the lower layer is 2:1 (8:4). For DB, the ratio of bisection bandwidth between the upper layer and the lower layer is 1:1. Only nodes at edge sides can consume packets, while center nodes are just used as switch.

It answers the reason why the lower layer of network becomes the bottleneck when the percentage of memory traffic is larger than 30 % for CMesh and 40 % for DB.

6. Latency-Injection rate

Figure 6 shows the performance comparison between CMesh, DB and CMesh2 in uniform traffic pattern. As shown in Fig. 6(a), when the memory traffic makes up 25 % of the total traffic, their performance are nearly the same. This is because the saturation of all three topologies are caused by the saturation of CPU layer network in 25 % memory traffic.

When the memory traffic accounts for 50 % of the total traffic, the performance of CMesh and CMesh2 are nearly the same, while the average performance gain of DB over CMesh is 54.5 %. Considering the performance bottleneck in high memory traffic, we can find that the performance gain of DB comes from overcoming the bottleneck of the edge portion network. A uniform and balanced network performs high efficiently. CMesh2 does not overcome the bottleneck of edge network. It shows that adding bandwidth in edge side is useless.

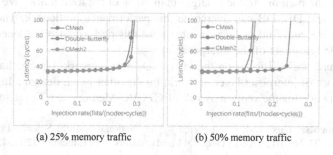

(a) 25% memory traffic   (b) 50% memory traffic

Fig. 6. Performance comparison

3.3 Summary and Design Goals of Interposer Network

Based on the comparison between CMesh and DB, we know that the link utilization of them are similar, link utilization is not the key factor of the performance bottleneck. Both single hop latency and zero load latency also have little impact on the bottleneck. In fact, the interposer network is similar to GPGPU network that the performance is more sensitive to interconnect bisection bandwidth rather than latency [14, 15]. On the contrary, the bisection bandwidth and average hops pose strong impact on the bottleneck. Larger bisection bandwidth makes larger throughput. Lower average hops reduce contention of the interposer network. Furthermore, compared with CMesh, DB improves the path diversity giving more routing choices to messages when being transferred. It leads the load to be balanced. When the workload increases in the interposer network, the high throughput highlights the advantage of lower contention and high bandwidth.

Therefore, we can conclude some design goals of the interposer network based on topologies analysis. First, in order to reduce the contention, we should try best to reduce average hops between the source and destination nodes. Leveraging long metal wires is a suitable way in interposer layer network, due to its abundant metal routing resource. Second, higher throughput needs higher bisection bandwidth. We should improve the bisection bandwidth through making connections between nodes as many as possible. Third, the interposer network should provide the path diversity as much as possible. As all nodes except memory nodes in the interposer network are switches, they are just used for transferring packets and cannot absorb packets. Thus, deterministic routing algorithms are not as suitable as minimal adaptive routing algorithms which provide more path diversity. It can balance the workload on the interposer network.

4 Conclusion

The 2.5D stacking technology leverages an interposer to stack chips and DRAMs. Making use of the metal layer on the interposer provides fascinating opportunities to explore new features on 2.5D NoC architecture. In this paper, first we find that the edge portion of interposer network in CMesh always lead the saturation of the whole 2.5D network when the memory traffic is larger than 30 % of the total traffic. We compare it with CMesh2 and DB. DB can overcome this performance bottleneck. Then we analyze their features and find out reasons that pose this performance bottleneck. At last, we propose design goals of the interposer network.

In the future, we will focus on the interposer layer network. On one hand, exploit the design space of interposer layer network; on the other hand, design a high efficient interposer network for the reply network of GPGPU-Memory 2.5D system.

Acknowledgements. This work is supported by the National Natural Science Foundation of China (No.6133007, No. 61303065), Doctoral Fund of Ministry of Education (20134307120028).

References

1. Wulf, W.A., McKee, S.A.: Hitting the memory wall: implications of the obvious. ACM SIGARCH Comput. Archit. News **23**(1), 20–24 (1995)
2. Xie, J., Zhao, J., Dong, X., Xie, Y.: Architectural benefits and design challenges for three-dimensional integrated circuits. In: 2010 IEEE Asia Pacific Conference on Circuits and Systems (APCCAS), pp. 540–543, December 2010
3. Deng, Y., Maly, W.P.: Interconnect characteristics of 2.5-d system integration scheme. In: Proceedings of the 2001 International Symposium on Physical design, pp. 171–175. ACM (2001)
4. Loh, G.H., Jerger, N.E., Kannan, A., Eckert, Y.: Interconnect memory challenges for multi-chip, silicon interposer systems. In: Proceedings of the 2015 International Symposium on Memory Systems, pp. 3–10. ACM (2015)
5. Bolsens, I., Xilinx, C.: 2.5D ICs: Just a stepping stone or a long term alternative to 3d? In: Keynote Talk at 3-D Architectures for Semiconductor Integration and Packaging Conference (2011)
6. AMD: Amd radeon r9 fury x graphics card (2015). http://support.amd.com/documents
7. Saban, K.: Xilinx stacked silicon interconnect technology delivers breakthrough FPGA capacity, bandwidth, and power efficiency. Xilinx White paper: Vertex-7 FPGAs (2011)
8. Jerger, N.E., Kannan, A., Li, Z., Loh, G.H.: Noc architectures for silicon interposer systems: Why pay for more wires when you can get them (from your interposer) for free? In: 2014 47th Annual IEEE/ACM International Symposium on Microarchitecture (MICRO), pp. 458–470. IEEE (2014)
9. Kannan, A., Jerger, N.E., Loh, G.H.: Enabling interposer-based disintegration of multi-core processors. In: Proceedings of the 48th International Symposium on Microarchitecture, pp. 546–558. ACM (2015)
10. Howard, J., Dighe, S., Hoskote, Y., et al.: A 48-core IA-32 message-passing processor with DVFS in 45 nm CMOS. In: 2010 IEEE International Solid-State Circuits Conference Digest of Technical Papers (ISSCC), pp. 108–109. IEEE (2010)
11. Wentzlaff, D., Griffin, P., Hoffmann, H., et al.: On-chip interconnection architecture of the tile processor. IEEE Micro **5**, 15–31 (2007)
12. Liu, C., Zhang, L., Han, Y., Li, X.: Vertical interconnects squeezing in symmetric 3d mesh network-on-chip. In: Proceedings of the 16th Asia and South Pacific Design Automation Conference, pp. 357–362. IEEE Press (2011)
13. Jiang, N., Becker, D.U., Michelogiannakis, G., Balfour, J., Towles, B., Shaw, D.E., Kim, J., Dally, W.J.: A detailed and flexible cycle-accurate network-on-chip simulator. In: 2013 IEEE International Symposium on Performance Analysis of Systems and Software (ISPASS), pp. 86–96. IEEE (2013)
14. Bakhoda, A., Kim, J., Aamodt, T.M.: Throughput-effective on-chip networks for manycore accelerators. In: Proceedings of the 2010 43rd Annual IEEE/ACM International Symposium on Microarchitecture, pp. 421–432. IEEE Computer Society (2010)
15. Bakhoda, A., Yuan, G.L., Fung, W.W., Wong, H., Aamodt, T.M.: Analyzing CUDA workloads using a detailed GPU simulator. In: Proceedings of the International Symposium on Performance Analysis of Systems and Software, April 2009

Micro-architectural Features
for Malware Detection

Huicheng Peng, Jizeng Wei$^{(\boxtimes)}$, and Wei Guo

Tianjin Advanced Network Key Lab, School of Computer Science and Technology,
Tianjin University, Yaguan Road. 135, Tianjin, China
{penghuicheng,weijizeng,weiguo}@tju.edu.cn

Abstract. As the variety and complexity of attacks continue to increase,
software-based malware detection can impose significant performance
overhead. Recent works have demonstrated the feasibility of malware detection using hardware performance counters. Therefore, equipping a malware detector to collect and analyze micro-architecture
features of CPUs to recognize malware at running time has become a
promising method. In comparison to the software-based malware detection, hardware-based malware detection not only reduces the cost of
system performance, but also possesses better detection capacity. However, hundreds of micro-architecture events can be monitored by hardware performance counters (HPCs) which are widely available in
prevailing CPUs, such as Intel, ARM and so on. In this paper, we take
Intel ivy bridge i3 processor as an example and examine most of these
micro-architectural features. Instead of relying on experience, the Lasso
algorithm is employed to reduce the dimensionality of feature vector to
6 elements. Furthermore, 4 classification methods based on supervised
learning are applied for the selected features. We improve the classification accuracy rate of 15 % on average. The results show that the micro-
architectural features of this paper can reveal the behaviors of malware
better.

Keywords: Malware detection · Performance counters · Micro-
architectural features

1 Introduction

Computer systems are becoming pervasive and improve the way of personal life
such as shopping, communication and work, not only promoting economic development but also bringing more threats. Malware, short for malicious software,
is created to damage or does other unwanted actions on a computer system. In
most cases, malware is designed because of the motivations of financial gains
[3]. Computer systems are continually under threat of malware. McAfee Labs
2016 Threats Predictions shows the cyber warfare capabilities of nation-states
will continue to grow in scope and sophistication. Cold and hot offensive cyber
attacks will affect political relationships [6].

© Springer Science+Business Media Singapore 2016
J. Wu and L. Li (Eds.): ACA 2016, CCIS 626, pp. 48–60, 2016.
DOI: 10.1007/978-981-10-2209-8_5

With the diversification of attack methods in malware, in response, the traditional software-based malware detection tools have grown in complexity. Especially, various of machine learning methods have been adopted to detect malicious programs on abundant collected software behavior features including system call, file using, memory footprint and et al. [4,5]. However, these software features are still difficult to directly reveal the characteristics of malware. Thus, some deliberate attackers can bypass the protection of software-based detection tools. And, protecting the system in real time is also difficult because of complicated detect/classification algorithms.

Demme et al. [1] recently showed that malware can be successfully detected with micro-architectural features, also called hardware events, obtained from hardware performance counters (HPCs) which are specialized registers implemented in modern processors. The cost of micro-architectural feature acquisition is much less than the software feature and the classification model based on these features has a very good detection rate. They demonstrated the feasibility of hardware detection methods and highlight the increased security from leveraging hardware. On the basis of this study, Meltem et al. [2] proposed malware-aware processors augmented with an online hardware-based detector. They explored hardware implementations and showed that this detector can effectively classify malware. However, Demme et al. provided little information about the concrete micro-architectural features and Meltem et al. paid more attention on features related to memory address and instructions rather than micro-architectural features.

Previous works put forward the use of instruction set architecture features and some micro-architectural features to carry out malicious software detection. But, they just selected micro-architectural features based on personal experiences. Hence, it is difficult to ascertain that if these features can exactly describe the characteristics of malware. The main contributions of this paper are as follows:

(1) We only use micro-architectural features, such as branch instructions references, D-TLB load misses, I-TLB misses and cache references, to build the detection model.
(2) In order to raise the accuracy and interpretability of classification models, we use the Lasso (Least Absolute Shrinkage and Selection Operator) method [7] to reduce the dimension of feature vectors.
(3) The efficiency of selected micro-architectural features are verified by four kinds of supervised machine learning algorithms and we improve the classification accuracy rate of 15 % on average.

The rest of the paper is organized as follows. We provide the background of malware types, attack methods, hardware performance counters and micro-architectural features of the Intel ivy bridge processor in Sect. 2. The experimental method and environment are presented in Sect. 3. We describe the Lasso-based feature selection in Sect. 4, and analyze the experimental results of various classification models in Sect. 5. We conclude this paper in Sect. 6.

2 Background

2.1 Malware

Malware can be broadly classified into the following types.

Viruses. A computer virus is a small program or piece of code that runs on our computer without our knowing and has ability to replicate itself. Viruses spread on their own by attaching their code to other programs, or transmitting itself across networks and bypassing security systems. They often perform harmful activity on infected computers, such as stealing hard disk space or CPU time, corrupting data and make the computer stop working.

Worms. A worm is a special type of virus that can replicate itself and spreads to other PCs, but cannot attach itself to other programs. They may spread using one or more of the following methods: email programs, instant messaging programs, file-sharing programs, social networking sites, network shares, removable drives and software vulnerabilities. Worms almost always cause some damage to the network by consuming bandwidth, but the virus always targeted computer corrupt or modify files.

Trojans. A Trojan is a program that attempts to look innocent, but in fact it is a malicious application. Different from viruses or worms, a trojan doesn't spread by itself. Instead, it tries to convince us to download and install them. Once installed, it can download more malware, or allow hackers to access our computers.

Adware. Adware refers to a computer program with advertisement, advertising as a profitable source software. Such software is often forced to install and can not be uninstalled, which collecting user information for profiting in the background, threatening user's privacy, frequent pop-up advertisement, consuming system resources, making the system run slower and so on.

Spyware. Spyware is a type of software that is installed on a computer and collects personal information, such as browsing history, email address, credit card number and key pressed by the user without the user's knowledge. These information will be illegally used by the attacker.

Botnet. A botnet is an interconnected network of computers infected with malware and controlled by a third party. Each computer in the botnet is called a bot, which is a type of malware that allows an attacker to take control over an affected computer. They're typically used to send spam emails, transmit viruses and engage in other acts of cybercrime.

2.2 Hardware Performance Counters

Hardware performance counters are a set of specialized registers about four to six in modern processor that provide detailed information about hardware and software events, such as cache misses, D-TLB load misses, I-TLB misses, branch instructions reference and so on. They were originally designed for the purpose of hardware verification and debugging, but nowadays, they can be used for CPU scheduling [8], integrity checking [9], performance monitoring [10], and workload pattern identification [11]. The function of those registers is to monitor and measure the processor's performance events. The information obtained from these counters can be used for tuning system and compiler performance.

Most modern processors provide a general concept of hardware performance counters and it has different specific names on different processors. Performance monitoring unit (PMU) was introduced in the Pentium processor with a set of model-specific performance-monitoring counters MSRs [12]. The performance monitoring mechanisms and performance events defined for the Pentium, P6 family, Pentium 4 and Intel Xeon processor are not architectural. They are all model specific. There are two categories of performance events in Intel processor. One is a set of architectural performance events and the other is a set of non-architectural performance events. The visible behavior of architectural performance events is consistent across processor implementations. But, the available events are very few only seven. In contrast, there are a large of non-architectural performance events that can be measured from four configurable performance counters. These events vary from on processor model to another and associated with the micro-architecture implement. Hence, we can use these rich micro-architectural information on mining useful features and train the classification models.

3   Experimental Setup

3.1   Date Set and Data Collection

In this study, we collect a large number of malware programs from the VirusSign website [13]. Using the VirusTotal malware classification tools [14], we identified different types and families of these malware programs. Note that some malware programs that can cause system crashes are removed from the data set. For sampling normal programs, SPEC2006 benchmarks are adopted. Finally, we analyze 253 malware programs and 180 normal programs in our experiments.

Previous experiments are carried out on a virtual machine environment. In this paper, we use the VTune tools [15] to collect data from the real machine, installed with 32-bit Windows 7 operating system and running an Intel Core i3-3220 (3.30GHz) CPU with 4 GB memory. We disabled the firewall and Windows security services to support malware operations. VTune provides a rich set of CPU and GPU performance events. Specific hardware event types that we take into consideration are listed in Table 1. The micro-architectural features are collected at a sampling rate of 1000 K instructions [16].

3.2   Machine Learning Method

There are a mass of available classifiers. In this paper, we use four different classification methods: logistic regression, decision tree, support vector machines and artificial neural networks.

Table 1. Types of hardware events.

Event type	Description
ARITH	Arithmetic operations
BR_INST	Branch instructions references
BR_MISP	Mispredicted branch instructions
DTLB_LOAD_MISSES	D-TLB load misses references
DTLB_STORE_MISSES	D-TLB store misses references
ITLB_MISSES	I-TLB misses references
LOAD	Load instructions
STORE	Store instructions
ICACHE	Instruction cache references
L2_LINES	L2 cache lines references
LLC	Last level cache references

(1) Logistic regression, a simple linear classification algorithm, is useful because it can take an input with any value from negative to positive infinity, whereas the output always takes values between zero and one and to convert this likelihood to a binary decision. The advantage of logistic regression is low computational cost and easy to implement in hardware.

(2) Decision tree uses a treelike model of decisions and their possible consequences. The final result is a tree with decision nodes and leaf nodes. A decision node has two or more branches and leaf node represents a classification or decision. The algorithm has low computing cost with good classifying accuracy, and the output result is easy to understand.

(3) Support vector machines are supervised learning models with associated learning algorithms that analyze data used for classification. A support vector machine performs classification by finding the hyperplane that maximizes the margin between the two classes. The vectors that define the hyperplane are the support vectors.

(4) Artificial neural networks are relatively crude electronic networks of neurons based on the neural structure of the brain. They process records one at a time, and learn by comparing their classification of the record with the known actual classification of the record. Artificial neural networks are advancing machine learning algorithms and their classification performance is better, but, they have higher computational complexity.

Construction and implementation of classifiers need to go through four steps. Firstly, all samples will be divided into two parts: training and testing data. And the ratio of train-test set is 70 %–30 %. Before model training, we need to process the data to optimize the input data. For support vector machines, they are better to use standardized data to build models. For neural networks, data normalization is a kind of processing method of data before building the neural network model. Secondly, basing on the training data, we respectively train four classification models by four machine learning algorithms. Thirdly, basing on these classification models, we use the testing data to make predictions. Finally, according the predictions, we calculate the necessary evaluation index and evaluate the performance of classification models.

4 Lasso-Based Feature Selection

4.1 Lasso Algorithm

The lasso is a shrinkage method, which shrinks the regression coefficients by imposing a penalty on their size [7]. It is introduced to improve the prediction accuracy and interpretability of regression models by altering the model fitting process. The lasso select only a subset of the provided variables for use in the final model rather than using all of them. The lasso estimate is defined by

$$\hat{\beta}^{\text{lasso}} = \operatorname*{argmin}_{\beta} \sum_{i=1}^{N}\left(y_i - \beta_0 - \sum_{j=1}^{P} x_{ij}\beta_j\right)^2 \text{ subject to } \sum_{j=1}^{P}|\beta_j| \leqslant t. \quad (1)$$

We can re-parameterize the constant β_0 by standardizing the predictors; the solution for $\hat{\beta}_0$ is $\bar{y}$, and thereafter we fit a model without an intercept. The x_{ij} is necessary input data, which are the collected micro-architectural features. Because of the nature of the constraint, making t sufficiently small will cause some of the coefficients to be exactly zero. Thus the lasso does a kind of continuous subset selection. If t is chosen larger than $t_0 = \sum_1^p |\hat{\beta}_j|$, then the lasso estimates are the $\hat{\beta}_j$'s. On the other hand, for $t = \frac{t_0}{2}$ say, then the least squares coefficients are shrunk by about 50 % on average.

We can also convert the lasso problem into the equivalent *Lagrangian form*

$$\hat{\beta}^{\text{lasso}} = \operatorname*{argmin}_{\beta}\left\{\frac{1}{2}\sum_{i=1}^{N}(y_i - \beta_0 - \sum_{j=1}^{P} x_{ij}\beta_j)^2 + \lambda\sum_{j=1}^{P}|\beta_j|\right\}, \quad (2)$$

which makes explicit shrinkage. Here $\lambda \geqslant 0$ is a complexity parameter that controls the amount of shrinkage: the larger the value of λ, the greater the amount of shrinkage. There is a one-to-one correspondence between the parameters t in (1) and λ in (2). Computing the lasso solution is a quadratic programming problem, although efficient algorithms are available for computing the entire path of solutions as λ is varied [21].

4.2 Feature Selection

When we use the data to train the classifier model, it is important to achieve a balance between over fitting and fitting. One way to prevent over fitting is to constrain the complexity of the model. Feature selection has become the focus

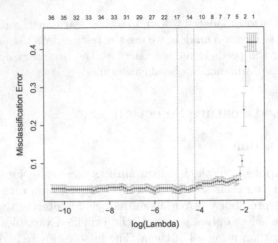

Fig. 1. Plot for Lasso Algorithm.

of much research in areas of application for which datasets with much more variables are available [17].

To pick out more representative micro-architectural features for classification, the Lasso algorithm is utilized to complete feature selection in this paper. The Intel processor permits hundreds of events to be monitored using hardware performance counters. According to previous researches in the literatures, we examine 65 micro-architectural features [18,19] and collect every event at the rate of 1000 K instructions by using VTune tools. We implement Lasso feature selection by using package of glmnet in R language [20]. Based on these configurations, we plot the result of feature selection in Fig. 1.

The horizontal axis is the logarithm of the lambda value, which is used to control the severity of the punishment. If it is set too large, the final model parameters will tend to zero. In contrast, if its value is too small, the effect of reducing the dimension will not be good. The vertical axis presents the misclassification error. The number of features is represented by the numbers above the curve. The value of each lambda is corresponding to the number of features and the error rate of classification. Each red dot in the graph shows the number of features corresponding to different lambda and the error rate of classification. For example, when the red dot represents that the logarithm of the lambda values is −2, we will get 3 features with 24 % misclassification error. From the Fig. 1 we can see that the best value of lambda is the lowest point in the red curve, i.e., the number of features is 17. Because the number of registers for collecting the micro-architectural features are very few, then picked out micro-architectural features should be down to a reasonable number if possible, as well as not increasing the classification errors. As a result, six features are enough to achieve a good classification and the misclassification error is still low.

These six events are listed in Table 2. The first one is speculative and retired branches and the second one is speculative and retired direct near calls.

Table 2. Selected hardware events marking malware.

Event number	Description
Event1[a]	Speculative and retired branches
Event2[b]	Speculative and retired direct near calls
Event3[c]	Load operations that miss the first DTLB level, but hit the second and do not cause a page walk
Event4[d]	Misses in all ITLB levels that cause completed page walk
Event5[e]	Instruction cache and victim cache misses
Event6[f]	L2 cache lines in E state filling L2

[a] Event1 is BR_INST_EXEC.ALL_BRANCHES.
[b] Event2 is BR_INST_EXEC.TAKEN_DIRECT_NEAR_CALL.
[c] Event3 is DTLB_LOAD_MISSES.STLB_HIT.
[d] Event4 is ITLB_MISSES.WALK_COMPLETED.
[e] Event5 is ICACHE.MISSES.
[f] Event6 is L2_LINES_IN.E.

Both of these two events are related to branch instructions. The other four events are related to memory access. DTLB_LOAD_MISSES.STLB_HIT is loading operations that missing the first D-TLB level, but hitting the second and not causing a page walk. This event is relevant only in case of multiple TLB levels. ITLB_MISSES.WALK_COMPLETED is missing in all I-TLB level that cause completed page walk. ICACHE.MISSES is instruction cache, streaming buffer and victim cache misses. L2_LINES_IN.E counts the number of L2 cache lines in the exclusive state. The execution paths of malicious software, in order to achieve the purpose of the attack, often occur very weird behaviors different from the normal program. Thus, the branch prediction unit will produce different judgments. To disguise malware as some legitimate software, attackers might use a file name of a legitimate Windows file or even inject code into a running legitimate process. No matter what they do, code has to run, which means it has to be in memory. Hence, malware program will cause different ways of memory access. Intel mainstream series processors, such as i3, i5 and i7, all have these six events. Therefore, our method can be widely applied to modern processors.

5 Experimental Results and Analysis

5.1 Experimental Results

According to the above analysis, we find that there are two types of micro-architectural feature that can be used to distinguish malware from normal programs. One is branch prediction relevant and the other is memory access relevant. Firstly, we respectively build classification models for these two types of hardware events by four classification algorithms. There are logistic regression, decision tree, support vector machines and artificial neural networks.

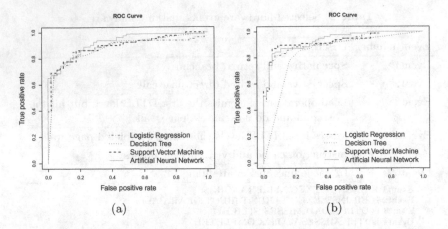

Fig. 2. ROC plots for branch prediction and memory access events.

The receiver operating characteristic (ROC) curve based on branch events is shown in Fig. 2(a) and the ROC curve based on memory access events is shown in Fig. 2(b). ROC curve is often used to evaluate the merits of a two value classifier. As shown in the Fig. 2, the horizontal axis is FP (false positive) rate and the vertical axis is TP (true positive) rate. In our experiment, FP rate is defined as Eq. 3,

$$(FPrate = \frac{FP}{FP+TN}),\tag{3}$$

where FP is an error classification for malicious software and TN is the true classification for the normal program. TP rate is defined as Eq. 4,

$$(TPrate = \frac{TP}{TP+FN}),\tag{4}$$

where TP is the correct classification for malicious software and FN is an error classification for the normal program. The upper left corner of an ROC graph (0,1) provides the best classification performance with no false positives and 100 % true positive rate. When the ROC curve is closer to the upper left corner, the better performance of the classifier is achieved.

The four classifiers of branch prediction events can correctly identify about 80 % of malware with about 23 % normal programs being classified as malware by mistake on average. The four classifiers of memory access events can correctly identify about 85 % of malware with only 10 % normal programs being classified as malware on average. It follows that the classifiers of memory access are better than branch prediction to recognize malware. Hence, we can infer that the ways of memory access of malware are very different from the normal programs. By theoretical analysis and experiments, we have proved the conclusions in previous works [2,16]. Further analysis of the results shows that malware attacks will change program flow and influence the way of memory access.

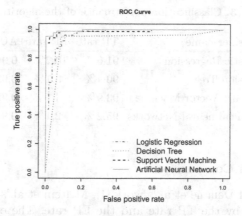

Fig. 3. ROC plot for combining features models.

Then, we combine these two types of events to build the classification models. The corresponding ROC curve of these models is depicted in Fig. 3. As expected, if we allow some false positives, classifiers can find more malicious software. The four classifiers can correctly identify about 93.8 % of malware with only 6.1 % normal programs being classified as malware on average. The results show that the collecting hardware events can be used to detect malicious software with high accuracy. As we can see in the Fig. 3, the classifiers of artificial neural networks and support vector machine have better classification ability than two other models. If we take into account the computational complexity, the classification efficiency of logistic regression and decision tree are also very good.

5.2 Analysis and Evaluation

In order to better evaluate the performance of the four classification models, we calculate the value of TP rate, FP rate and AUC (Area under the ROC curve), which are listed in Table 3. Taken the artificial neural network as an example, the TP rate represents that 95.2 % real malware are successfully picked up and the FP rate shows that only 2.1 % normal programs are classified as malware by mistake. The TP rate of logistic regression also reaches up to 91.6 %, but its FP rate is relatively high (about 10.2 %), which is the highest in the four classification models.

The reason of using AUC value as the evaluation criteria is that most of the time ROC curve does not clearly indicate that the effect of which classifier is better. But as a numerical value, the corresponding AUC is bigger classifier is better. From the last column of the table, we can see that the classification performance of artificial neural networks is the best. From TP rate, FP rate and the ROC curve, we cannot judge which is better between logistic regression and decision tree. However, according the AUC, we can confirm that the model of logistic regression is better.

Table 3. Classification performance of the algorithms.

Classifier name	TP rate	FP rate	AUC
Logistic Regression	91.6%	10.2%	0.968
Decision Tree	90.4%	8.1%	0.920
Support Vector Machine	93.9%	4.1%	0.988
Artificial neural Networks	95.2%	2.1%	0.995

5.3 Performance Comparison

The performances of Demme et al.'s work [1], Meltem et al.'s work [2], and our work are evaluated by the TP rate and the FP rate. The overall comparison results of the approaches are shown in Table 4. Our logistic regression classifier has a much higher TP rate than Demme et al.'s work and Meltem et al.'s at the same FP rate. The TP rate of our artificial neural networks is higher than the Meltem et al.'s, while the FP rate is much lower than the Meltem et al.'s. There are mainly two reasons why we greatly improve the performance of classification. First, we only use micro-architecture features, so it is more essential to reflect the behavior of malicious software on hardware level. Second, the micro-architecture features that lasso algorithm selects are better to distinguish between malicious software and normal software. The comparison results imply that our classifiers can identify more malware programs. In other words, they are also possible to identify the malicious software that other classifiers can not detect.

Finally, we have drawn the conclusion that the behavior of malware at micro-architectural level has a strong relativity with branch instructions and memory access and this may help us to directly detect malicious software at the hardware level. The performance of the classification model trained by micro-architectural features which is collected at low overhead is effective.

Table 4. Performance comparison of the approaches.

Works	Algorithms	TP rate	FP rate
Demme et al.	Decision Tree	82.3%	10%
	KNN	73.3%	10%
	Random Forest	68.9%	10%
Meltem et al.	Logistic Regression	70%	10%
	Artificial Neural Networks	88%	20%
Our work	Logistic Regression	91.6%	10.2%
	Decision Tree	90.4%	8.1%
	Support Vector Machine	93.9%	4.1%
	Artificial Neural Networks	95.2%	2.1%

6   Conclusion

A promising approach to detect malicious software is to build malware detectors in hardware. In this paper, we want to make sure that some micro-architectural performance events collected by hardware performance counters can be used to detect malicious software with low overhead. We use a statistical approach to identify the 6 most easily distinguishable micro-architectural features for normal programs and malicious software. These features can be divided into two categories, one of which is related to branch instructions, and the other is related to memory read and write especially D-TLB, I-TLB and cache relevant. We demonstrate that there is a difference between malware and normal program in the relevant behavior of D-TLB, I-TLB, cache and branch prediction. In conclusion, our experimental results show that it can train a very good classification model by only using the hardware events to detect the malware. The classifier of artificial neural networks can detect malware with a high detection rate 95.2 % and an acceptable false positive rate of 2.1 %.

Acknowledgment. This work is supported by the Natural Science Foundation of China (No. 61402321) and the Natural Science Foundation of Tianjin (No. 15JCQNJC00100).

References

1. Demme, J., Maycock, M., Schmitz, J., et al.: On the feasibility of online malware detection with performance counters. ACM SIGARCH Comput. Archit. News **41**(3), 559–570 (2013)
2. Ozsoy, M., Donovick, C., Gorelik, I., et al.: Malware-aware processors: a framework for efficient online malware detection. In: 2015 IEEE 21st International Symposium on High Performance Computer Architecture, pp. 651–661 (2015)
3. Stone-Gross, B., Abman, R., Kemmerer, R., Kruegel, C., Steigerwald, D., Vigna, G.: The underground economy of fake antivirus software. In: Schneier, B. (ed.) Economics of Information Security and Privacy III, pp. 55–78. Springer, New York (2013)
4. Lanzi, A., Balzarotti, D., Kruegel, C., Christodorescu, M., Kirda, E.: Accessminer: using system-centric models for malware protection. In: Proceeding of the 17th ACM Conference on Computer and Communications Security, pp. 399–412 (2010)
5. Christodorescu, M., Jha, S., Kruegel, C.: Mining specifications of malicious behavior. In: Proceedings of the 6th Joint Meeting of the European Software Engineering Conference and the ACM SIGSOFT Symposium on the Foundations of Software Engineering, ESEC-FSE 07, p. 514 (2007)
6. McAfee Labs Report 2016 Threats Predictions. http://www.mcafee.com/us/resources/reports/rp-threats-predictions-2016.pdf
7. Tibshirani, R.: Regression shrinkage and selection via the lasso. J. Roy. Stat. Soc.: Ser. B (Methodol.) **58**, 267–288 (1996)
8. Bulpin, J.R., Pratt, I.: Hyper-threading aware process scheduling heuristics. In: USENIX Annual Technical Conference, General Track, pp. 399–402 (2005)
9. Malone, C., Zahran, M., Karri, R.: Are hardware performance counters a cost effective way for integrity checking of programs. In: Proceedings of the Sixth ACM Workshop on Scalable Trusted Computing, pp. 71–76. ACM (2011)

10. Contreras, G., Martonosi, M.: Power prediction for intel XScale processors using performance monitoring unit events. In: Proceedings of the 2005 International Symposium on Low Power Electronics and Design, ISLPED 2005, pp. 221–226. IEEE (2005)
11. Cohen, I., Chase, J.S., Goldszmidt, M., et al.: Correlating instrumentation data to system states: a building block for automated diagnosis and control. In: OSDI, p. 16 (2004)
12. Guide, P.: Intel 64 and IA-32 Architectures Software Developers Manual. Volume 3B: System programming Guide, Part 2. Chaps. 18,19 (2011)
13. VirusSign. http://www.virussign.com/index.html
14. VirusTotal. https://www.virustotal.com/
15. Intel   VTune   Amplifier   2016.   https://software.intel.com/en-us/intel-vtune-amplifier-xe
16. Tang, A., Sethumadhavan, S., Stolfo, S.J.: Unsupervised anomaly-based malware detection using hardware features. In: Stavrou, A., Bos, H., Portokalidis, G. (eds.) RAID 2014. LNCS, vol. 8688, pp. 109–129. Springer, Heidelberg (2014)
17. Guyon, I., Elisseeff, A.: An introduction to variable and feature selection. J. Mach. Learn. Res. **3**, 1157–1182 (2003)
18. Shen, K., Zhong, M., Dwarkadas, S., et al.: Hardware counter driven on-the-fly request signatures. ACM SIGARCH Comput. Archit. News **36**(1), 189–200 (2008)
19. Hoste, K., Eeckhout, L.: Comparing benchmarks using key microarchitecture-independent characteristics. In: 2006 IEEE International Symposium on Workload Characterization, pp. 83–92. IEEE (2006)
20. Ihaka, R., Gentleman, R.: R: a language for data analysis and graphics. J. Comput. Graph. Stat. **5**(3), 299–314 (1996)
21. Friedman, J., Hastie, T., Tibshirani, R.: The Elements of Statistical Learning. Springer Series in Statistics. Springer, New York (2001)

An Energy Efficient Algorithm for Virtual Machine Allocation in Cloud Datacenters

Ahmad Ali, Li Lu, Yanmin Zhu$^{(\boxtimes)}$, and Jiadi Yu

Department of Computer Science and Engineering,
Shanghai Jiao Tong University, Shanghai, China
{ahmadali,luli_jtu,yzhu,jiadiyu}@sjtu.edu.cn

Abstract. In cloud datacenters, virtual machine (VM) allocation in a power efficient way remains a critical research problem. There are a number of algorithms for allocating the workload among different machines. However, existing works do not consider more than one energy efficient host, thus they are not efficient for large scale cloud datacenters. In this paper, we propose a VM allocation algorithm to achieve higher energy efficiency in large scale cloud datacenters. Simulation result shows that, compared with BRS, RR and MPD algorithms, our algorithms can achieve 23 %, 23 % and 9 % more power efficiency in large scale cloud environment.

Keywords: Cloud computing · Dynamic Voltage and Frequency Scaling (DVFS) · Data centers · Bin packing

1 Introduction

Cloud computing [1] is a popular computing service model. Users can easily access and manage a pool of computing resources like storage, networks, servers and other client applications in the cloud. This on-demand technology service helps user speedily release with trivial management efforts [2]. Clouds try to decrease the price of software and hardware management.

Managing infrastructures cost-efficiently [3] is one of the important tasks in the cloud. Many famous information technology organizations and companies have installed big scale datacenters with thousands of computing servers to provide cloud computing services, such as Google, IBM, Amazon and Microsoft. The incredible growth in the amount and size of datacenters leads to substantial power consumption. According to the report of Environmental Protection Agency (EPA) in USA, datacenters consume around 61TWH of energy in 2006 i.e. 1.5 % of the entire power usage. The report estimated that the power consumption will double in each five years. Inside datacenters 40 % power is consumed by computing infrastructures, 45 % is consumed for the cooling machines and 15 % is lost in the power generation units. The EPA report shows that 70 % power consumption can be saved by applying state-of-art efficiency methods at the cooling, power units and computing infrastructure. Table 1 compares the

© Springer Science+Business Media Singapore 2016
J. Wu and L. Li (Eds.): ACA 2016, CCIS 626, pp. 61–72, 2016.
DOI: 10.1007/978-981-10-2209-8_6

Table 1. Annual saving in 2011 using state-of-art methods

ICT apparatus	2011 energy usage	Power consumption under state-of-art technique
Infrastructure	42.1	18.1
Network devices	4.1	1.7
Storage	4.1	18
Servers	33.7	14.5
Overall	84.1	36.1

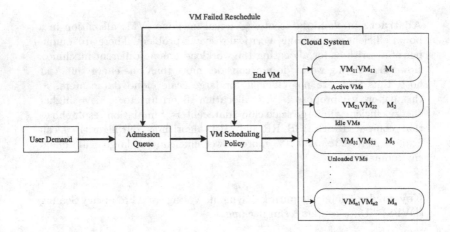

Fig. 1. VM allocation in cloud computing

power consumption of datacenters in 2011 with that under applying the state-of-art methods [4].

VM allocation and placement technique is one of the background technology to achieve this efficiency in cloud infrastructure. VM allocation and placement technique is a method of mapping VMs to physical hosts. After users finish selecting VMs, they'll be allocated to different physical hosts for executing user application. Figure 1 shows that the procedure of VM allocations. VM allocations have a direct impact on the energy consumption since it is one of important parts in the Resource Management (RM). The main purpose of the allocation policy is to allocate the available resources efficiently, i.e., the resource utilization is maximized to reduce power consumption. Providers can shutdown physical host as more as possible while ensure their service needs. Thus the power consumption would be minimized.

To ensure quality of service (QoS), only unused hosts can be shutdown. Thus the critical step is to allocate VMs efficiently, i.e., increasing the utilization of hosts. Since the workload is dynamic and future workload is hard to predict, allocating VM to hosts efficiently is difficult to decide.

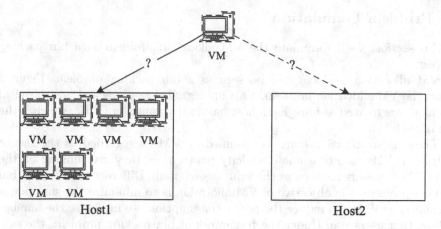

Fig. 2. VM allocation problem as bin packing problem

Efficient VM allocation remains a critical problem. In [5] authors describe VM allocation as a bin packing problem. They propose a best-fit decreasing on VM allocation i.e. power-aware BFD (PABFD). PABFD allocate a VM to a host that will raise least power consumption, it also allocate VMs to a host that has less cores based on CPU utilization. In [6] authors proposed allocation of VMs scheduling algorithm to minimized power consumption during task execution in cloud datacenters environment. In [7] authors proposed VM allocation method. If request does not map to any VM then they focus on near that most suitable VM pattern to the customer to check remain in queue. However, these works do not discuss the condition when more than one energy efficient hosts are available.

In this paper, we concentrate on IaaS clouds, e.g., Amazon EC2. We formulate the problem of VMs allocation as a bin packing problem. The objective is to minimize energy consumption in a datacenters. To overcome the disadvantage of just choosing one host, we proposed Energy Efficient (EE) algorithm by select most energy efficient host first. The proposed algorithm focus on decreasing the power consumption in cloud datacenters. To achieve this goal, we adopt Power Aware (PA), Non-Power Aware (NPA), and Dynamic Voltage Frequency Scheduling (DVFS) techniques to our algorithm. The experiment result shows that our algorithm achieves 23 %, 23 % and 9 % higher power efficiency than BRS, RR and MPD algorithms.

The rest of this paper is organized as follows: we formulate the VM allocation problem as a bin packing problem in Sect. 2. In Sect. 3 we propose a novel VM allocation algorithm to achieve higher energy efficiency. In Sect. 4, we evaluate the proposed technique, and compare the performance with traditional heuristics in an event driven simulator. Sects. 5 and 6 show some related works and conclusion respectively.

2   Problem Fomulation

In this section, we'll formulate the VM allocation problem as a bin packing problem.

VM allocation problem can be seen as a bin packing problem. Figure 2 shows the VM allocation problem. VMs are regarded as items and host physical machines are treated as bins. Each host has fixed volumes of CPUs, which is the size of each bin.

The computational resources consumed by VMs is regarded as the size of each item. VMs also consume electricity power when they are running on the hosts. These powers are seen as the value of each item. Different from typical bin packing problem, the objective of VM allocation is to minimize the sum power consumed by VMs. To reduce the power consumption, we minimize the number of host that users use. Under the framework of bin packing problem, the sum size of items cannot exceed the capacity of bins, i.e., the sum computational resources consumed by VMs cannot exceed the capacity of hosts. Thus, VM allocation problem is formulated as:

$$min \ z = \sum_{j=1}^{n} Y_j \tag{1}$$

$$s.t. \ \sum_{i=1}^{n} w_i x_{ij} \leq c_j \tag{2}$$

$$\sum_{j=1}^{n} x_{ij} = 1, \tag{3}$$

where w_i is the computational resources consumed by the ith VM, and c_j denotes the capacity of the jth host. Y_j is a binary variable, meaning whether bin_j is used or not. x_{ij} denotes the decision variable, meaning if $item_i$ is placed in bin_j.

$$Y_j = \begin{cases} 1, & if \ bin_j \ is \ used \\ 0, & otherwise \end{cases} \tag{4}$$

$$x_{ij} = \begin{cases} 1, & if \ item_i \ is \ placed \ in \ bin_j \\ 0, & otherwise. \end{cases} \tag{5}$$

So far, the VM allocation problem is formulated as a bin packing problem. We treat VMs as items and hosts as bins. The objective of VM allocation is to minimize the power consumption, i.e., minimize the number of used hosts. The constraint is to ensure quality of service.

3   Proposed Algorithm

In this section, we propose the Energy Efficient allocator (EE) algorithm to achieve high energy efficient.

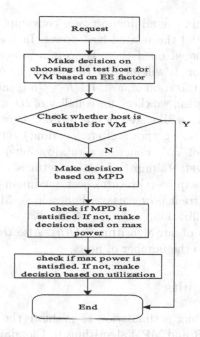

Fig. 3. Flow chart of the EE algorithm

The basic idea of EE algorithm is greedy, i.e., we always select the most energy efficient host to place our VMs. If there are more than one EE hosts, then the allocation is implemented using PABFD. In case PABFD returns more than one energy efficient hosts, then the more utilized host is nominated to reduce the number of migrations. The last step is divided into two different steps. The first one is to select a host that is more utilized to reduce the number of migrations. The second option is to choose a less utilized host to balance the utilization. Figure 3 shows the main procedures of EE algorithm.

To show energy efficiency, we first define a metric to evaluate the energy efficiency. The energy efficiency is the ratio between CPU capacity and energy.

$$H_{EE} = \frac{C_{host}}{P_{max}}, \tag{6}$$

where C_{host} is the entire CPU capacity and P_{max} is the maximum energy consumption of the host.

Algorithm 1 shows details of the Energy Efficient allocator algorithm. First in line 4 we check all hosts whether the VM is suitable or not. If it is suitable, the process will be end. In line 11 we find the most energy efficient host if we have more hosts available. If this condition is not satisfied, we check the most efficient host according to MPD. But this step is very expensive because if we do not have VM but still the author proposed this algorithm and we consider this algorithm and merge with our proposed algorithm to find the best efficient hosts for VM allocation. In line 17, we calculate the minimum power consumption. In line 21, if the power difference and the minimum power consumption are equal, we can find the allocated host and the related host power. In line 27–29, we calculate decision on utilization based on if there is no min power available. When we take decision on utilization, it will increase the utilization of hosts. In line 30, we check the condition for utilization of host. If $Uh > Ua$ is satisfied, we assign host to allocated host. Otherwise, we check for equality of Uh and Ua, and check the total mips of host. Then we allocate the host if line 34 condition is satisfied.

In Algorithm 1, function getpowerafterallocation() returns the total power of host after allocation of VM. Function getutalization() returns CPU current percentage used while gettotalmips() function returns total MIPS that CPU supports. Function getmaxpower() returns host maximum power while getpower function returns host current power usage. Function getMIPS() returns host or VM maximum MIPS utilization.

The time complexity of our algorithm is $O(n)$. Also the space complexity is $O(n)$, and n is related to the number of hosts.

4   Evaluation Results

In this section, we conduct a simulation to evaluate the performance our EE algorithm with BRS, RR and MPD algorithms in CloudSim. We combine these four algorithms with three techniques, i.e., NPA, PA and DVFS to evaluate the performance.

4.1   Simulation Setup

To evaluate our proposed allocation algorithm, we conduct several simulations in an event driven simulation environments, i.e., CloudSim. In CloudSim, the workloads are represented by cloudlets which are submitted to VMs. VMs are placed on the available servers (i.e., hosts) in the datacenter. The processing speed of servers is evaluated by Millions of Instructions Per Second (MIPS) rating.

To analyze the performance of proposed algorithm, we conduct the simulations with small, medium and large size datacenters having heterogeneous machines (Table 2).

- In case of small size datacenters, we choose 10 hosts, 20 VMs and 20 tasks.
- In case of medium size datacenter we have selected 100 hosts, 200 VMs and 200 tasks.
- In case of large size we choose 1000 hosts, 2000 VMs and 2000 tasks.

The detailed configurations for hosts and VMs are as following:

- Hosts: each host has 1 TB of storage, 24 GB RAM, 1 processing entity (PE) and gigabit Ethernet. And hosts adopt Linux and Xen as operating system and virtual machine monitor respectively.
- VMs: each VM requires 1 PE; the processing capacity of each VM are 500, 750, and 1000 MIPS which are create in a round-robin fashion.

Algorithm 1. Allocator EE

Input hostlist, VM

Output allocatedhost

1: Best=0
2: allocatedhost=host
3: **for** each host in list **do**
4:    **if** host is suitable for vm **then**
5:        Powerafterallocation= host.getPowerafterallocation()
6:        **if** Powerafterallocation is not null **then**
7:            MIPS=host.getmips()
8:            Maxp=host.getmaxpower()
9:            Powerefficiency=MIPS/MaxPower
10:            MinPower=max_value
11:            **if** Powerefficiency >Best **then**
12:                Best=Powerefficiency
13:                allocatedhost=host
14:            **end if**
15:            **if** Powerefficiency==Best **then**
16:                Powerdiff=Powerallocation-host.getPower ()
17:                **if** Powerdiff <MinPower **then**
18:                    MinPower=Powerdiff
19:                    allocatedhost=host
20:                **end if**
21:                **if** Powerdiff==MinPower **then**
22:                    Pa=allocatedhost.getPower()
23:                    Ph=host.getPower()
24:                    **if** Ph <Pa **then**
25:                        allocatedhost=host
26:                    **end if**
27:                    **if** Ph==Pa **then**
28:                        Ua=allocatedhost.getutalization()
29:                        Uh=host.getutalization()
30:                        **if** Uh >Ua **then**
31:                            allocatedhost=host
32:                        **end if**
33:                        **if** Uh==Ua **then**
34:                            **if** host.gettotalmips() >allocatedhost.gettotalmips() **then**
35:                                alloactedhost=host
36:                            **end if**
37:                        **end if**
38:                    **end if**
39:                **end if**
40:            **end if**
41:        **end if**
42:    **end if**
43: **end for**
44: **return** allocatedhost

Table 2. Example for heterogeneous datacenter

Hosts	Host1	Host2	Host3	Host4	Host5
MIPS	1000	1500	2000	2500	3000
Power	200	250	300	350	400

– Tasks: every task has 300 bytes of data before and after the processing (Generalized Cloudsim model); every task consists of 10,000, 15,000, 20,000 and 25,000 MIPS which are create in a round-robin fashion.

In our simulations, we evaluate the performance of algorithms combined with three datacenter techniques: (1) NPA (which do not support to shutdown unused machines), (2) PA (which support to shut down unused machines) and (3) DVFS idle machine consumes 70 % of its energy and totally used machine consumes 100 % of the energy.

4.2 Simulation Results

To validate our proposed algorithm, the results were compared with two classic scheduling algorithms i.e. Best Resource selection (BRS), Round Robin (RR) and MPD, which is one Cloudsim power management algorithm in terms of cloudlets completion time and power consumption [7]. In the BRS policy the machine with the peak ratio (MIPS in Use/Total no-of-MIPS) is chosen for any VM next in line. This ensure reducing no-of migrations and have affinity to achieve quicker outcomes. In case of RR policy, every VM is allocated to a different machine using circular policy. Machines that can allocate VM are avoided. In case there is no machines talented to accommodate VMs, the allocation is postponed. MPD is used as the vital model of power savings in Cloudsim environment. Each coming VM is allocated to the machine which will consume less power to run the VM.

Figure 4(a), (b) and (c) show the evaluation result under NPA and PA techniques. Figure 4(a) shows the result for small size datacenter. Our proposed algorithm achieves 21 %, 21 % and 3.7 % higher power efficiency than RR, BRS and MPD combined with PA technique. Figure 4(b) shows the result for medium size datacenter. Our proposed algorithm saves 17 %, 16 %, and 6 % more power than RR, BRS and MPD combined with PA technique in this case. Figure 4(c) shows the result for large size datacenter. Our proposed algorithm works 19 %, 16 % and 7.1 % better than RR, BRS and MPD combined with PA technique respectively. Since under NPA technique, all existing algorithms could not make significant progress, we do not show the improving ratio.

Figure 5(a), (b) and (c) show the evaluation result under DVFS technique. Figure 5(a) shows the result for small size datacenter. Our proposed algorithm saves 23 %, 23 % and 9 % more power than RR, BRS and MPD. Figure 5(b) shows the result for medium size datacenter. Our proposed algorithm works 18 %, 13 % better than RR, BRS. But MPD performs the same to our proposed algorithm. Figure 5(c) shows the result for large size datacenter. Our proposed algorithm

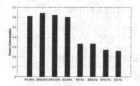 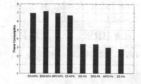 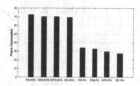

(a) Power consumption evaluations for Small data center

(b) Power consumption evaluations for Medium data center

(c) Power consumption evaluations for Large data center

Fig. 4. Power consumption evaluations among different algorithms for different size data center under NPA and PA techniques

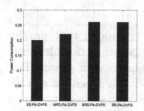 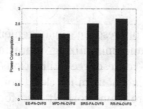 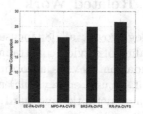

(a) Power consumption evaluations for Small data center

(b) Power consumption evaluations for Medium data center

(c) Power consumption evaluations for Large data center

Fig. 5. Power consumption evaluations of different algorithms for different size data center under DVFS techniques

show better performance than RR, BRS, and MPD at the ratio of 20 %, 14 % and 1.1 % respectively.

To evaluate the performance and stability of our algorithm and other three algorithms, we compare the average power consumption and standard deviation among them. From Table 3 we can see, our proposed algorithm achieves better result in both average power consumption and standard deviation than other three algorithms in case of large size datacenter. Smaller standard deviation shows higher stability of algorithms. Similarly, from Table 4 we can also see that, our proposed algorithm works better than other three existing techniques both in the average and standard deviation.

Table 3. Comparative table for power aware simulation

Experiments	RR		BRS		MPD		EE	
Large size	33.82	0.084	31.77	0.068	29.25	0.036	27.49	0.032
Small size	0.33	0.0074	0.32	0.0088	0.26	0.0057	0.26	0.0057

Table 4. Comparative table for large size DVFS simulation

Experiments	RR		BRS		MPD		EE	
Large size	26.48	0.057	24.97	0.046	21.44	0.038	21.11	0.034

From the above experiments we can see that the proposed method can save 12.8 % power in case of PA and 12.2 % in the case of DVFS enabled techniques. From the analysis, we find that our method saves more power in large scale systems.

5 Related Work

Beloglazov et al. [8] focused on resource management technique that provide quality-of-service constraint and minimizing operating costs. Performing consolidation of VMs according to resource utilization help to save power. Berl et al. [9] used energy efficient mechanism for cloud computing, specifically in the area of networks and hardware framework. It also focuses on decreasing power consumption in software and hardware, improving the load balancing and minimizing communication power consumption. Suri et al. [10] design an allocation algorithm that decrease the load on servers needs to achieve minimum power consumption. In [11], the authors propose a technique that allocates VMs to achieve the goal of decreasing power consumption in virtualized cloud datacenters.

In [5,12–17] power-aware VM allocation techniques for energy efficient RM in cloud datacenters were proposed. In [5] authors proposed allocation of VMs scheduling algorithm to minimized power consumption during task execution in cloud datacenters environment. This paper also concentrate on to shutdown of underutilized hosts and DVFS. In [7] authors proposed VM allocation method. If request does not map to any VM then they focus on near that most suitable VM pattern to the customer to check remain in queue. They also focused on to describe concept of cloud to choose an efficient VM to facilitate customers as well as maintaining QoS and SLA. VM placement are NP-hard problem and still there is no optimal solution. Also, in [18,19] discuss the VM placement and [20,21] discuss affinity aware solution to solve complicated problems. In a datacenters power saving increases by keeping VMs on a physical hosts in an optima way.

In [22] authors formulated score-based scheduling method as hill-climbing algorithm, also focus on principle map searching (host, VM) pairs. Where, the score of each (host, VM) pair is the addition of numerous factors, including resource requirement, power consumption, software and hardware fulfilment. A clouds scheduler can use the metric of performance-per-watt to assign VMs to hosts for energy efficiency. Their proposed approach, i.e. EPOBFs [23] allocates a host that has maximum MIPS/Watts. In [22] authors discussed PA VM allocation heuristics for power-efficient resource management in cloud datacenter. A hybrid VM provisioning method is proposed in [24], which is based on two methods, (i) On Demand (OD) and (ii) Spare Resources (SR). OD policy start the resources when they are wanted. To avoid the requests timeout issue, the authors implemented SR policy to decrease energy consumption on private clouds and avoid SLA violation.

Our proposed solution differs from these existing techniques. We select a more energy efficient host for the VM placement.

6   Conclusion

Cloud computing services enable developers and companies flexibly manage their infrastructure since it provides infinite resources and adopt the pay-as-you-go pricing model. There are certain risks related to cloud computing such as energy cost minimization and carbon dioxide emissions reduction. We formulate the VM allocation problem as a bin packing problem. To achieve power efficiency, we proposed a VM allocation algorithm to place VMs requests on most energy efficient physical hosts. We evaluated the proposed method with three existing algorithms, including BRS, RR and MPD. By using NPA, PA and DVFS enabled techniques in a simulation environment, our algorithms can achieve 23 %, 23 % and 9 % more power efficiency than other algorithms.

References

1. Zakarya, M., Khan, A.A.: Cloud QoS, high availability & service security issues with solutions. IJCSNS **12**, 71 (2012)
2. Malik, S.U.R., Khan, S.U., Srinivasan, S.K.: Modeling and analysis of state-of-the-art VM-based cloud management platforms. IEEE Trans. Cloud Comput. **1**, 1 (2013)
3. Hussain, H., Malik, S.U.R., Hameed, A., Khan, S.U., Bickler, G., Min-Allah, N., Qureshi, M.B., Zhang, L., Yongji, W., Ghani, N., et al.: A survey on resource allocation in high performance distributed computing systems. Parallel Comput. **39**, 709–736 (2013)
4. Shuja, J., Bilal, K., Madani, S.A., Khan, S.U.: Data center energy efficient resource scheduling. Clust. Comput. **17**, 1265–1277 (2014)
5. Beloglazov, A., Buyya, R.: Energy efficient allocation of virtual machines in cloud data centers. In: 10th IEEE/ACM International Conference on Cluster, Cloud and Grid Computing (CCGrid) (2010)
6. Lago, D.G.d., Madeira, E.R., Bittencourt, L.F.: Power-aware virtual machine scheduling on clouds using active cooling control and DVFS. In: Proceedings of the 9th International Workshop on Middleware for Grids, Clouds and e-Science (2011)
7. Shah, M.D., Prajapati, H.B.: Reallocation and allocation of virtual machines in cloud computing (2013)
8. Beloglazov, A., Buyya, R.: Energy efficient resource management in virtualized cloud data centers. In: Proceedings of the 10th IEEE/ACM International Conference on Cluster, Cloud and Grid Computing (2010)
9. Berl, A., Gelenbe, E., Di Girolamo, M., Giuliani, G., De Meer, H., Dang, M.Q., Pentikousis, K.: Energy-efficient cloud computing. Comput. J. **53**, 1045–1051 (2010)

10. Binder, W., Suri, N.: Green computing: energy consumption optimized service hosting. In: Nielsen, M., Kučera, A., Miltersen, P.B., Palamidessi, C., Tůma, P., Valencia, F. (eds.) SOFSEM 2009. LNCS, vol. 5404, pp. 117–128. Springer, Heidelberg (2009)
11. Hu, L., Jin, H., Liao, X., Xiong, X., Liu, H.: Magnet: a novel scheduling policy for power reduction in cluster with virtual machines. In: IEEE International Conference on Cluster Computing (2008)
12. Beloglazov, A., Abawajy, J., Buyya, R.: Energy-aware resource allocation heuristics for efficient management of data centers for cloud computing. Future Gener. Comput. Syst. **28**, 755–768 (2012)
13. Beloglazov, A., Buyya, R.: Energy efficient resource management in virtualized cloud data centers. In: Proceedings of the 10th IEEE/ACM International Conference on Cluster, Cloud and Grid Computing (2010)
14. Buyya, R., Beloglazov, A., Abawajy, J.: Energy-effcient management of datacenter resources for cloud computing: a vision, architectural elements, and open challenges (2010). arXiv preprint arXiv:1006.0308
15. Beloglazov, A., Buyya, R.: Optimal online deterministic algorithms and adaptive heuristics for energy and performance efficient dynamic consolidation of virtual machines in cloud data centers. Concurr. Comput. Pract. Exp. **24**, 1397–1420 (2012)
16. Qian, H., Lv, Q.: Proximity-aware cloud selection and virtual machine allocation in IaaS cloud platforms. In: IEEE 7th International Symposium on Service Oriented System Engineering (SOSE) (2013)
17. Schmidt, M., Fallenbeck, N., Smith, M., Freisleben, B.: Efficient distribution of virtual machines for cloud computing. In: 18th Euromicro International Conference on Parallel, Distributed and Network-Based Processing (PDP) (2010)
18. Corradi, A., Fanelli, M., Foschini, L.: VM consolidation: a real case based on OpenStack Cloud. Future Gener. Comput. Syst. **32**, 118–127 (2014)
19. Kousiouris, G., Cucinotta, T., Varvarigou, T.: The effects of scheduling, workload type and consolidation scenarios on virtual machine performance and their prediction through optimized artificial neural networks. J. Syst. Softw. **84**, 1270–1291 (2011)
20. Sonnek, J., Greensky, J., Reutiman, R., Chandra, A.: Starling: minimizing communication overhead in virtualized computing platforms using decentralized affinity-aware migration. In: 39th International Conference on Parallel Processing (ICPP) (2010)
21. Sudevalayam, S., Kulkarni, P.: Affinity-aware modeling of CPU usage for provisioning virtualized applications. In: IEEE International Conference on Cloud Computing (CLOUD) (2011)
22. Goiri, I., Julia, F., Nou, R., Berral, J.L., Guitart, J., Torres, J.: Energy-aware scheduling in virtualized datacenters. In: IEEE International Conference on Cluster Computing (CLUSTER) (2010)
23. Quang-Hung, N., Thoai, N., Son, N.T.: EPOBF: energy efficient allocation of virtual machines in high performance computing cloud. In: Hameurlain, A., Küng, J., Wagner, R., Thoai, N., Dang, T.K. (eds.) TLDKS XVI. LNCS, vol. 8960, pp. 71–86. Springer, Heidelberg (2015)
24. Geronimo, G.A., Werner, J., Westphall, C.B., Westphall, C.M., Defenti, L.: Provisioning and resource allocation for green clouds. In: 12th International Conference on Networks (ICN) (2013)

Research on Virtual Machine Cluster Deployment Algorithm in Cloud Computing Platform

Zheng Yao, Wen-Sheng Tang[✉], Sheng-Chun Wang, and Hui Peng

The Department of Computer Teaching, Hunan Normal University, Changsha, 410081, China
154976552@qq.com

Abstract. To address the virtual machine cluster deployment issues in cloud computing environment, a novel MCSA (Min-cut segmentation algorithm) of virtual machine cluster is proposed with resource and communication bandwidth constraints. In this paper, the basic idea is based on the fully consideration on the CPU, memory, hard-disk and other resource constraints between virtual machine cluster and physical host, as well as the communication bandwidth constraints between the virtual machine. We quantified the virtual machine cluster constructed an undirected graph. In the undirected graph, the nodes represent the virtual machine, so the weight of a node represents the value of resources, and the edges represent the communication bandwidth, so the weight of the edge represents the value of communication bandwidth. Base on the above transformations, the resources and bandwidth constrained optimization problem is transformed into the graph segmentation problem. Next we segment the undirected graph by minimum cut algorithm, and computing the matching degree of physical machines. Last we obtained the approximate solution. To validate the effectiveness of the new algorithm, we carried out extensive experiments based on the CloudSim platform.

Keywords: Cloud computing · Virtual machine cluster deployment · Graph partitioning · Communication bandwidth

1 Introduction

Cloud computing is a product of the development and convergence of conventional computer technologies and network technologies, such as grid computing, distributed computing, parallel computing, utility computing, network storage technologies, virtualization, load balance etc. [1]. To ensure that the users can easily and quickly use resources through various kinds of terminals, Cloud computing provides available, convenient, and on-demand network access method to manage the various resources from cloud effectively and safely according to the demands of users. As the growing user demands, how to effectively manage resources and make it quickly available to users becomes the key technology of cloud computing needed to be addressed.

Virtualization technology is the foundation of cloud computing, it is a kind of infrastructure and the upper system and software to coupling separation technology, Virtualization technology through the upper service package to the virtual machine, and

© Springer Science+Business Media Singapore 2016
J. Wu and L. Li (Eds.): ACA 2016, CCIS 626, pp. 73–84, 2016.
DOI: 10.1007/978-981-10-2209-8_7

manage resources through the deployment of virtual machines. Virtual machine deployment is to map the physical resource based on the virtual machine deployment request according to a reasonable allocation rules. The whole process is to seek optimal deployment of physical hosts under a multi-constraint optimization problem. Therefore, effective virtual machine deployment model and algorithm will be the key point of the efficient use of resources.

With in-depth studies on virtual machine deployment algorithms, the resource mapping of Virtual machine and physical host is developed from earlier one-on-one to later more-on-one relationship. Besides, Virtual machine deployment also changed from a single virtual machine mode to the virtual machine cluster. Virtual machine cluster refers to the communication needs and deployment restrictions of multiple virtual machine deployment limitation [2]. However, the deployment of the virtual machine cluster still faces many problems, such as high network communication consumption between the virtual machine, physical host resources waste problem and so on.

Many researchers have carried out extensive research on the virtual machine clusters deployment. For different application requirements of users, Paper [3] presents the sequence deployment strategy and balanced deployment strategy, however, these strategies only considering CPU resource constraints between virtual machines and physical host, wasting the physical host resources significantly. To solve the problem, paper [4] presents a resource matching strategy based on CPU and memory. Compared to paper [3], the strategy improves the usage of the physical host resources. However, it did not fully take into account the composition of virtual machines from a variety of resources, so this strategy cannot meet the needs of users in a variety of applications. To satisfy the various requirements of users, Paper [5] proposed a performance vector-based algorithm for virtual machine deployment. However, the deployment process only considers a single resource constraint of virtual machine and physical hosts. When more virtual machines exist, although the resource waste reduction in the rate of a single physical host, the waste of resources in the rate of the overall system does not reduce. Paper [6] presents a heuristic algorithm based on graph decomposition, which only considers the deployment of virtual machines on a single physical host. To cope with the problem, paper [7] proposed a decomposition algorithm. Throughout the deployment process, the overall rate decreased waste of resources. Paper [8] proposed a decomposition algorithm. The paper has associated physical resources as a deployment target, but only considers the communication bandwidth factor.

For the virtual machine cluster deployment issues, we proposed a MCSA based on constraint of resources and communication bandwidth. The algorithm firstly quantifies the virtual machines cluster resources and bandwidth, so that the virtual machines cluster can construct a weighted directed graph. As the weights of the nodes depict resources and the weight of each edge represents the value of the communication bandwidth. The double constrained optimization problem of resources and communication bandwidth can be translated to sub-chart graph partitioning problem. With minimum cut algorithm, the virtual machine is divided into small clusters from virtual cluster. For each virtual machines cluster, if its external communication is larger, the internal communication is smaller and vice versa. Then we calculate the cluster resource matching distance of the virtual machine cluster and the physical host, which can be determined the approximate optimal solution of deployment issues.

2   Related Works

Virtual machine is composed of resources (CPU, memory, hard disk and other resources) which are required by the user. We can consider the virtual machine as entities consisted of all kinds of resources, in which physical host is serving as containers. Virtual machine deployment is to establish a resource mapping between virtual machines and physical host, then under the constraint of related resources, the virtual machine will looking for the best physical host to deploy. With the Deeping of the study, virtual machine deployment has developed from a single virtual machine deployment to the virtual machine clusters deployment, as shown in Fig. 1 [5].

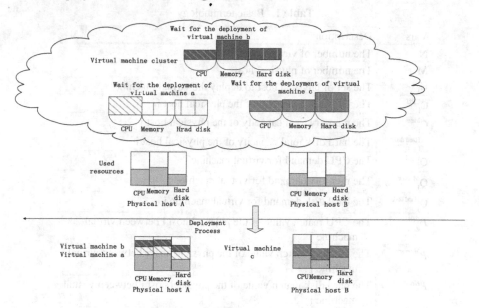

Fig. 1. Virtual machine cluster deployment model

In the cloud computing environment, application providers usually deployed services in the physical hosting, and these services are generally made by the end user to a virtual machine. In order to efficiently provide service to users, Virtual machines need to collaborate with each other to jointly complete the user's needs. Thus, a plurality of virtual machines with communication requirements and deployment restrictions constitute a virtual machine cluster. Figure 1 describes the virtual machine cluster deployment model. Multiple virtual machines constitute a virtual machine cluster, virtual machines and physical host are component with the CPU, memory, hard disk, and other resources. In standby mode, the physical host requires certain resources to run the initial state, removing the physical hosts in the standby state of the resource, by calculating the remaining available resources of the physical host resources available to meet the physical host in the case of virtual machine resources required, will deploy a virtual machine to a physical host. Different deployment constraints, the results for the entire deployment will have greater impact.

3   Virtual Machine Cluster Deployment Algorithm

3.1   Related Terms

Virtual machine cluster deployment description: n mutually between communication bandwidth demand virtual machine cluster, m need to deploy to the physical host.

In order to better describe the problem, we introduce the following symbols (Table 1).

Table 1. Basic terminology

Vars	Description
N	The number of virtual machines
M	The number of physical hosts
H_j	The set of physical host to deploy the virtual machine
C_i^{CPU}	The CPU total capacity of the physical host i
C_i^{Memory}	The memory total capacity of the physical host i
$C_i^{Hard\ disk}$	The hard disk total capacity of the physical host i
Q_j^{CPU}	The CPU demand for virtual machine j
Q_j^{Memory}	The memory demand for virtual machine j
$Q_j^{Hard\ disk}$	The hard disk demand for virtual machine j
P_{ij}^{CPU}	The CPU match value of the physical host i between virtual machine j
P_{ij}^{Memory}	The memory match value of the physical host i between virtual machine j
$P_{ij}^{Hard\ disk}$	The hard disk match value of the physical host i between virtual machine j
E_{ij}	the figure of the edge weights for virtual machine i between virtual machine j
D_{ij}	The Resource matching vector for virtual machine j between physical host i
K_{ij}	The desired physical host Weighted match vector for virtual machine j between physical host i

3.2   Virtual Machine Cluster Deployment Model

Virtual machine cluster for physical host deployment process works as follows: first, according to the communication bandwidth constraints segmented virtual machine cluster, getting a virtual machine cluster divided. Second, calculating resource matching between the virtual machine and physical host clusters, and searching for the best physical host deployment. The deployment process of resources and communication bandwidth constraints need to be considered at the same time.

1. According to the communication bandwidth constraints, we use the minimum-cut algorithm [9] for virtual machine cluster segmentation. After segment, it forms the plurality of virtual machine cluster. The Segmentation strategies are as follows:

   (1) Virtual machine is represented as a vertex graph.
   (2) Communication bandwidth relationship between virtual machines is defined as the Edges.
   (3) The virtual machine's resources (such as CPU, memory, hard disk) is expressed as the figure of peak value $V_i\left(Q_j^{CPU}, Q_j^{Memory}, Q_j^{Hard\ disk}\right)$, the communication bandwidth between the virtual machine is expressed as the figure of the edge weights E_{ij}. Through the above quantitative, the problem of Virtual machine cluster can be converted into a problem of weighted undirected graph.
   (4) The division process of virtual machine cluster is transformed into segmentation process of diagram. The segmentation of process is divided by the minimum-cut algorithm, so graph G can be divided into a plurality of sub-graph G1, G2… Gn. As shown in Fig. 2.

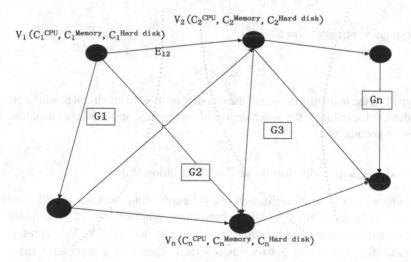

Fig. 2. Weighted undirected graph

2. Computing resource requirements of the virtual machine cluster, according to the physical host resources condition, seeking the best physical host through resource constraints.

The virtual machine cluster converted into a weighted undirected graph, we use the minimum-cut algorithm to divide weighted undirected graph, and get a number of weighted undirected graph after divided. The weighted undirected graph represents the virtual machine cluster. Next, Virtual machine cluster choose physical host to deploy.

In order to improve resource utilization, we should choose the optimal physical hosts to deploy. In this paper, we use the Euclidean distance cluster to represent the virtual machine and physical host resources matching degree.

The various resources matching:

$$P_{ij}^{CPU} = \sqrt{C_i^{CPU^2} - Q_j^{CPU^2}} \tag{1}$$

$$P_{ij}^{Memory} = \sqrt{C_i^{Memory^2} - Q_j^{Memory^2}} \tag{2}$$

$$P_{ij}^{Hard\ disk} = \sqrt{C_i^{Hard\ disk^2} - Q_j^{Hard\ disk^2}} \tag{3}$$

Calculating the virtual machine and the physical hosts a variety of cluster resources match, getting resources match vector $D_{ij} = (P_{ij}^{CPU}, P_{ij}^{Memory}, P_{ij}^{Hard\ disk})$.

In order to meet the needs of users for different resources, we weighted distance vector to represent user demand for resources. Weighted vector $\alpha = (\alpha_1, \alpha_2, \alpha_3)$. Finally, get the desired physical host Weighted match vector:

$$K_{ij} = \alpha * (P_{ij}^{CPU}, P_{ij}^{Memory}, P_{ij}^{Hard\ disk}) \tag{4}$$

Destination physical host Match:

$$L = \sum_{j=0}^{m} K_{ij} \tag{5}$$

Type L is the matching degree of the physical host between virtual machine clusters. With the L value reduced, the match degree of the physical host between virtual machine clusters is become well.

3.3 System Communication Bandwidth Utilization Rate

Communication bandwidth utilization rate (The communication bandwidth occupancy rate) R refers to the value of virtual machine cluster bandwidth utilization and the ratio of the communications bandwidth in the whole system. $B_w(V_i, V_j)$ represents the communication bandwidth between two virtual machines, T represents the virtual machine cluster deployment environment. On the process of virtual machine deployment to host, some virtual opportunities deployed on the same host, for the external communication bandwidth of the virtual machine transformed the internal communication of the host. The communication of the whole system will not result in a greater impact. Therefore, when the virtual machine is deployed to the different physical host, T is 1, when the virtual machine is deployed in the same physical host, T is 0. And B_n represents the total bandwidth. So Communication bandwidth utilization rate is expressed as:

$$R = \sum_{i=1}^{n} B_w(V_i, V_j) * T / B_n \tag{6}$$

3.4   The Analysis of System Resource Waste Rate

Because of different deployment strategies, there are large differences in Virtual Machine Deployment Results. For example, when the distribution of resources on the physical host is uneven, it is like to cause the entire system to waste resources. So, in this article, we calculate the physical host resources waste rate to reduce the waste of the resources of the system. Wastage rate $Waste_p$ refers to the average ratio value between different resources and the whole physical server, as shown in Equation.

$$\text{Waste}_{P_j}^{CPU} = (p_j^{cpu} - Q_j^{CPU})/p_j^{cpu} \tag{7}$$

$$\text{Waste}_{P_j}^{Memory} = (p_j^{Memory} - Q_j^{Memory})/p_j^{Memory} \tag{8}$$

$$\text{Waste}_{P_j}^{Hardisk} = (p_j^{Hard\ disk} - Q_j^{Hard\ disk})/p_j^{Hard\ disk} \tag{9}$$

Optimized resource wastage rate can be expressed as:

$$\min\text{Waste}_P = \sum_{j=0}^{m}(\text{Waste}_{P_j}^{CPU} + \text{Waste}_{P_j}^{Memory} + \text{Waste}_{P_j}^{Hard\ disk})/3 \tag{10}$$

3.5   Virtual Machine Cluster Deployment Algorithm Process

In this paper, algorithm is based on double constraints of the resources and communication bandwidth, and we quantify the resources and bandwidth to form a weighted undirected graph, where the vertex weights graph represents the resources, right side of the figure represents the value of the communication bandwidth, the double constraints of resources and communication bandwidth optimization problem can be transform into a graph of graph partition problems, we use the minimum cut algorithm to break up the Weighted undirected graph. Next, calculate the approximate solution of the problem.

(1)   Initialize the data center, randomly generated virtual machine and the physical host. Get resource requirements of the virtual machine cluster R_{VM}, communication bandwidth between the virtual machine W_{VM}, the list of hosts' available resources of all hosts H_{PM}.

(2)   Modeling for virtual machine cluster deployment problem, quantify the virtual machine cluster, get weighted undirected graph.

(3)   Converted the virtual machine cluster to weighted undirected graph and use the minimum-cut algorithm to divide weighted undirected graph.

(4)   After segmentation, calculate the resources matching distance of virtual machine cluster and physical host calculation, if physical host can be deployed it, we will build the virtual cluster to deploy on physical host. If there is no, then jump step (3).

(5)   Cycle all virtual machines cluster list, until all the virtual machines clusters deployed over.

The deployment process is shown in Fig. 3 below:

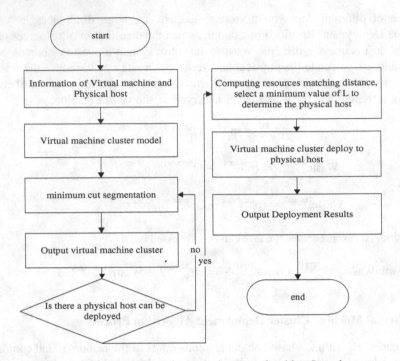

Fig. 3. Virtual machine cluster deployment algorithm flow chart

The Algorithm is described as follows:

For every VM

Get VM resource requirements data list R_{VM}, the communication bandwidth of VM array W_{VM}

For every PM

Get PM performance data list H_{PM}

Label 1 : **For** W_{VM}, R_{VM}

Min-Cut algorithm ()

VM clusters R_{VM} Divided into R_{VMi}, R_{VMj}

Array W_{VM} Divided into W_{VMi} and W_{VMj}

For R_{VMi} or R_{VMj} resource requirements data matching to H_{PM} performance data

If match success, get current matching degree list L

Get the L_{min}

Then get the best match PM, and return deployment result

Else match failure

Goto label 1

Return all deployment result

4 Simulation and Analysis

In this paper, we conduct simulations based on the Cloudsim 3.0 [10] with the operation of windows 7 64-bit. The JDK version adopted in the paper is jdk1.6.0_43. We compare greedy algorithm, a single resource constraint algorithm and article of virtual machine cluster allocation algorithm to analyst is System resources waste rate and Communication bandwidth occupancy rate. Simulation results validate that the algorithm has a good performance compared to other algorithms.

4.1 Simulation Platform

For the simulation platform, according to this paper, we have expanded our simulation platform by recompiling CloudSim3.0.3, and the writing simulation programs. First, we initialize a data center, and each data center contains a number of physical hosts. In the data center, we use using a random way to produce physical resources and virtual machine hosts. At the same time, by expanding the classes, Datacenter, Host, virtual machine and DataCenteBoker, we realize the underlying physical and virtual machine simulation. The experiment procedure of physical machines and virtual machine strategies are as follows:

(1) Virtual machine
Using random strategy, generate virtual machine allocation request queue, in which the CPU is generated randomly from 1 to 6 nuclear, memory and hard disk are also randomly generated. For each generation of virtual machine memory, the quantity is 512 M integer times and hard disk is the integer times of 16 G.
(2) Physical host
Custom Datacenter Characteristics class, generate the corresponding Datacenter and physical Host. Including CPU, memory, hard drive 10 integer times randomly generated by the virtual machine.
(3) The communication bandwidth of virtual machine.
Using randomly generated strategy, generate virtual machine communication bandwidth matrix between 0–9.

4.2 Results Analysis

1. System resources waster rate
System resources waste rate refers to the average resources waste rate of the physical hosts deployed with virtual machines. It is to note that in the paper, we only consider the CPU, memory and hard disk. This can measure the system resource utilization. Figure 4 depicts the physical host resources waste rate differences between the various algorithms. The Fig. 4 shows that with the increasing of virtual machine requests, the algorithm proposed in this paper can gradually reduce system resource waste rate and tends to be stable. For the three kinds of algorithms, the resource waste rate of MCSA algorithm is the lowest, followed by the single resource constraints algorithm, greedy algorithm is the worst. As we can see from the figure,

MCSA algorithm has good performance lies in that when allocating resources, we taken the approximation degree of virtual machine cluster between physical hosts into consideration. Specifically, if the degree is closer, it means more balanced use of resources after the distribution of the physical host, the greater the variety of resources available extent and the smaller the rate of physical hosts waste of resources. As the greedy algorithm does not adopt any optimization mechanism in resources allocation, it has the highest waste rate.

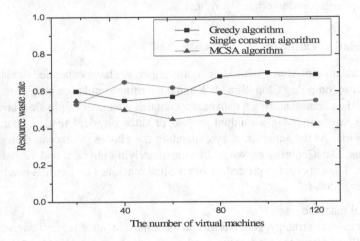

Fig. 4. system resources waste rate

2. System bandwidth occupancy rate
    Communication bandwidth occupancy rate refers to the ratio between the communication bandwidth of each virtual machine cluster and communication bandwidth needed for the whole system in the physical host. It represents communication bandwidth occupying degree of the whole system when running a virtual machine cluster. As it can be seen from the Fig. 5, with the increasing number of virtual machines, MCSA algorithm can keep the communication bandwidth occupancy rate at a low level. The reason lies in that it divides the virtual machine cluster with into several virtual machines cluster with a minimum cut algorithm which has lower communication and bandwidth demands. Meanwhile the virtual machine cluster with larger communications bandwidth demands redeployed on the same physical host. The single constraint algorithms occupy larger communication bandwidth as it only considers the resources of the virtual machine between cluster and physical host. The greedy algorithm did not consider any allocation optimization. It has the largest communication bandwidth occupied.

To sum up, in the situation where the virtual machine in the cluster requires frequent communication, the proposed virtual machine cluster deployment algorithm in the paper can keep a low system resource waste rate, stays small system communication bandwidth, and achieves high network utilization.

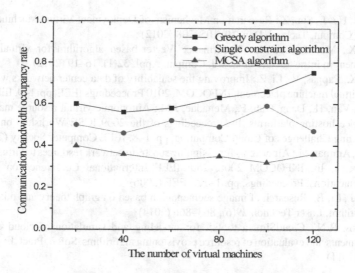

Fig. 5. System bandwidth occupancy rate

5   Conclusions

In this paper, to cope with the Virtual machine cluster deployment issues in cloud computing platform, we translate the virtual machine cluster deployment into optimization problems under multiple constraints. We presented a MCSA algorithm based on the double constraints of virtual machine resources and communication bandwidth. The algorithm firstly quantifies the resources and the communication bandwidth in the virtual machine cluster and separates the virtual machine cluster by minimum cut algorithm of graph theory. Then based on the segmentation of virtual machine cluster, the algorithm can effectively select the target physical host. The simulation results validate that it can reduce the resource waste rate and the system communication bandwidth utilization rate significantly. For further research, we aim to explore the combination of virtual machine energy consumption and resource equilibrium problems.

Acknowledgment.   The authors would like to thank the anonymous reviewers for their helpful and constructive comments. This work is supported by education reform Item of Hunan Normal University (Grant [2014]75). Program for Excellent Talents in Hunan Normal University (Grant no.ET61008).

References

1. Tu, H.-K., Zhou, H., Lin, R.-H.: Design and implementation of enhanced parallel computing framework system in cloud. New Ind. **12**, 33–40 (2012)
2. Wang, G., Ma, Z., Sun, L.: Deployment of virtual machines with clustering method based on frame load awareness. J. Comput. Appl. **33**(5), 1271–1275 (2013)
3. Yuan, J.: The Research on Multi-VM Fast Deployment Mechanism. Huazhong University of Science & Technology, Wuhan (2008)

4. Cao, W., He, J., Sun, Z.: Research on Mechanism of Deployment Virtual Machine in Mode of IaaS. Comput. Technol. Dev. **10**, 105–108 (2012)
5. Yang, X., Ma, Z., Sun, L.: Performance Vector-based algorithm for virtual machine deployment in infrastructure clouds. J. Comput. Appl. **32**(1), 16–19 (2012)
6. Meng, X., Pappas, V., Li, Z.: Improving the scalability of data center networks with traffic-aware virtual machine placement. INFOCOM, 2010 Proceedings IEEE, pp. 1–9. IEEE (2010)
7. Nguyen Van, H., Dang Tran, F., Menadue, J.M.: Autonomic virtual resource management for service hosting platforms. In: Proceedings of the 2009 ICSE Workshop on Software Engineering Challenges of Cloud Computing, pp. 1–8. IEEE Computer Society (2009)
8. Zhu, Y., Ammar, M.: Algorithms for assigning substrate network resources to virtual network components. In: INFOCOM 2006, 25th IEEE International Conference on Computer Communications, Proceedings, pp. 1–12. IEEE (2006)
9. Zhang, J., Li, B.: Research of image segmentation based on graph theory and minimum cut set algorithm. Laser Technol. **29**(6), 863–866 (2014)
10. Calheiros, R.N.: CloudSim: a toolkit for modeling and simulation of cloud computing environments and evaluation of resource provisioning algorithms. Softw. Pract. Exper. **41**(1), 23–50 (2011)

H-TDMS: A System for Traffic Big Data Management

Xingcheng Hua[1], Jierui Wang[1], Li Lei[1], Bin Zhou[2], Xiaolin Zhang[2],
and Peng Liu[1(✉)]

[1] College of Information Science & Electronic Engineering, Zhejiang University,
Hangzhou 310027, China
{hua2009x,jrw,leili,liupeng}@zju.edu.cn
[2] Zhejiang Uniview Technologies Co., Ltd., Hangzhou 310051, China
{zhoubin,zhangxiaolin}@uniview.com

Abstract. Massive traffic data is produced constantly every day, causing problems in data integration, massive storage, high performance
processing when applying conventional data management approaches.
We propose a cloud computing based system H-TDMS (Hadoop based
Traffic Data Management System) to capture, manage and process the
traffic big data. H-TDMS designs a configurable tool for data integration, a scalable data scheme for data storage, a secondary index for fast
search query, a computing framework for data analysis, and a web-based
user-interface with data visualization service for user interaction. Experiments on actual traffic data show that H-TDMS achieves considerable
performance in traffic big data management.

Keywords: Traffic big data · Cloud computing · Data integration ·
Secondary index · Data analysis

1 Introduction

The last few years have witnessed an explosion of traffic data due to the rapid
improvement in Intelligent Transportation System (ITS). Surveillance system
plays an important role in modern intelligent traffic management and produces
massive and complex traffic data every day. Usually traffic data is stored as
records, which are metadata extracted from the collected media information
such as images and videos. The volume of records of a big city in China may
exceed one hundred billion in a year.

In order to fully exploit traffic big data potential, there remain many technical challenges that must be addressed. The most critical challenges of traffic big data management system are: (1) integrating data from heterogeneous
sources in different formats to solve the problem of Data Island (data sets in iso-
lated storages with different specifications); (2) providing high availability and
scalability to support large volume of collected data; (3) equipping enormous
processing capacity to handle the analyzing of the traffic data; and (4) providing

J. Wu and L. Li (Eds.): ACA 2016, CCIS 626, pp. 85–96, 2016.
DOI: 10.1007/978-981-10-2209-8_8

diverse mining algorithms and models for deep analysis, such as criminal detection and risk pre-alarming [6,10,14,20]. All these problems call for well-adapted infrastructures which can efficiently handling traffic big data integration, indexing and query, and mining and analysis.

Cloud computing in current era plays a critical role when conventional data platforms fail in the "Big Data" scenario. Hadoop [1] is a popular framework for cloud computing running on commodity hardware. With the advantage of Hadoop, we propose a cloud computing based system H-TDMS, providing traffic big data management to support decision making and knowledge discovery. This proposed system has several key features:

(1) Flexible data import and distributed data storage
    H-TDMS integrates a flexible and efficient tool to capture and extract data from various databases and provides a storage system for massive traffic data with high performance and sufficient scalability based on a distributed database.
(2) Fast data indexing and query
    H-TDMS adopts a secondary index structure to build a lightweight and powerful search engine. The answer of a search query is returned back within a tolerable response time limit, usually in seconds.
(3) Intelligent analysis and mining
    H-TDMS integrates and encapsulates diverse algorithms and models for traffic characteristics analysis and criminal detection. It provides both on-line and off-line data processing services to support traffic management and public security issues.
(4) Web-based user-interface and data visualization
    H-TDMS provides a web-based user-interface to hide the complexity for accessing and managing data. Analysis results are interpreted by data visualization to help produce and comprehend insights from massive traffic data.

The rest of the paper is organized as follows. Section 2 outlines the the background and related work. Section 3 presents our design in detail. Section 4 gives the evaluation results based on the prototype system and Sect. 5 concludes.

2   Related Work

Big data and cloud computing have brought great opportunities for managing data. Hadoop is a framework for cloud computing, including a distributed file system HDFS (Hadoop Distributed File System) and a parallel processing framework MapReduce. Based on HDFS, HBase [2] is developed as a scalable, distributed database that supports data storage for large tables. Sqoop [4] is an open source software used for efficiently transferring data between Hadoop and structured relational databases (e.g., PostgreSQL [5]). Spark [3] is a fast framework for large-scale data processing. Compared with MapReduce, Spark runs some programs faster due to its in-memory computing.

Hadoop was proven to be an efficient framework for big data storage and query. Hadoop-GIS [7] stored large scale spatial data in HDFS and built a spatial index to support high-performance spatial queries. SpatialHadoop [9] was designed specifically to handle huge datasets of spatial data, which employed a two-level spatial index structure and some efficient spatial operations. Lee et al. [11] presented a lightweight spatial index for big data stored in HBase. Le and Takasu [15] proposed a scalable spatio-temporal data storage for ITS based on HBase and a spatio-temporal index structure using a hierarchical text-encoding algorithm. However these systems supported limited query constraints. As we know, more complex search queries should be provided for traffic big data.

Data mining has attracted wide attention as an approach to discovering information from traffic data. Moriya et al. [13] developed an algorithm using feature-based non-negative matrix factorization to predict the number of accidents and cluster roads to identify the risk factors. Benitez et al. [8] presented a two-step trajectory pattern recognition process including a k-means clustering and a classification over a Self-Organizing Map. Yue et al. [19] proposed a multi-view attributes reduction model for discovering the patterns to manage traffic bottleneck. Lv et al. [12] utilized a deep learning approach considering the spatial and temporal correlations inherently to predict the traffic flow. Xu and Dou [17] implemented an assistant decision-supporting method for urban transportation planning. Since so many works studied accident detection, pattern recognition, traffic flow prediction, investment decision, etc., diverse data mining approaches could be adopted in H-TDMS.

Several traffic big data platforms, based on cloud computing, were researched in recent years. RTIC-C [18] was a system designed to support traffic history data mining based on MapReduce framework. Kemp et al. [10] presented a big data infrastructure for managing data and assisting decision making for transport systems using service oriented architecture. Xiong et al. [16] discussed the design of ITS, including the current situation and future trend of related research and development areas. Different from these solutions, H-TDMS focuses more on how to provide data integration, search query, data analysis and user interaction in one system for traffic big data management, and achieve considerable performance based on cloud computing techniques.

3   System Design

Cloud computing is an inevitable trend for traffic data processing due to its great demands on big data analysis and mining. H-TDMS constructs three layers to meet these demands, as shown in Fig. 1. The data layer stores all the massive traffic data and provides high read/write performance when supporting transparent usage of physical resources. The processing layer provides diverse modular functions for upper layer services, and helps improve performance by parallel-based data processing. The application layer provides the entrances for users to call functions of the lower layers as well as http-based services for end users to access and use H-TDMS.

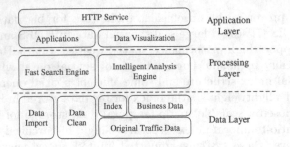

Fig. 1. H-TDMS architecture

3.1 Data Collection and Storage

Traffic data is stored as records in heterogeneous databases in different formats due to historical reasons (e.g., different times of construction, different application scenarios, and different equipment manufacturers). H-TDMS aims to integrate all kinds of data into one distributed database to fully exploit their potential. There is a critical need to flexible import data from various databases. A data import tool is designed as shown in Fig. 2. Though the process of crawling real-time data from the surveillance system is not shown in the figure, H-TDMS supports collecting real-time data into its storage system directly as well.

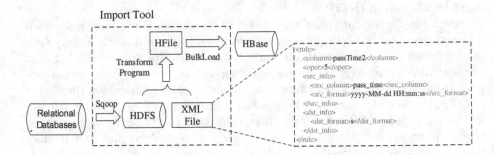

Fig. 2. Data import tool

Sqoop is used for transferring data between HDFS and structured relational databases, which are frequently applied to store traffic data. The transform program is capable of transforming the data to the target format and storing it in the low-level storage files of HBase called HFiles. The HFiles are moved to the regions of a table by BulkLoad, which is a function native supported by HBase. Both Sqoop and the transform program are based on MapReduce to accelerate their processes. An XML file which specifies the transform rules including the target field of a record, the source field of a record and the transform operation between them, is another input used in the transform program to guarantee the flexibility of the import tool. An example of time transformation is shown in Fig. 2.

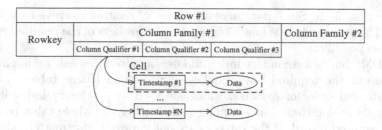

Fig. 3. HBase four-dimensional data model

H-TDMS builds a storage system based on HBase due to its high performance and scalability. The HBase data model is shown in Fig. 3. A well-adapted data scheme is designed to store traffic record data. A complete record consists of a list of fields including the information about a vehicle and its passing events. Table 1 shows the format of the obtained record. Every day all records are stored in a table named by date (e.g., *Table_20160101*) for management reasons. Each record is indexed with a unique rowkey calculated according to the *recordId* and stored in a row of the table. Some key fields such as *PlateCode* and *TollgateCode* are stored in a cell separately and others like *pic1Name* and *relateVideoAddr* are concatenated and stored in one cell to obtain the most considerable performance. Because there is a trade-off between one-column based and multi-column based table structures. The former achieves faster import speed but less access flexibility while the latter is just the opposite.

Table 1. Record format

Field	Example	Field	Example
recordId	1	backendPlateCode	浙A12345
tollgateCode	222051	vehicleColor	A
laneIndex	4	vehicleSpeed	10
passTime	00:00:00	pic1Name	...
plateCode	浙A12345	relateVideoAddr	...
plateColor	1	...	...

There is a lot of business data to be stored while the system is running, including fundamental data like road network information and result data generated by some applications. As a result, many different HBase tables are constructed to hold the corresponding data for maintenance and extension.

3.2   Fast Search Engine

A fast search engine is implemented to support search query, especially multi-condition search and fuzzy search. Equipped with this engine, user could search out the records whose fields containing the specified values within a tolerable response time limit. Since data access is done by relating rowkeys to values in HBase. The problem here is how to figure out the rowkeys of the required records as soon as possible.

H-TDMS builds a secondary index and uses a customized calculation method to figure out the required rowkeys. Logically data in HBase tables is stored in alphabetical order of rowkeys, which are used as a primary index in fact. However there is no way but scanning and filtering the whole table to search out the required records if the rowkeys are not known. Unfortunately, the filter operation in HBase is quite slow and inefficient. HBase would get all the records in a table and then check the content to find out the records that contain the specified values. Instead of using filter operation, a secondary index is designed to relating the specified values to their rowkeys. Figure 4 (a) shows the construction of table *Index_Tollgate* for instance. There is one index table for one specified field of a record and all index information for that field goes into the same index table. When a row is put into the record table, the index information is put into the corresponding index tables. Table *Index_Time* is constructed in another way shown in Fig. 4 (b), utilizing the timestamps generated by a convert function. Any time interval can be specified by setting the range of timestamp. To support fuzzy search of *plateCode*, table *Index_PlateX* is constructed similar as table *Index_Tollgate*, but a special management is employed. When a row is put into the record table, seven rows of index data are generated and put into table *Index_PlateX* at the same time as shown in Fig. 4 (c). A fuzzy search of *plateCode* can be decomposed into several scans, in which the prefixes can be obtained by shifting the *plateCode*. As the rowkeys with the same prefix are stored at a near place in HBase, the scans can be completed very soon. Other index tables such as table *Index_Color* and table *Index_Speed* are constructed in a similar way as table *Index_Tollgate*.

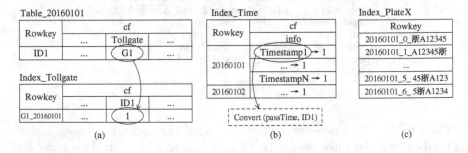

Fig. 4. Construction of index tables

Based on the index tables, the fast search engine defines two basic operations "OR" and "AND" to calculate the index information. Index information is obtained from the index tables and stored in bit sequences, in which the positions of "1"s represent the rowkeys in record tables. "OR" and "AND" are bit-wise operations which are quite fast for processor to perform. The whole process is divided into several sub-processes according to the time condition, usually by the day. In a sub-process, a multi-condition search is decomposed into several steps. Firstly, the search engine decomposes the conditions to get the corresponding index data from the index tables. For each kind of index information, each row of the index data is stored as a bit sequence, which is initialized with "0"s and inserted with "1"s according to the index data. Then all bit sequences are calculated by "OR"/"AND" operations to generate a unique bit sequence for each kind of index information. The calculating logic is determined based on the search conditions in advance. Finally the result bit sequence is generated by calculating the bit sequences of all kinds of index information and the rowkeys of required records are obtained by figuring out the offsets of the "1"s. All of the sub-processes are performed in parallel but commited sequential to make sure that the response can be returned as quickly as possible.

The fast search engine composes of the secondary index and the fast calculation method as discussed above. The secondary index is constructed when the original record data is imported and only sparse "1"s are stored in the index tables. The calculation method takes full advantage of processor's basic bit operations to improve the performance. Both of them make the engine lightweight and powerful.

3.3   Intelligent Analysis Engine

In modern society, people's everyday life has a close connection with traffic issues. In other words, a lot of knowledge can be achieved from the massive traffic data and then be used in traffic management and public security areas. To mine and utilize the knowledge, an intelligent analysis engine is developed based on the fusion of physical, cyber and cognitive spaces. The three-dimensional space model is shown in Fig. 5 (a).

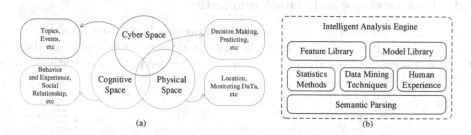

(a)   (b)

Fig. 5. (a) Three-dimensional space model. (b) Intelligent analysis engine

The conventional analysis methods of pattern recognition and data mining usually collect related data from the physical space which is consisted of fundamental data such as location and monitoring data and process them in the cyber space to form events and topics such as traffic jams. However human's

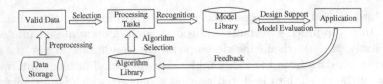

Fig. 6. General process model

experience and judgements are very important and useful in the traffic management and public security areas. Human's feedback will help evaluate and improve the models generated/used during the data processing. So we introduce the human cognitive space which is consisted of human's knowledge into the analysis process. The intelligent analysis engine is hierarchical with three layers as shown in Fig. 5 (b). The semantic parsing layer is applied to define and describe technical terms such as the congestion level of the road section, the speed limit, peak accident times, etc. The algorithm layer integrates and encapsulates various algorithms, including data mining techniques, statistics methods, and human experience. The library layer is adopted to store the features of the traffic and analysis models for prediction, classification, etc.

The intelligent analysis engine is constructed based on Spark instead of MapReduce, because data mining and statistics algorithms benefit a lot from Spark's in-memory computing. Since there is no general one fits all solution in Hadoop, application development is always ad hoc. However, the general process can be modeled as shown in Fig. 6. Human plays an important role during the process, providing professional experience, evaluating results and returning feedback to H-TDMS. Some of the H-TDMS's applications are illustrated and evaluated in detail in Sect. 4.

3.4   User-Interface and Data Visualization

A web-based user-interface is implemented to provide interaction between user and H-TDMS. A set of RESTful web services are created to exchange data. End users access and use H-TDMS through web browsers. Many operations are

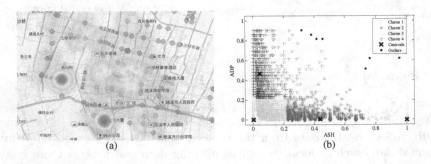

Fig. 7. (a) Sunburst view for a vehicle's activities. (b) Vehicle cluster analysis

defined to allow users to combine their flexibility and creativity. In order to gain insights from the complex analysis results, data visualization is applied to transform various types of data into appropriate visual representations. Figure 7 illustrates two examples of data visualization. Figure 7 (a) is the sunburst view for a vehicle's activities and Fig. 7 (b) shows the result of vehicle cluster analysis.

4   System Evaluation

A prototype system is built on a Hadoop cluster using 3 nodes. One master node takes charge of both cluster management and data processing while the other two slave nodes are only responsible for data processing. The system environment is shown in Table 2. We evaluate our design using actual traffic data of a city in south China, which contains more than 100 million records with a size about 40 GB per month.

Table 2. System environment

Hadoop environment	
Hadoop version	2.6.0
Sqoop version	1.4.5
HBase version	1.0.0
Spark version	1.3.0
Node environment	
CPU	Intel(R) Core(TM) i7-3770 @ 3.40 GHz
Memory	32 GB
OS	Ubuntu Server 12.04 LTS (64-bit)

4.1   Data Import and Preprocessing

The actual traffic data is imported from a PostgreSQL database. Several record sets with different sizes are selected to evaluate the import tool. The performance is shown in Fig. 8 (a). As is evident from the linear regression line, the speed of data import keeps stabile and exceeds 15 million records per minute when the number of records ranges from 20 to 400 million. The main reason for this stability is that the import tool fully utilizes all the processor resources of the cluster during its MapReduce process.

The traffic data is organized and categorized by the intelligent engine, utilizing statistics methods, to extract necessary information for later use. For instance, many spatial and temporal features of vehicle activities and the information about road conditions are summarized based on the historical vehicle trajectory data, which is generated by combining the relating records.

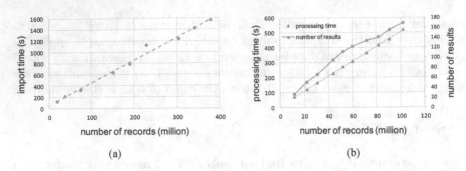

Fig. 8. (a) Performance of data import. (b) Fake plate vehicle detection

4.2 Search Query

Several typical query groups are executed to demonstrate the performance of the search engine. The response times of the queries in the same group differ only tens of milliseconds and an example of each group and its result are listed in Table 3. Query1, Query2 and Query3 are used to get the records of a specified time interval, a specified vehicle and a specified tollgate, respectively, and their response times are less than 300 milliseconds. Query4 to Query9 are the most frequently used search query types, in which the plate number of a vehicle is known or partly known. For a search query with a complete plate number such as Query4 and Query5, the response times are less than 500 milliseconds. The response time of the search queries with more tollgates increases a little as more index information is calculated. Although complex fuzzy search queries like Query6, Query7, Query8, and Query9 have longer response times, they can still return results in just a few seconds. Compared Query9 with Query8, the response time does not increase exponentially along with the time interval's growth because of the process division and parallel computing of the search engine.

Table 3. Performance of the search engine. (The Dash (-) represents an unspecified value, the Question Mark (?) indicates an unknown character, and the Star (*) depicts at least an unknown character.)

	Time interval (hour)	Number of Tollgates	Plate number	Response time (ms)	Numeber of required records
Query1	24	-	-	248	4974959
Query2	24	-	浙BRU683	285	16
Query3	24	1	-	289	6092
Query4	24	1	浙BRU683	287	1
Query5	24	10	浙BRU683	488	9
Query6	24	-	浙B*68?	2298	16037
Query7	24	1	浙B*68?	4924	28
Query8	24	10	浙B*68?	5116	288
Query9	168	10	浙B*68?	7721	2757

4.3 Fake Plate Vehicle Detection

A fake plate vehicle is a vehicle using a plate number that is the same as another legal one. Based on the idea that a vehicle can not appear in more than one location within a short time, H-TDMS employs an application, utilizing trajectory data and road conditions, to detect fake plate vehicles. The number of records analyzed ranges from 12 to 102 million. Figure 8 (b) shows the processing time of the application and the number of fake plate vehicles detected. It takes H-TDMS less than 10 minutes to process 100 million records, revealing the high data processing capability of H-TDMS. The result can be verified by checking the related image and video data.

4.4 Vehicle Cluster Analysis

A case in point to show the usability and scalability of H-TDMS based on users' flexibility and creativity is the vehicle cluster analysis, which can be applied to support risk pre-alarming through outlier detection. The user-interface of H-TDMS provides entrances for users to access data and call functions to construct their own applications. We firstly define a feature vector and then apply rules and precedence to the data to create it. The feature vector is consisted of a vehicle's activity of daily period (ADP) and activity of specified hours (ASH), which represent the temporal features of the vehicle. Then a k-means clustering algorithm is applied to classify 1 million vehicles' feature vectors. The result is shown in Fig. 7 (b). It is convenient for users to construct, run and tune their own applications through the web-based user-interface of H-TDMS.

5 Conclusion

Big data has brought great opportunities for resolving transportation problems. In this paper, we provide H-TDMS for traffic big data management based on cloud computing. Our evaluation shows that H-TDMS achieves considerable performance in data integration, search query, data analysis, and provides usability and scalability for users to combine their flexibility and creativity. In our future work, we plan to develop more customized mining services and encapsulate more open interfaces to support more application functionalities.

References

1. Apache hadoop. http://hadoop.apache.org. Accessed 10 Apr 2016
2. Apache hbase. http://hbase.apache.org. Accessed 10 Apr 2016
3. Apache spark. http://spark.apache.org. Accessed 10 Apr 2016
4. Apache sqoop. http://sqoop.apache.org. Accessed 10 Apr 2016
5. Postgresql. https://www.postgresql.org. Accessed 10 Apr 2016
6. Adiba, M., Castrejon-Castillo, J.C., Oviedo, J.A.E., Vargas-Solar, G., Zechinelli-Martini, J.L.: Big data management challenges, approaches, tools and their limitations. In: Yu, S., Lin, X., Misic, J., Shen, X.S., (eds.) Networking for Big Data, pp. 43–56. Chapman and Hall/CRC, February 2016

7. Aji, A., Wang, F., Vo, H., Lee, R., Liu, Q., Zhang, X., Saltz, J.: Hadoop GIS: a high performance spatial data warehousing system over mapreduce. Proc. VLDB Endowment **6**(11), 1009–1020 (2013)
8. Benitez, I., Blasco, C., Mocholi, A., Quijano, A.: A two-step process for clustering electric vehicle trajectories. In: IEEE International Electric Vehicle Conference (IEVC), pp. 1–8. IEEE (2014)
9. Eldawy, A., Mokbel, M.F.: A demonstration of spatialhadoop: an efficient mapreduce framework for spatial data. Proc. VLDB Endowment **6**(12), 1230–1233 (2013)
10. Kemp, G., Vargas-Solar, G., Da Silva, C.F., Ghodous, P., Collet, C., Lopezamaya, P.: Towards cloud big data services for intelligent transport systems. In: ISPE International Conference on Concurrent Engineering, vol. 2, pp. 377. IOS Press (2015)
11. Lee, K., Ganti, R.K., Srivatsa, M., Liu, L.: Efficient spatial query processing for big data. In: ACM International Conference on Advances in Geographic Information Systems, pp. 469–472. ACM (2014)
12. Lv, Y., Duan, Y., Kang, W., Li, Z., Wang, F.Y.: Traffic flow prediction with big data: a deep learning approach. IEEE Trans. Intell. Transp. Syst. **16**(2), 865–873 (2015)
13. Moriya, K., Matsushima, S., Yamanishi, K.: Traffic risk mining from heterogeneous road statistics. In: IEEE International Conference on Data Science and Advanced Analytics (DSAA), pp. 1–10. IEEE (2015)
14. Shah, N.K.: Big data and cloud computing: pitfalls and advantages in data management. In: International Conference on Computing for Sustainable Global Development (INDIACom), pp. 643–648. IEEE (2015)
15. Van Le, H., Takasu, A.: A scalable spatio-temporal data storage for intelligent transportation systems based on hbase. In: IEEE International Conference on Intelligent Transportation Systems (ITSC), pp. 2733–2738. IEEE (2015)
16. Xiong, G., Zhu, F., Dong, X., Fan, H., Hu, B., Kong, Q., Kang, W., Teng, T.: A kind of novel its based on space-air-ground big-data. IEEE Intell. Transp. Syst. Mag. **8**(1), 10–22 (2016)
17. Xu, X., Dou, W.: An assistant decision-supporting method for urban transportation planning over big traffic data. In: Zu, Q., Hu, B., Gu, N., Seng, S. (eds.) HCC 2014. LNCS, vol. 8944, pp. 251–264. Springer, Heidelberg (2015)
18. Yu, J., Jiang, F., Zhu, T.: Rtic-c: a big data system for massive traffic information mining. In: International Conference on Cloud Computing and Big Data (CloudCom-Asia), pp. 395–402. IEEE (2013)
19. Yue, X., Cao, L., Chen, Y., Xu, B.: Multi-view actionable patterns for managing traffic bottleneck. In: Workshops at the Twenty-Ninth AAAI Conference on Artificial Intelligence (2015)
20. Zheng, X., Chen, W., Wang, P., Shen, D., Chen, S., Wang, X., Zhang, Q., Yang, L.: Big data for social transportation. IEEE Trans. Intell. Transp. Syst. **17**(3), 620–630 (2016)

GLDA: Parallel Gibbs Sampling for Latent Dirichlet Allocation on GPU

Pei Xue[1], Tao Li[1,2(✉)], Kezhao Zhao[1], Qiankun Dong[1], and Wenjing Ma[3]

[1] College of Computer and Control Engineering,
Nankai University, Tianjin 300071, China
litao@nankai.edu.cn
[2] State Key Lab. of Computer Architecture, Institute of Computing Technology,
Chinese Academy of Sciences, Beijing, China
[3] Laboratory of Parallel Software and Computational Science,
State Key Laboratory of Computing Science, Institute of Software, Chinese Academy
of Sciences, Beijing, China

Abstract. With the development of the general computing ability of
GPU, more and more algorithms are being run on GPU, to enjoy much
higher speed. In this paper, we propose an approach that uniformly accelerate Gibbs Sampling for LDA (Latent Dirichlet Allocation) algorithm on
GPU, which makes the data load to the cores of GPU evenly to avoid the
idle waiting for GPU, and improves the utilization of GPU. We use three
text mining datasets to test the algorithm. Experiments show that our
parallel methods can achieve about 30x speedup over sequential training
methods with similar prediction precision. Furthermore, the idea that
uniformly partitioning the data bases on GPU can also be applied to
other machine learning algorithms.

Keywords: CUDA · Parallel LDA · Topic model · Data partition ·
Machine learning

1 Introduction

With the development of social networks, huge amount of text messages are produced every day. Text mining algorithms can extract and analyze useful information from a large collection of texts. Among them, LDA (Latent Dirichlet
Allocation) algorithm based on Gibbs sampling [3] is a mature topic clustering algorithm. Gibbs sampling is a Markov-chain Monte Carlo method to perform inference. We simply call LDA algorithm based on Gibbs sampling as LDA
algorithm in this paper. LDA algorithm can accurately extract the text theme
and latent semantic [12,18], and it has been widely used in the field of micro
blog recommendation, news search, semantic analysis, etc. However, due to the
increasing amount of data on the Internet, running it on a CPU is usually time-
consuming. Thus how to accelerate the LDA algorithm efficiently has become a
hot topic.

© Springer Science+Business Media Singapore 2016
J. Wu and L. Li (Eds.): ACA 2016, CCIS 626, pp. 97–107, 2016.
DOI: 10.1007/978-981-10-2209-8_9

LDA does not take the order of words and documents into account, so it can be parallelized on multiple platforms. There are two common ways to do it: parallelize LDA algorithm based on distributed platform or based on shared memory multi-core platform. In the first scenario, with the increase of node number, the communication cost is also increased [22], which has a bad effect on performance. Also, the amount of work on a single node in a distributed cluster is still large. The problems of node communication and computation of the loose coupled line are solved by tightly coupled shared memory platform. However, the traditional data partition according to documents leads to severe load imbalance on different cores. Thus, all the cores have to carry out data synchronization after each iteration (all have to wait for the core with largest amount of data), which lead to a lot of idle waiting or even stagnation. In addition, LDA parallel sampling will cause data writing and reading conflict on tightly coupled shared memory platform. Therefore, how to make full use of multi-cores computing power and avoid large idle waiting time is also a big problem.

With the development of hardware architecture, GPU (Graphics Processing Unit) [1] has super computing power with multi-cores and high memory bandwidth. Every core has equal computing power and memory bandwidth, and all cores share one global memory in GPU [23]. NVIDIA Kepler [1] compute architecture of GPU has a high performance on parallel computing. Also, throughput of global memory atomic operations on Kepler is substantially improved. We use CUDA (Compute Unified Device Architecture) programming model for GPU parallel computing. CUDA is designed by NVIDIA, and provides a good programming framework for accelerating the LDA topic clustering algorithm.

In this paper, we propose a new parallel LDA model based on the GPU architecture. This model is able to partition the data uniformly to different threads, and thus can avoid idle waiting and improve the utilization of the GPU cores. We propose a double data rotation method with atomic operation to solve data reading and writing conflicts, which improves the performance. We use different datasets to test the performance of this model, and prove that this model can achieve the same prediction accuracy as their sequential method on CPU.

The rest of the paper is organized as follows. Related works are introduced in Sect. 2. Section 3 present the basic introduction to LDA model using Gibbs sampling. In Sect. 4, we introduce our new parallel model based on GPU. In Sect. 5, we used different datasets to test the speedup and perplexity of the new algorithm. We conclude this paper in Sect. 6.

2   Related Work

The parallel methods of LDA algorithm fall in two main categories: (1) LDA parallel algorithm based on loosely coupled distributed platform [13,19]. (2) LDA parallel algorithm based on tightly coupled shared memory platform [9,12]. The main loosely coupled distributed parallel LDA algorithm is as follows. Newman et al. [16] proposed to Approximate Distributed LDA algorithm (AD-LDA).

Asynchronous Distributed LDA model (AS-LDA) proposed by Asuncion et al. [17]. AD-LDA algorithm was improved with Message Passing Interface (MPI) and MapReduce by Chen et al. [5]. There are also some tightly shared memory parallel LDA algorithms. Yan et al. [21] introduced a parallel model of Gibbs sample inference for LDA on GPU, Masada T et al. [14] introduced a parallel model of Collapsed Variational Bayesian (CVB) inference for LDA on GPU.

Parallel LDA algorithm based on loosely distributed platform partitions the documents to different nodes. Each sampling consists of two parts: (1) every node in distributed form samples its own data; (2) Communication between different nodes, so that the data of each node can be updated. With the number of nodes increasing, communication costs between different nodes will also gradually increase [13,16,17,19]. In addition, the calculation ability of one single node is still large. These two aspects will affect acceleration performance seriously. Parallel LDA algorithm based on tightly coupled shared memory platform can solve the communication problem in distributed platform. Yan et al. [21] proposed a data partition scheme running on GPU where documents and words are both divided into P disjoint subsets, and loading to P threads. To avoid access conflict in parameter matrices, the input document-word matrix is partitioned into independent data blocks with non-overlapping rows and columns. A pre-processing algorithm is used to balance the number of words in data blocks so that different threads can scan with no-conflict in blocks and do a synchronization step. However, the number of words in one document may be several times of another document and there may be uneven distribution of different words in one document. Therefore, it is difficult for absolute data block balancing, and faster threads need to wait for the slowest one, which causes longer locking time or even stagnation. The preprocessing algorithm running on GPU adds some extra time. In this paper, we propose a new partition scheme that data can be truly and evenly loaded to the threads of GPU's kernel. Moreover, We propose a double data rotation method with atomic operation to solve data reading and writing conflicts.

3   LDA Algorithm Based on Gibbs Sampling

We briefly review the LDA model based on Gibbs sampling now. LDA [4] is an unsupervised classification algorithm, which can be used to identify the hidden topic information of large-scale document sets. It uses the bag of words method, taking each document as a vector of word frequency, and converting text information to numerical vectors which are easier to be modeled. Document j of D documents is a multinomial distribution denoted by θ as a mixture over T latent topics, and each topic k is a multinomial distribution with a word vocabulary having W distinct words, denoted by φ. Both θ and φ have Dirichlet prior distribution [4] respectively with super parameters α and β, the formula is denoted as:

$$\theta_{k|j} \sim Dirichlet[\alpha], \varphi_{w|k} \sim Dirichlet[\beta] \tag{1}$$

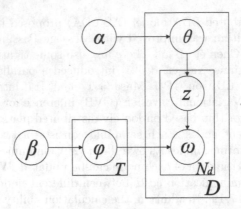

Fig. 1. LDA topic generation model diagram

Gibbs sampling process is to produce every word of documents with prior distribution θ and φ. This generation process can be represented by Fig. 1.

As is shown in Fig. 1, the document set D is a collection of T topics. Each document represents a probability distribution over the topics, and each topic represents a probability distribution over the words. So the probability of the document j on topic k is θ_{jk}. When word x_{ij} is assigned to topic z_{ij}, the probability of the word w on topic z_{ij} can be denoted as $\varphi_{z_{ij}w}$. When sampling the word w_{ij} (the ith word in document j) in LDA, the current topic z_{ij} of word w_{ij} is sampled by the conditional probability formula:

$$P(z_{ij} = k \mid z^{\neg ij}, x, \alpha, \beta) \propto \frac{n_{x_{ij}k}^{\neg ij} + \beta}{n_k^{\neg ij} + W\beta}(n_j^{\neg ij}k + \alpha) \qquad (2)$$

In formula (2), $n_{x_{ij}k}$ denotes the number of ith word in document j assigned to the topic k, n_{jk} denotes the number of words in document j assigned to topic k, and $n_k^{\neg ij} = \sum_w n_{kw}^{\neg ij}$. Superscript $\neg ij$ means the variable is calculated as if word x_{ij} is removed from the training data. Paramter W Parameter.

The precess of LDA algorithm is described as follows:

Step 1: For each document and each word in the document, assign a topic randomly.
Step 2: According to Formula (2), sample the words of the documents.
Step 3: Repeat step 2, until the subject distribution convergences.

It is assumed that the algorithm get converge after n iterations, in each iteration it needs to sample N words in documents D, and each time of sampling should traverse T topics, so the time complexity of the algorithm is close to $O(n \times N \times T)$. When the dataset is large, the corresponding N and T is relatively large, so the total time complexity is relatively large, therefore parallel algorithm is needed.

4   Parallel LDA Training on GPU

4.1   Data Partition

In LDA algorithm, we need not consider the order of documents in a dataset and the order of words in a document. This provides a good theoretical basis to parallelize LDA algorithm. The common data partition scheme is to divide the documents into a number of partitions, and distributing the partitions to different nodes or cores, then all the nodes or cores update their data after synchronization and communication. However, as mentioned in Sect. 2, the number of words in one document may be several times of another document. For synchronization, we must wait for the node or core which has the documents with the most number of words. On GPU architecture, we also face this problem of load imbalance. Therefore, we propose a partition scheme that distribute the data evenly on the threads.

Our data partition scheme is motivated by the following observation: When we sample the documents dataset, we are sampling the words in it, since a document is a vector of words frequency in LDA. So we just put the words in different documents into the same dataset. In each iteration, we just count the number of words of the dataset, denoted as N, and distribute them over K threads. We do not consider the document subscript of the word, so each thread loads N/K words. In CUDA, a kernel can be executed by multiple equally-shaped blocks, and every block has its blockId; one block can have many threads, and every thread has its threadId [10, 11]. the number K of total threads in kernel is calculated by $blockDim \times gridDim$. We count the thread's id with $blockIdx.x \times blockDim + threadIdx.x$, every thread loads N/K words ranging form $id \times N/K$ to $(id + 1) * N/K$.

Actually the data partition scheme may cause a problem that the words from one document may be distributed to different threads. So when different threads sample the data on GPU in parallel, it may cause writing conflict. Multiple threads may access the same value of document-topic matrix N_{dk} at the same time when they occasionally process the words of one document simultaneously. We call this document-topic conflict. Besides document-topic conflict, multiple threads may access the same value of the word-topic matrix N_{wk} or topic vector Z_k at the same time. When they occasionally process the same word or the same topic simultaneously, we call it word-topic conflict and topic-vector conflict respectively. This issue may lead to wrong inference results and operation failure. In this paper, we use atomic operation to solve this problem, and more details will be described in the next section.

4.2   GLDA Algorithm

In the processing of the LDA algorithm, the most time consuming part is Gibbs sampling, so the main goal of parallelizing LDA algorithm is to parallelize Gibbs sampling. On GPU, the words in the document set D are equally divided into

S part, with each part denoted as $V_1, V_2, ..., V_S$. Each thread processes approximately N/S words. In Gibbs sampling on GPU, the topic matrix of words N_{wk}, the topic matrix of documents N_{dk}, topic capacity matrix Z_k (the number of words assigned to topic k), are all stored in the global memory of one GPU. Since data are divided evenly, the matrix N_{wk}, N_{dk}, Z_k may all encounter reading conflict and writing conflict. Writing conflict has been illustrated in Sect. 4.1. When we use atomic operation to sample N_{wk}, N_{dk}, Z_k, it means this operation is performed without interference from other threads, when we used the atomic operation to write other threads could not read from it, we call it reading conflict. So we adopt double data rotation strategy to reduce the waiting time. We adopt double data rotation strategy to solve reading conflict problem. Each of these three matrices has a "reading copy" $N_{dk}^{"}, N_{wk}^{"}, Z_k^{"}$ respectively in each iteration. The data of each thread s is sampled from:

$$P(Z_{ijs} = k \mid z^{"ij}, x, \alpha, \beta) \propto \frac{n_{x_{ij}k}^{"ij} + \beta}{n_k^{"ij} + W\beta}(n_j^{"ij}k + \alpha) \qquad (3)$$

where superscript $"ij$ denotes the variable word x_{ij} is from the reading copy matrix. Since the data in the "reading copy" are from the last iteration, they are not affected by the updating operation of the threads, therefore we can ensure that all the threads are seeing consistent values of the 3 matrices. When writing the sampling result to the matrices in each thread, we use *atomic* operation to avoid writing conflict. Atomic operation is completed by hardware in only a few clock cycles, and therefore very efficient. The overhead is almost neglectable on NVIDIA Kepler [1] compute architecture of GPU. Each time the Gibbs sample is completed, the reading matrix is updated by the result of the sampling with threads and the process is very fast. The pseudo code of this algorithm is shown in Algorithm 1.

Algorithm 1. Parallel Gibbs Sampling

Input: Document data collection
Count words number of dataset: N
Equally divide the words into S part:$V_1, V_2, ..., V_S$
Initialized the matrix N_{dk}, N_{wk}, Z_{ij} for writing.
Initialized the matrix $N_{dk}^{"}, N_{wk}^{"}, Z_{ij}^{"}$ for reading.
repeat
for each Processor s in parallel with data V_s **do**
   for each Word in V_s **do**
      read from matrix $N_{dk}^{"}, N_{wk}^{"}, Z_{ij}^{"}$
      atomic sample writing matrix N_{dk}, N_{wk}, Z_{ij} according to Formula (3)
   end for
end for
Synchronization step for N_{dk}, N_{wk}, Z_{ij}
Update $N_{dk}^{"} \leftarrow N_{dk}, N_{wk}^{"} \leftarrow N_{wk}, Z_{ij}^{"} \leftarrow Z_{ij}$
until convergence
Output: N_{dk}, N_{wk}, Z_{ij}.

In the pseudo code, we divide the words into S disjoint subsets according to the number of words, and distribute them to S threads. In each iteration, S threads parallelly read data from matrix $N_{dk}^{''}, N_{wk}^{''}, Z_{ij}^{''}$ and sample the results into N_{dk}, N_{wk}, Z_{ij} with atomic operation, and then we update $N_{dk}^{''}, N_{wk}^{''}, Z_{ij}^{''}$ with N_{dk}, N_{wk}, Z_{ij}. Finally the results is convergent.

5   Experiments

5.1   Experimental Environment

Hardware Environment. We used a machine with an Inter(R) Core(TM) i7-2600 CPU with frequency of 3.40 GHz. The host memory size is 6 GB. Our GPU is an NVIDIA Tesla K40, which has 2880 cores and each core at 745 MHz. The K40 GPU has 12 GB global memory, and the memory bandwidth is 288 GB/s.

Software Environment. We adopted CUDA toolkit [8] as our GPU development environment, and CUDA programs run on a Single Program Multiple Threads (SPMT) fashion [7]. Our program is written in C language, and we used an NVCC compiler to compile the program. The toolkit and compiler run on Ubuntu 14.04 with 64-bit Linux kernel.

In this paper, we used three common data sets of different sizes to test the performance of our algorithm. These three data sets are commonly used in natural language processing. They are KOS data set, RCV1 data set, and Enron data set. The attribute of the data sets is shown in Table 1. We randomly extracted 90 % of all word tokens as the training set, and the remaining 10 % of word tokens are the testing set.

Table 1. Datasets used in the experiments

dataset	Number of documents (D)	Vocabulary Size (W)	Number of word tokens (N)
KOS	3430	6906	467700
RCV1	23149	47151	2798000
Enron	39861	28102	6400000

Tesla K40 adopted the NVIDIA Kepler compute architecture. According to the number of SM(Streaming Multiprocessor) and SP(Streaming Processor) in K40 [2,6], we set the thread block number to 192 and thread number in each block to 256.

For each dataset, we set $\alpha = 0.5$ and $\beta = 0.01$ in all experiments, which results in good quality in practice. For each dataset, we also tested the impact of different number of the topics. We set the number of topics K to 20, 40, and 60 in each dataset. In addition, we set the number of iterations L to 100, 150, 200, and 250, in order to test the impact of different iterations.

5.2 Speedup in Experiments

We compared our parallel method with the serial code on a single core on the CPU. All CPU implementations are compiled by gcc compiler with -O3 optimization. We did our best to optimize the code of the original C language serial program, such as using better data layout and reducing redundant computation. The run time of the final CPU code is almost twice as fast as the initial code. The parallel and serial experimental results for each data set are shown in Fig. 2.

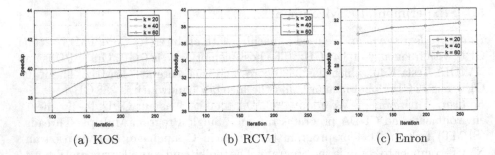

(a) KOS   (b) RCV1   (c) Enron

Fig. 2. Speedup

The results prove that more than 30x speedup is achieved for parallel algorithm with all the three datasets. For example, the running time of RCV1 dataset ($K = 40, L = 200$) in serial is 379.76 s, while our parallel algorithm on GPU only takes 11.48 s. As is shown in the experimental results, our method on the KOS dataset can achieve almost 38x speedup under different topic numbers and different iterations, on the RCV1 data set can achieve almost 35x speedup, and on the Enron data set can achieve almost 30x speedup. We can see that the larger the data set, the lower the speedup. Our analysis is that when we use GPU to deal with the data set, we must first copy the data set from host memory to the global memory in GPU. Then, after running the algorithm in GPU, we copy the result from the global memory to host memory. The data transmission between the CPU-GPU heterogeneous system is through the PCIe bus, whose bandwidth can only reach 5–6 G/s. The time of data copy is proportional to the size of data set. Thus we can infer that the copy time of a bigger data set is longer, so the speedup is a little smaller. However, the time of data transmission only accounts for a small part of the total running time when the amount of data is large enough. As shown in the Fig. 2, with more iterations, the proportion of data transmission decreases, so the speedup increases. In summary, our algorithm can achieve a high performance from different data sets we tested, and at least 25x speedup can be achieved.

5.3 Perplexity in Experiments

We measure the performance of the parallel algorithms using test set perplexity [15, 20]. Perplexity is usually used to measure the quality of the data mining model.

The smaller the perplexity finally converges to, the better the quality of the model is. Test set perplexity is defined as $\exp\left(-\frac{1}{N^t_{est}}\log p(X^{test})\right)$ [20]. For LDA algorithm model, we compute the likelihood $p(X^{test})$ by averaging $M = 10$ samples at the end of 250 iterations from different chains. The log likelihood $\log p(X^{test})$ is defined as:

$$\log p(X^{test}) = \sum_{j,w} \log \frac{1}{M} \sum_M \sum_k \theta^S_{k|j}\varphi^S_{w|k}, \tag{4}$$

where

$$\theta^S_{k|j} = \frac{\alpha + n^S_{k|j}}{K\alpha + n^S_j}, \varphi^S_{w|k} = \frac{\beta + n^S_{w|k}}{W\beta + n^S_k}. \tag{5}$$

Each data set is split into a training set and a test set. When running the test set after each iteration, we copy the current sample results from the global memory in GPU to the host memory, and then calculate the perplexity value according to Formula (2) in each iteration. The perplexity results of the three data sets is shown in Fig. 3.

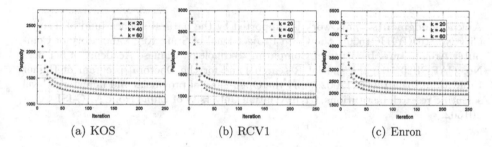

(a) KOS   (b) RCV1   (c) Enron

Fig. 3. Perplexity

For each data set, we computed the perplexity value of different number of topics ($K = 20, 40, 60$), and in each test we set the iterations to 250. We observe that the perplexity values of KOS generally converge to 1300 by 100 iterations, the perplexity values of RCV1 generally converge to 1200 by 50 iterations, and the perplexity of Enron generally converge to 2500 by 100 iterations. On the one hand, the perplexity values of the three data set are all convergent, and for each data set, the value the perplexity converges to with different topic numbers is not of much difference. On the other hand, the convergent speed of different data set is approximately the same, but the convergent value is different. That is mainly because that different data sets have distinctive internal structures.

In conclusion, we calculated the perplexity value with different data sets and different topic numbers in our parallel algorithm, and the perplexity values in our experiment are convergent and reasonable, which verified the correctness and accuracy of our algorithm. We also compared the perplexity values of our parallel method with that of the serial method under the same parameter conditions, and the results of serial algorithm are basically the same. We did not show the serial perplexity results in the figures, because their images are overlapped.

6   Conclusions

LDA algorithm is commonly used in the field of text mining with high time complexity. In this paper we simply introduced the background of the GPU structure and the CUDA Programming Model, and then simply reviewed the LDA algorithm, and finally we proposed a new parallel LDA algorithm of partition data uniformly. We used different data sets to test the speedup and perplexity of this new algorithm and achieved good result. There are two main contributions of our new algorithm: (1) a new data partition scheme which can load the data evenly on each thread, and (2) a new way to solve the reading and writing conflict in GPU.

In the future, we can use multiple GPUs to parallelize the LDA algorithm, and further improve the data copy strategy of CPU-GPU heterogeneous to reduce the time of data transmission in the heterogeneous system as far as possible.

Acknowledgments. This work is supported by the natural science fund of Tianjin City No. 16JCYBJC15200, the Open Project Fund of State Key Laboratory of Computer Architecture, Institute of Computing Technology, Chinese Academy of Sciences No. CARCH201504, the special Research Fund for the Doctoral program of Higher Education No. 20130031120029, and the Open Fund of provincial and ministerial level scientific research institutions, Civil Aviation University of China No. CAAC-ISECCA-201502.

References

1. Nvidia cuda. http://www.nvidia.com/cuda
2. Aila, T., Laine, S.: Understanding the efficiency of ray traversal on GPUs. In: Proceedings of the Conference on High Performance Graphics 2009, pp. 145–149. ACM (2009)
3. Blei, D.M.: Introduction to probabilistic topicmodels. http://www.cs.princeton.edu/blei/papers/Blei2011.pdf
4. Blei, D.M., Ng, A.Y., Jordan, M.I.: Latent dirichlet allocation. J. Mach. Learn. Res. **3**, 993–1022 (2003)
5. Chen, W.Y., Chu, J.C., Luan, J., Bai, H., Wang, Y., Chang, E.Y.: Collaborative filtering for orkut communities: discovery of user latent behavior. In: Proceedings of the 18th international conference on World wide web, pp. 681–690. ACM (2009)
6. Cook, S.: CUDA programming: a developer's guide to parallel computing with GPUs. Newnes (2012)
7. Wu, E., Liu, Y.: General calculation based on graphics processing unit (in Chinese). J. Comput. Aided Des. Comput. Graph. **16**(5), 601–612 (2004)
8. Zhang, H., Li, L., Lan, L.: Research on the application of the general calculation of GPU (in Chinese). Comput. Digit. Eng. **33**(12), 60–62 (2005)

9. Leischner, N., Osipov, V., Sanders, P.: GPU sample sort. In: 2010 IEEE International Symposium on Parallel & Distributed Processing (IPDPS), pp. 1–10. IEEE (2010)

10. Li, T., Liu, X., Dong, Q., Ma, W., Wang, K.: HPSVM: Heterogeneous parallel SVM with factorization based ipm algorithm on CPU-GPU cluster. In: 2016 24th Euromicro International Conference on Parallel, Distributed, and Network-Based Processing (PDP), pp. 74–81. IEEE (2016)

11. Li, T., Wang, D., Zhang, S., Yang, Y.: Parallel rank coherence in networks for inferring disease phenotype and gene set associations. In: Wu, J., Chen, H., Wang, X. (eds.) ACA 2014. CCIS, vol. 451, pp. 163–176. Springer, Heidelberg (2014)

12. Liu, X., Zeng, J., Yang, X., Yan, J., Yang, Q.: Scalable parallel em algorithms for latent dirichlet allocation in multi-core systems. In: Proceedings of the 24th International Conference on World Wide Web, pp. 669–679. International World Wide Web Conferences Steering Committee (2015)

13. Liu, Z., Zhang, Y., Chang, E.Y., Sun, M.: Plda+: parallel latent dirichlet allocation with data placement and pipeline processing. ACM Trans. Intell. Syst. Technol. (TIST) 2(3), 26 (2011)

14. Masada, T., Hamada, T., Shibata, Y., Oguri, K.: Accelerating collapsed variational Bayesian inference for latent dirichlet allocation with nvidia CUDA compatible devices. In: Chien, B.C., Hong, T.P., Chen, S.M., Ali, M. (eds.) IEA/AIE 2009. LNCS, vol. 5579, pp. 491–500. Springer, Heidelberg (2009)

15. Nallapati, R.M., Ahmed, A., Xing, E.P., Cohen, W.W.: Joint latent topic models for text and citations. In: Proceedings of the 14th ACM SIGKDD international conference on Knowledge discovery and data mining, pp. 542–550. ACM (2008)

16. Newman, D., Smyth, P., Welling, M., Asuncion, A.U.: Distributed inference for latent dirichlet allocation. In: Advances in Neural Information Processing Systems, pp. 1081–1088 (2007)

17. Smyth, P., Welling, M., Asuncion, A.U.: Asynchronous distributed learning of topic models. In: Advances in Neural Information Processing Systems. pp. 81–88 (2009)

18. Tang, J., Huo, R., Yao, J.: Evaluation of stability and similarity of latent dirichlet allocation. In: Software Engineering (WCSE), 2013 Fourth World Congress on. pp. 78–83. IEEE (2013)

19. Tora, S., Eguchi, K.: Mpi/openmp hybrid parallel inference for latent dirichlet allocation. In: Proceedings of the Third Workshop on Large Scale Data Mining: Theory and Applications. pp. 5. ACM (2011)

20. Wang, Y., Bai, H., Stanton, M., Chen, W.Y., Chang, E.Y.: PLDA: Parallel Latent Dirichlet Allocation for Large-Scale Applications. In: Goldberg, A.V., Zhou, Y. (eds.) AAIM 2009. LNCS, vol. 5564, pp. 301–314. Springer, Heidelberg (2009)

21. Yan, F., Xu, N., Qi, Y.: Parallel inference for latent dirichlet allocation on graphics processing units. In: Advances in Neural Information Processing Systems. pp. 2134–2142 (2009)

22. Yan, J.F., Zeng, J., Gao, Y., Liu, Z.Q.: Communication-efficient algorithms for parallel latent dirichlet allocation. Soft Computing 19(1), 3–11 (2015)

23. Zhang, S., Li, T., Dong, Q., Liu, X., Yang, Y.: Cpu-assisted gpu thread pool model for dynamic task parallelism. In: Networking, Architecture and Storage (NAS), 2015 IEEE International Conference on. pp. 135–140. IEEE (2015)

High Performance Stencil Computations for Intel® Xeon Phi™ Coprocessor

Luxia Feng, Yushan Dong, Chunjiang Li[✉], and Hao Jiang

School of Computer, National University of Defence Technology,
Changsha, Hunan, China
932744732@qq.com, yushandong@hotmail.com,
{chunjiang,haojiang}@nudt.edu.cn

Abstract. Stencil computations are a class of computational kernels which update array elements according to some stencil patterns, and they have drawn more attentions recently. The Intel Xeon Phi coprocessor, which is designed for high performance computing, has not been fully evaluated for stencil computations. In this paper, we present a series of optimizations to accelerate the 3-D 7-point stencil code on Intel Xeon Phi coprocessor. We focus on how to exploit the performance potential of many cores and wide-vector unit in each core. In order to exploit data locality, we use loop tiling and we propose a method for calculating the block size while tiling. The achieved performance brings a speedup of 211.6 in comparison with the serial code.

Keywords: Stencil computation · Intel® Xeon Phi™ coprocessor · Vectorization · Loop tiling

1 Introduction

Stencil computations [1,2] are an important class of code, and they are commonly found in a variety of applications. Stencil computations described a structured grid of points in N dimensions. The fixed set of neighboring points whose values are required to calculate the new value of one point is usually called a stencil. The stencil [3] defines how the value of a point should be computed from the values of itself and its neighbors.

Intel Xeon Phi Coprocessor [4] is the very first product of the Intel Many Integrated Core (MIC) architecture [5]. Intel Xeon Phi coprocessor offers more than 50 cores and more than 200 hardware threads, and each core contains a 512-bit vector unit (SIMD). It can deliver peak performance of 1 teraFLOP/s for double precision floating point calculations. Intel Xeon Phi coprocessors were already deployed in the fastest supercomputer Tianhe-2 [7]. Programming for the Intel Xeon Phi coprocessors is mostly like programming for a shared memory multi-processing system. But, when transplant stencil code to Intel Xeon Phi, lots of performance tuning is still inevitable. In this paper, we evaluate the performance of a 3-D 7-point stencil computation on Intel Xeon Phi coprocessors

© Springer Science+Business Media Singapore 2016
J. Wu and L. Li (Eds.): ACA 2016, CCIS 626, pp. 108–117, 2016.
DOI: 10.1007/978-981-10-2209-8_10

with a serious of optimizations. In summary, our work makes the following contributions:

1. Multi-level parallelism (multi-threading for outermost loop and vectorization for the innermost loop) is leveraged to make use of the massively parallel processing power of Intel Xeon Phi.
2. In order to exploit data locality, loop tiling is used for further optimization. And a tile size calculation suitable for Intel Xeon Phi is also devised.

The rest of this paper is organized as follows. Section 2 analyzes the target stencils. Section 3 presents an overview of the Intel Xeon Phi architecture. Section 4 describes various performance optimization techniques we applied. Section 5 gives the performance evaluation. Section 6 introduces some related works. In Sect. 7, a summary of our work and some directions for future work are presented.

```
1    for (t = 0; t < niter; t++) {
2      for (z = 0; z < nz; z++) {
3        for (y = 0; y < ny; y++) {
4          for (x = 0; x < nx; x++) {
5            cur[z,y,x] = cc*old[z,y,x] + cw*old[z,y,x-1] + ce*old[z,y,x+1]+
6              cn*old[z,y-1,x] + cs*old[z,y+1,x] + cb*old[z-1,y,x]+
7              ct*old[z+1,y,x] ;
8    } } }
9      swap (cur, old) ;
10   }
```

Fig. 1. 3-D 7-point stencil code

2   Target Stencils

As Fig. 1 shows, We choose 3-D 7-point stencil code as the target because it's typical stencil code with medium complexity. The `old[]` array contains the current volume data and the `cur[]` array is used to store the results of the current time step iteration. The outermost loop is the number of time steps requested and the inner triple loops (lines 2–8) applies the stencil calculations to each dimension using the previous value of the target point and six nearest neighboring points. After being processed for current time step, the two array pointers are swapped (line 9). Besides, the data type of all arrays is double-precision floating-point, and the weights should satisfy the Eq. 1.

$$cc + cw + ce + cn + cs + cb + ct = 1 \tag{1}$$

From the stencil code shown in Fig. 1, it is obvious that there is no data dependence for each iteration of time step, so the outmost loop can be parallelized. And there is no data dependence in the innermost loop, so the innermost loop can be vectorized. Besides, each update of a signal point requires 13 double-precision float-point operations, so $(nx \times ny \times nz) \times 13 \times count$ operations are performed in all. Meanwhile, $(nx \times ny \times nz) \times sizeof(double) \times 3 \times count$ bytes data is loaded or stored. Hence, the compute/fetch ratio is calculated as Eq. 2. The ratio clearly indicates that the stencil code is memory-intensive.

$$\frac{(nx \times ny \times nz) \times 13}{(nx \times ny \times nz) \times sizeof(double) \times 3 \times count} = 0.54 Flops/B \qquad (2)$$

3   Architecture of the Intel Xeon Phi

The Intel Xeon Phi coprocessor is composed of a silicon chip (containing the cores, caches and memory controllers), GDDR5 memory chips, flash memory, system management controller, miscellaneous electronics and connectors to attach into a computer system. The x86-based cores, the memory controllers, and the PCI Express system I/O logic are interconnected with a high speed ring-based bidirectional on-die interconnect. Figure 2 illustrates the architecture of Intel Xeon Phi [6]. Each core supports SIMD, and the vector processing unit (VPU) executes the newly introduced Intel Initial Many Core Instructions (IMCI) with 512-bit vector length. And each core also supports four hardware threads. Each core has 32 KB private L1 instruction cache, 32 KB private L1 data cache and 512 KB shared L2 cache. The L2 caches are fully coherent and they can supply data to each other on-die. The memory subsystem is comprised of high speed GDDR5 memory. Besides, the Intel Xeon Phi coprocessor runs Linux operating system (OS) that is a minimal and embedded Linux environment with the Linux Standard Base core libraries.

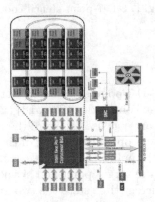

Fig. 2. Architecture of Intel® Xeon Phi™ coprocessor

Intel Xeon Phi coprocessor supports three working modes, including native, offload and symmetric. In the native mode, it runs as a share-memory many-core processor. In the offload mode, it acts as a coprocessor. In the symmetric mode, it behaves just like an equivalent node with the general purpose host processor.

4 Performance Optimizations

As an x86-based SMP-on-a-chip, we can still use the code shown in Fig. 1 without any modification, and put it as the baseline for subsequent performance optimizations and evaluations.

4.1 Parallelization and Vectorization

As a share-memory many-core processor, parallelizing the code to execute on all cores is the first challenge. Fortunately, the simple and powerful OpenMP [8], which is the prevalent standard API for shared memory multiprocessing, brings us convenience. As the analysis shown in Sect. 2, each iteration of the time steps of the 3-D 7-point stencil code can be parallelized. Then an OpenMP `parallel for` loop pragma can be added before the z loop. Line 2 of the code shown in Fig. 3 displays the method of parallelization. THNUM parameter is used to specify the number of thread in parallelization.

```
1    for (t = 0; t < niter; t++) {
2    #pragma omp  parallel for num_threads(THNUM) private(x,y)
3        for (z = 0; z < nz; z++) {
4            for (y = 0; y < ny; y++) {
5    #pragma simd
6    #pragma vector nontemporal
7                for (x = 0; x < nx; x++) {
8                    boundary processing and indices linearizing
9                    cur[c] = cc*old[c] + cw*old[w] + ce*old[e] +
10                           cs*old[s] + cn*old[n] + cb*old[b] + ct*old[t];
11       }  }  }
12       swap (cur, old) ;
13   }
```

Fig. 3. 3-D 7-point stencil code with parallelizing optimizations

Each core in Intel Xeon Phi coprocessor has a 512-bit VPU and its crucial to effectively utilize it for achieving high performance. Because there is no dependency in the innermost loop, SIMD directives that force the compiler to vectorize the iterations in the innermost loop (line 5 in Fig. 3). However, alignment of the store addresses is required. When the length of the array is not the multiples of 64, the `malloc()` are replaced with `_mm_malloc()` with a second parameter of 64 specifying the byte alignment of the arrays.

4.2 Loop Tiling for Data Locality

Another important optimization is to exploit data locality for L2 cache. We applied multi-level loop tiling [9] to exploit data locality. In this scheme, a signal sweep of the grid is partitioned into cubic blocks. Within a single iteration of the time-step loop t, it partitions the 3-D domain of size $(nx \times ny \times nz)$ into blocks of size $(tx \times ty \times tz)$, so that grid points which are close in space are grouped to be modified together. Each grid point in every block can remain in cache to compute new values of points without fetching from memory. And the size of the block should satisfy the Eq. 3.

$$(tx \times ty \times tz) \times sizeof(DType) \times T_p \times N_m < S_{cache} \qquad (3)$$

Where $DType$ represents the data type, T_p is the number of thread in each core, N_m is the amount of array read from memory, and S_{cache} represents the capacity of cache. For example, the capacity of L2 cache in each core of Intel Xeon Phi coprocessor is 512 KB. While running two threads on a core with streaming store, the number of double-precision floating-point grid point in each block is 32 K at most. Leopol [10] have found that when the 3-D domain of size N^3 is tiled to achieve higher performance, the suggested size of blocks is $(N \times s \times (s \times \frac{L}{2}))$. Where L is the size of cache line (64 B), and s is the only parameter calculated to satisfy the target platform. Keeping the x not to be partitioned can achieve preferable vectorization of the inner loop. Corresponding to the Eq. 3, Eq. 4 can be achieved.

$$(N \times s \times (s \times \frac{L}{2})) \times T_p \times N_m < S_{cache} \qquad (4)$$

Figure 4 illustrates the result of applying conventional loop tiling to improve cache reuse of the 3-D 7-point stencil code shown in Fig. 1, where the partitioned blocks with a single sweep of the grid are assigned to different threads to be evaluated simultaneously.

```
1    for (t = 0; t < niter; t++) {
2    #pragma omp  parallel for num_threads(THNUM) private(xx, yy, x, y, z)
3
4      for (yy = 0; yy < ny; yy+=ty) {
5        for (zz = 0; zz < nz; zz+=tz) {
6          for (xx = 0; xx < nx; xx+=tx {
7            for (z = zz; z < zz+tz; z++) {
8              for (y = yy; y < yy+ty; y++) {
9    #pragma simd
10   #pragma vector nontemporal
11               for (x = xx; x < xx+tx; x++) {
12                 //boundary processing and indices linearizing
13                 cur[c] = cc*old[c]+cw*old[w]+ce*old[e]+
14                         cs*old[s]+cn*old[n]+cb*old[b]+ct*old[t];
15   } } } } } }
16     swap (cur, old) ;
17   }
```

Fig. 4. 3-D 7-point stencil code with loop tiling

5 Performance Evaluation and Analysis

5.1 Hardware and Software Configuration

To evaluate the effectiveness of the optimization methods presented in this paper, we measure performance of the 3-D 7-point stencil code on two kinds of platforms: Intel Xeon Phi coprocessor and Intel Xeon processor. The basic specifications of the platforms are listed in Table 1.

Table 1. The specifications of experiment platform

	Intel Xeon E5-2670 (Sandy bridge)	Intel Xeon Phi 31S1P coprocessor (Knights corner)
Cores	16 (8 × 2)	57
Logical core count	32 (16 × 2)	228 (57 × 4)
SIMD width(64-bit)	2(SSE), 4(AVX)	8 (IMCI)
Clock frequency	2.6 GHz	1.1 GHz
Memory size/type	128 GB/DDR3	8 GB/GDDR5
Peak DP/SP FLOPs	345.6/691.2 GFLOP/s	1.065/2.130 TFLOP/s
Peak memory bandwidth	85.3 GB/s	320 G/s
Cache	32 KB L1-D 32 KB L1-1, 256KB L2, 20 MB L3	32 KB L1-D, 32KB L1-1, 512 KB/Core L2
Host OS	Linux Redhat 4.4.5-6	
Compiler	Intel Compiler Version 15.0.0	

5.2 Performance Results

For performance evaluation, we define the N as 512, and the performance of the stencil code in Fig. 1 is used as the baseline. About the size of tiling, Eqs. 3 and 4 have shown the method of calculation. For the evaluation on Intel Xeon Phi 31S1P, s is 4 while running two threads for a core.

Figure 5 shows the run time and speedup of 3-D 7-point stencil code achieved with different optimization techniques. We can find that significant improvements in performance over the baseline are achieved for Intel Xeon Phi after applying the optimizations we devised. With the basic optimizations, 3-D 7-point stencil code achieves performance speedup of 160.51. The loop tiling gives another 32 % improvement over the basic optimization. That is about 212 times improvement from the original single-threaded baseline. Besides, we can find that the parallel code with SIMD achieves much higher performance than the code without SIMD optimization.

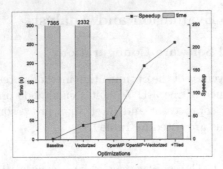

Fig. 5. Performance of the baseline and the optimized code on Intel® Xeon Phi™ 31S1P

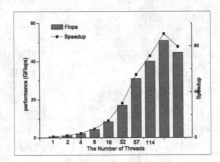

Fig. 6. Performance of stencil code on Intel® Xeon Phi™ 31S1P with different core counts

5.3 Scalability

In order to investigate the effectiveness of our parallel strategy, we evaluate the performance of our stencil code with incrementally increasing the number of logical threads from 1 to 224. When the size of 3-D domain is 512^3, the performance of stencil code with different count of threads is shown in Fig. 6. The relative speedup is compared with serial code. We can see that the performance of stencil computations increases proportionally with the number of threads. Three threads per core provide the best performance, and it achieves the speedup of 90.66. When the number of thread is 228, the performance decreased. The main reason might be that more context switch of threads involves more overhead. However, the speedup of the optimized kernel demonstrates good scalability of parallelization.

5.4 Overall Performance Comparison

Using the stencil code in Fig. 5, the performance comparisons between Intel Xeon Phi coprocessor and Intel Xeon processor with different optimization techniques and thread counts is shown in Fig. 7. In Fig. 7(a), 'base' means the performance of the serial code; 'openmp' means using OpenMP for task parallelism; 'simd' means using vectorization for data parallelism; 'tiling' means using loop tiling to improve data locality. The number on top of each bar represents the speedup of performance improvement achieved compared to the corresponding optimization of Xeon processor. We find our optimization strategies achieve better performance on both Xeon processor and Xeon Phi coprocessor. Although Xeon achieves a higher performance of base stencil code than Xeon Phi, the performance of Xeon processor is 1.292 times and 4.210 times lower than Xeon phi coprocessor for parallelization and vectorization. The main reason is that Xeon processor has a higher clock frequency, and Xeon Phi coprocessor has wider vector processing unit and more cores. Figure 7(b) shows the performance of stencil code over increasing numbers of cores on Xeon and Xeon Phi. Except for the increasing performance with more parallelism, the main difference is the flattening of performance on Xeon after initial scaling due to the memory-bound nature of the problem. Based on these results, in terms of performance for our stencil code, we conclude that one Xeon Phi card is 5.1 times faster than one Xeon processor.

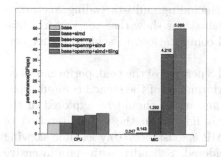

(a) Performance with Different Optimizations

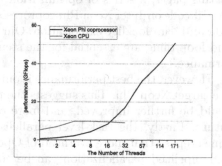

(b) Performance with Different Thread Counts

Fig. 7. Performance comparisons between Xeon and Xeon Phi

6   Related Work

As a class of popular iterative kernels in scientific and engineering computation, stencil computations have received considerable attention. Since 2014, *International Workshop on High-Performance Stencil Computations* (HiStencils) [1] is convened each year. HiStencils focuses on the optimizations of stencil computations involving all fields. The target platforms have been changed from the traditional single core CPU to symmetric multiprocessing on-a-chip, even to some kinds of accelerators, such as NVIDIA GPU [11,12]. Rahman [14] et al. modeled the relationship between performance improvements achieved by different optimizations and their efficiency of utilizing various hardware components on multi-core architectures, which can be used to effectively guide the optimization of different stencil kernels. Schäfer A and Fey D [11] chose the Jacobi method to evaluate a set of algorithms on NVIDIA GPGPU. Maruyama N. and Aoki T. [12] evaluated the performance of 3-D 7-point stencil on NVIDIA Fermi GPU with a series of memory access optimizations, such as spatial blocking and Temporal Blocking. Also, there were lots of work about optimizing application kernels on Intel MIC. Yang You et al. [13] accelerated the wave propagation forward modeling on the CPU, GPU, and MIC with various optimizations. Qinglin Wang [15] and Xiantao Cui accelerated a kind of parallel algorithm on Intel MIC respectively, and achieved a considerable speedup compared with Intel Xeon CPU. Gao T. et al. [16] evaluated the performance of the graph search algorithm on MIC.

But for Intel Xeon Phi, few optimization work for stencil computation has been published yet. Furthermore, GPU and Xeon Phi are quite different on architecture and programming, the optimization method for GPU can not be transplanted to Xeon Phi directly.

7   Conclusions and Future Work

In this paper, a series of optimization techniques were devised for 3-D 7-point stencil code on Intel Xeon Phi coprocessor, including multi-threading, vectorization and data locality exploitation. Our evaluations show that the vectorization and loop tiling are essential for the stencil computations to achieve higher performance.

However, the best performance is only 4.8 percent of the peak performance on the target Xeon Phi. This suggests the performance of the stencil computations could be further improved, and more optimizations should be explored in the future. Firstly, the task-level parallelism is limited in the signal iteration of time step, so that more overhead of OpenMP is existence. Maybe, time skewing and pipelined parallelization can be considered. Secondly, as a data-intensive application, data prefetch might be applied to stencil codes for hiding memory latency.

Acknowledgments. The work described in this paper is partially supported by the project of National Science Foundation of China under grant No.61170046 and No.61402495.

References

1. HiStencils. http://www.exastencils.org/histencils/. Accessed 15 Apr 2015
2. Stencil code. http://en.wikipedia.org/wiki/Stencil_code/. Accessed 15 Apr 2015
3. Michael, M., Reinders, J., Robison, A.: Structured Parallel Programming: Patterns for Efficient Computation. Elsevier, Amsterdam (2012)
4. Intel Corporation. Intel® Xeon Phi™ coprocessor system software developers guide, March 2014
5. Duran, A., Michael, K.: The Intel® many integrated core architecture. In: International Conference on High Performance Computing and Simulation (HPCS). IEEE (2012)

6. James, J., Reinders, J.: Intel® Xeon Phi™ Coprocessor High-performance Programming. Newnes, Oxford (2013)
7. Top 500 list. http://www.top500.org/. Accessed 1 June 2016
8. Chapman, B., Jost, G., Van Der Pas, R.: Using OpenMP: Portable Shared Memory Parallel Programming, vol. 10. MIT press, Massachusetts (2008)
9. Xue, J.: Loop Tiling for Parallelism. Springer Science & Business Media, Berlin (2000)
10. Leopold, C.: Tight bounds on capacity misses for 3D stencil codes. In: Sloot, P.M.A., Tan, C.J.K., Dongarra, J., Hoekstra, A.G. (eds.) ICCS-ComputSci 2002, Part I. LNCS, vol. 2329, pp. 843–852. Springer, Heidelberg (2002)
11. Schäfer, A., Fey, D.: High performance stencil code algorithms for GPGPUs. Procedia Comput. Sci. **4**, 2027–2036 (2011)
12. Maruyama, N., Takayuki, A.: Optimizing stencil computations for NVIDIA Kepler GPUs. In: Proceedings of the 1st International Workshop on High Performance Stencil Computations, Vienna (2014)
13. You, Y., et al.: Evaluating multi-core, many-core architectures through accelerating the three-dimensional LaxCWendroff correction stencil. Int. J. High Perform. Comput. Appl. **28**(3), 301–318 (2014)
14. Rahman, S.M., Faizur, Q.Y., Apan, Q.: Understanding stencil code performance on multicore architectures. In: Proceedings of the 8th ACM International Conference on Computing Frontiers. ACM (2011)
15. Wang, Q., et al.: Accelerating embarrassingly parallel algorithm on Intel MIC. In: International Conference on Progress in Informatics and Computing (PIC). IEEE (2014)
16. Tao, G., et al.: Using the intel many integrated core to accelerate graph traversal. Int. J. High Perform. Comput. Appl. **28**(3), 255–266 (2014)

RLDRPSO: An Efficient Heuristic Algorithm for Task Partitioning

Xiaofeng Qi[✉], Xingming Zhang, and Kaijian Yuan

National Digital Switching System Engineering and Technological R&D Center,
Zhengzhou 450000, China
qxxxxf@gmail.com

Abstract. Task partitioning is the critical step in the co-design of reconfigurable embedded system. Particle Swarm Optimization (PSO) has been used for fast task partitioning. However, PSO has the problems of local extremum and low precision, leading to the poor partitioning quality and unsatisfied performance. In this paper, Reverse Learning Dynamic Radius Particle Swarm Optimization (RLDRPSO) task partitioning algorithm was proposed to solve these problems. Firstly, the fitness function was designed according to the system model. Then, DRPSO was proposed to extend the solution space and improve the accuracy. Finally, reverse learning strategy was proposed to degenerate solution periodically and solve the problem of local extremum. Experimental results show that RLDRPSO increases the partitioning quality by 20 %–45 % and the average performance of system by 7 %–9 %.

Keywords: Task partitioning · Radius particle swarm optimization · Reverse learning

1 Introduction

Task partitioning is the critical step in the co-design of reconfigurable embedded system, which has a dominant effect on the system performance. It determines which components of the system are implemented on hardware and which ones on software [1]. Traditional methods of task partitioning are made by hand. As the embedded system becomes more and more complex, it is difficult for task partitioning in embedded system. Then many researchers put attention on task partitioning algorithms, turning to use automatic methods to solve this problem [2].

Task partitioning is a problem of multi-objective optimization. Using Mixed Integer Linear Programming(MILP) [3] and Dynamic Programming(DP) [4] could find global optimal solution in theory to achieve the best system performance. However, these methods search for the whole solution space blindly. Particularly in the case of large-scale amount of tasks, these methods run for a long time.

Then, many researchers used heuristic methods [5], like Genetic Algorithm(GA) [6], Simulated Annealing(SA) [7], Ant Colony Optimization (ASO) [8]

© Springer Science+Business Media Singapore 2016
J. Wu and L. Li (Eds.): ACA 2016, CCIS 626, pp. 118–129, 2016.
DOI: 10.1007/978-981-10-2209-8_11

and Particle Swarm Optimization(PSO) [9], as the partitioning strategy. PSO in these heuristic methods has simple parameters, executes rapidly and costs less [9]. So, we choose PSO to solve the problem of task partitioning in this paper.

While, the disadvantages of PSO are the unsatisfied approximate solution and local extremum. To solve inherent defects of PSO, early literatures proposed the optimized parameters. In the initial stage of PSO, the convergence is accelerated by the individual learning factor. In the latter part, the search is performed by the global learning factor. The improvement of this strategy is not obvious. Yang [10] proposed CLPSO task partitioning algorithm, which changed the structure of PSO and led the population to converge on the global optimal solution by a alterable leader. CLPSO is unreliable for unstable results. Luo [11] proposed ICPSO task partitioning algorithm, which combines the PSO and immune clone algorithm to extend the solution space through cloning and mutation. Hu [12] combined PSO and simulated annealing algorithm, which delays the convergence to avoid the local extremum. These methods have the problems of premature and poor accuracy and result in unsatisfied task partitioning quality.

Above all, we propose RLDRPSO task partitioning algorithm to improve the task partitioning quality system performance. RLDRPSO includes the optimized parameters, structure and combined algorithm. DRPSO algorithm is used to search for optimum solution dynamically, which expands the solution space and improves the accuracy. When judging the results falling into the local extremum, the algorithm uses reverse learning mechanism to degenerate solution in a certain extent, so as to overcome the problem of local extremum and search for better solution on this basis. Experimental results show that the proposed algorithm can effectively improve the partitioning quality and performance of the system.

This paper is organized as follow. Section 2 introduces the task partitioning model. In Sect. 3, we propose RLDRPSO task partitioning algorithm. Then the proposed algorithm is compared with typical algorithms in Sect. 4. The fifth section points out shortcomings of the proposed algorithm and the direction for further study.

2   Problem Definition

2.1   System Structure

The general structure of configurable embedded system model is presented in Fig. 1 [13].

CPU is the processor for software tasks, which contains the local memory(LM). FPGA or ASIC is the processor for hardware tasks. The communication among tasks is realized by bus and shared memory. We suppose that execution time, energy consumption, area of hardware resources and the communication time and energy consumption in CPU or FPGA are known. In this model, tasks oriented two-way division.

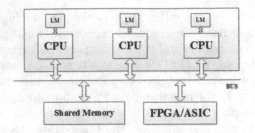

Fig. 1. Embedded system model [13]

2.2 Generalized Task Partitioning

According to the task granularity, an application needs to be decomposed into a number of tasks, which is represented by Data Flow Graph(DFG):

$$G = \{V, E\} \tag{1}$$

DFG G is a directed acyclic graph that contains a set of nodes V and edges E. Each node $v_i \in V$ represents a task that needs to be performed in processor cores. Each side $e_{ij} \in E$ indicates that the data is transferred from v_i to the task v_j via the bus. The number of tasks is n. $\forall v_i, i \in [1, n]$ contains multiple attributes:

$$v_i = \{x_i, TS_i, TH_i, ES_i, EH_i, A_i\} \tag{2}$$

x_i is the candidate partitioning location of v_i. For the task is divided into two directions, $x_i \in \{0, 1\}$. $x_i = 1$ means v_i performed in the CPU and $x_i = 0$ means v_i performed in the FPGA. TS_i, TH_i are the execution time of v_i in CPU or FPGA respectively. ES_i, EH_i are the energy consumption of v_i in CPU or FPGA respectively. A_i indicates the hardware area resources needed to perform v_i in FPGA. The hardware area resources usually mean the cost of the system design.

Generally speaking, the goal of task partitioning is to minimize the execution time and energy consumption of the system under system constraints, so as to achieve the goal of improving the system performance. For the problem of two-way partitioning in heterogeneous embedded systems, the target is to solve the optimal solution X:

$$X = \{x_1, x_2, ..., x_n\} \tag{3}$$

In G, V is divided into $\{V_s, V_h\}$. V_s represents a collection of tasks performed in CPU, and V_h represents a collection of tasks performed in FPGA or ASIC, $V_s \cup V_h = V$ and $V_s \cap V_h = \emptyset$. In the co-design of embedded system, the hardware area resource is limited. For the generalized task partitioning, the principle is to make full use of limited area resource and at the same time minimize the execution time and energy consumption. Therefore, in this paper we will not focus on tasks sensitive to time and energy, but discuss the limited area resource under this generalized principles. At the same time, the communication time and energy consumption between each task are ignored in the bus structure. The objective function to describe the task partitioning problem is in formula (4):

$$
\begin{cases}
\min \left[\sum_{i=1}^{n} TH_i \cdot x_i + \sum_{i=1}^{n} TS_i \cdot (1 - x_i) \right] \\
\min \left[\sum_{i=1}^{n} EH_i \cdot x_i + \sum_{i=1}^{n} ES_i \cdot (1 - x_i) \right] \\
\sum_{i=1}^{n} A_i \cdot x_i < A_{\max}
\end{cases}
\tag{4}
$$

$T(x), E(x), A(x)$ respectively represent the time, energy consumption and area overhead of a particular application. $A_{\max}$ is the largest area on the FPGA for performing tasks.

2.3 PSO Task Partitioning Algorithm

In the classical PSO task partitioning algorithm, each particle represents a candidate partition solution. PSO randomly generated m candidate partition solutions, $X_1, X_2, ..., X_m$. Number of tasks is n. $X_i = \{x_{i1}, x_{i2}, ..., x_{id}, ..., x_{in}\}$ is n-dimensional vector in Euclidean space R^n and x_{id} is the dth element. PSO updates partitioning solutions by iteration. The number of iterations is $K \in N^*$. The current iteration number is $k \in [1, K]$. Each x_{id} corresponds to an updating rate of v_{id}. Updating speed vector is $V_i = \{v_{i1}, v_{i2}, ..., v_{id}, ..., v_{in}\}$, meaning the updating speed of candidate partition solution, which should be controlled within a certain range $|v_{id}| < v_{\max d}$. Velocity threshold vector is $V_{\max} = \{v_{\max 1}, ..., v_{\max d}, ..., v_{\max n}\}$. PSO uses the fitness function $f(X)$ to evaluate the candidate partitioning solution, so as to find the optimal partitioning solution. $f(X)$ is determined by the target of the system, as shown in formula (4). It is used to measure the degree of the candidate solution to adapt to the system constraints. $X_1^*, X_2^*, ..., X_n^*$ are the optimal partition solutions in the updating processes of X_i. $X_g^* = \{X_{g1}^*, X_{g2}^*, ..., X_{gn}^*\}$ is the optimal partition solution in $X_1^*, X_2^*, ..., X_n^*$. In each iteration, the candidate partition solution is guided by X_i^* and X_g^*. In the kth generation, x_{id} and v_{id} correspond to x_{id}^k and v_{id}^k. The updating formula is as follow:

$$
\begin{cases}
v_{id}^{k+1} = \omega \cdot v_{id}^k + c_1 r_1 (X_{id}^* - x_{id}^k) + c_2 r_2 (X_{gd}^* - x_{id}^k) \\
x_{id}^{k+1} = x_{id}^k + v_{id}^{k+1}
\end{cases}
\tag{5}
$$

The updating formula of PSO task partitioning algorithm is composed of three parts. The first part is the inertia part, ω is the inertia factor, which is used to measure the effect of the current updating rate. The second part is the part of self-cognition, which reflects the memory of the particle's own historical experience. The third part is the social cognitive part, which reflects the historical experience of the cooperation and knowledge sharing among the particles. c_1 and c_2 are learning factors, which respectively indicate the effect of the individual optimal solution and the global optimal solution on the direction of population updating. r_1 and r_2 are random number between [0,1].

3 RLDRPSO Task Partitioning Algorithm

In RLDRPSO task partitioning algorithm, we first design learning factors and the fitness function. With the idea of "divide and conquer", DRPSO selects regional optimal value and global optimal solution from the regional optimal solution. In the latter part of the algorithm, if the candidate partitioning solution falls into local optimal solution, this algorithm triggers reverse learning mechanism to degenerate partitioning solution, jumping out of local extremum. On the basis, the optimal solution is solved.

3.1 Learning Factors and Fitness Function

ω, c_1 and c_2 in PSO are in linear form, expressed as follows:

$$\omega = \omega_{\min} + \frac{(\omega_{\max} - \omega_{\min})(K - k)}{K} \tag{6}$$

$$c_1 = (c_{1\max} - c_{1\min}) \cdot \frac{k}{K} + c_{1\min} \tag{7}$$

$$c_2 = (c_{2\max} - c_{2\min}) \cdot \frac{K - k}{K} + c_{2\min} \tag{8}$$

In the initial stage of the algorithm, ω and c_1 are larger and c_2 is smaller. V_i and X^* have a great influence on solution updating, which not only ensures the solution space but also increases the speed of updating. At the later stage of the algorithm, c_2 increases, which means the impact of X_g^* on the updating process is larger. ω and c_1 decrease, which means the impact of X^* on the updating process is small. As a result, the updating speed is reduced and the accuracy of the solution increases.

According to formula (4), we evaluate candidate partitioning solutions from three aspects, the hardware area, task execution time and energy consumption. After that, we normalize the processing and design fitness function. Generally, if the hardware area of partitioning solution needed is larger than the area system provided, the task will not be performed. So, the fitness function is designed in the formula (9):

$$f(x) = a \cdot e^{\frac{A(x) - A_{\max}}{\delta_A} \cdot m_a} \cdot \left| \frac{A(x) - A_{\max}}{\delta_A} \right| + b \cdot \frac{T(x)}{\delta_T} + c \cdot \frac{E(x)}{\delta_E} \tag{9}$$

$A(x)$, $T(x)$ and $E(x)$, respectively, are the hardware area, execution time and energy consumption in one partitioning solution. δ_A, δ_T and δ_T, respectively, are the normalization factor of area, execution time and energy consumption. $\delta_A = \max\{\max A - A_{\max}, A_{\max} - \min A\}$, $\delta_T = \max T - \min T$, $\delta_E = \max E - \min E$. a, b and c are influence factors. Punishment factor is shown as follow:

$$m_a = \begin{cases} 1, A(x) \leq A_{\max} \\ k, A(x) > A_{\max} \end{cases} \tag{10}$$

In this penalty mechanism, if the candidate partitioning solution is not in excess of the hardware area system provided, the fitness value decreases in the form of the exponential function. Otherwise, the fitness value increases rapidly according to current iteration number. When the iteration is small, the punishment is light, offering an opportunity for the candidate partitioning solution correcting the error. When the number of iterations is larger, the punishment is large. Penalty mechanism no longer tolerates the wrong candidate partitioning solution. The fitness function is in good agreement with the actual situation.

3.2 Reverse Learning

In order to solve the problem that PSO algorithm is easy to fall into the local extremum, which makes the system cannot reach the prospective performance, we design a reverse learning mechanism (RL) for the task partitioning algorithm. The idea of reverse learning is to jump out of the local extremum when algorithm predicates solution falling into local extremum. The reverse learning mechanism first initializes x_i and v_i of each partitioning solution, the initial location of the worst solutions W_i^0 and the worst location of each individual solution W_i^k. After Lth reverse learning, the result jumps out of local extremum. In the reverse learning mechanism, l indicates the number of the current reverse learning iteration. RL's updating formula is as shown in (11):

$$\begin{cases} v_{id}^{l+1} = \omega \cdot v_{id}^l + c_3 r_3 (x_{id}^l - W_{id}^l) + c_4 r_4 (x_{id}^l - W_{id}^0) \\ x_{id}^{l+1} = x_{id}^l + v_{id}^{l+1} \end{cases} \tag{11}$$

The distance between solutions is in the Euclidean distance. The distance between W_i^0 must be large enough in order to ensure that the W_i^0 can pull the result out the local extreme value. When choosing W_i^0, their distance is greater than the preset distance $R = \sqrt{n}$.

In the reverse learning mechanism, the updating speed threshold changes to $RV_{\max} = 2 \cdot V_{\max}$, making the candidate partitioning solution jumping out of local extremum rapidly under the leading of W_i^0 and W_i^k (Table 1).

Table 1. RL mechanism

Algorithm 1. RL mechanism
INPUT: X_i^k, W_i^k, W_i^0 and L
OUTPUT: X_i^k
1. initialize $l = 0$, $X_i^l = X_i^k$, $V_i^l = V_i^k$
2. **for** $l < L$
3.   randomly select initial worst partition scheme from W_i^0
4.   update X_i^{l+1} and V_i^{l+1}
5.   calculate fitness value $f(X_i^{l+1})$
6.   select max $f(X_i^{l+1})$, updating $W_i^{l+1} = X_i^{l+1}$
7. **endfor**
8. **return** $X_i^k = X_i^L$

3.3 RLDRPSO

In this paper, we improve RPSO [14] algorithm to solve the problem of task partitioning. Generally speaking, at the initial stage of the algorithm, X_i is far from the optimal solution. Using a larger radius to search X_i is conducive for fast convergence. In the late stage of the algorithm, X_i is near from the optimal solution. Reducing radius can improve the search accuracy. The basic idea of DRPSO is to dynamically adjust the region size of each candidate partition solution according to the number of iteration. The global optimal solution is selected from these region optimal solutions. Set radius r. r varies linearly with the number of iteration, as shown in formula (12):

$$r = \frac{K - k}{K} \cdot n \tag{12}$$

The distance between solutions is in the Euclidean distance. Firstly, Choose the optimal individual solution location as the center of the circle, whose radius is r. Then randomly select neighbor solutions in this circle. Find the region optimal solution $X_i^R = \{X_{i1}^R, ..., X_{id}^R, ..., X_{id}^R\}$. DRPSO's updating formula is shown as follow:

$$\begin{cases} v_{id}^{k+1} = \omega \cdot v_{id}^k + c_1 r_1 (X_{id}^R - x_{id}^k) + c_2 r_2 (X_{gd}^* - x_{id}^k) \\ x_{id}^{k+1} = x_{id}^k + v_{id}^{k+1} \end{cases} \tag{13}$$

Combined with the reverse learning mechanism mentioned in the last subsection, when the solution falls into local extremum, RL helps the result to jump out of local extremum (Table 2).

Table 2. RLDRPSO task partitioning algorithm

Algorithm 2. RLDRPSO task partitioning
INPUT: K
OUTPUT: X_g^*
1. Initialize X_i^0, W_i^0
2. **for** $k<K$
3.   calculate current X_i^k 's fitness value $f(X_i^k)$, select X_i^*
4.   initialize dynamic radius r
5.   randomly select X_i^R ensuring $|X_i^* - X_i^R| < r$
6.   updating X_i^{k+1} and V_i^{k+1}
7.   updating X_i^*, W_i^{k+1}, X_g^*
8.   **if** X_g^* falling into local extremum
9.   trigger Algorithm 1
10.   **endif**
11. **endfor**
12. **return** X_g^*

4 Experimental Results

4.1 DFG Data and RLDRPSO Parameters

Researchers usually use TGFF [15] to generate DFG and attributes as the test-bench for task partitioning algorithm. According to the research [10], we use TGFF to generate the DFG and the hardware area, execution time and power consumption of each task. The range of the specified task attributes is shown in Table 3.

Table 3. Task attributes' value [8,10]

	Task attribute	Range
FGPA	area/unit	[50,150]
	power consumption/W	[0.15,0.55]
	time/ns	[75,225]
CPU	area/unit	0
	power consumption/W	[0.25,0.65]
	time/ns	[200,400]

Task partitioning algorithms run in Visual Studio 2010, Xeon Intel 2680 CPU 2.8 GHz, RAM 4 GB, Window7. Besides RLDRPSO task partitioning algorithm, we also select the standard PSO task partitioning algorithm [9], ICPSO task partitioning algorithm [8] and CLPSO task partitioning algorithm [10] for comparison. In order to ensure the comparability, the experiment uses the same PSO parameters. The parameters are shown in Table 4.

Table 4. RLDRPSO constant parameters

DRPSO		RL	
K	100	R	10
ω_{max}	0.9		
ω_{min}	0.4	ω	0.7
$c_{1\,max}$	2	c_3	0.7
$c_{1\,min}$	1.85		
$c_{2\,max}$	2	c_4	0.3
$c_{2\,min}$	1.85		
v_{max}	0.8	rv_{max}	1.6

4.2 Results

To evaluate the performance of the system, the algorithm is designed to punish the task sensitive to area. So we first study the performance of the algorithm under different area. HAR refers to the ratio of the hardware area restriction to the total hardware area. MR is the probability that the task partitioning solution cannot satisfy the system constraints. When the task partitioning solution cannot meet the requirements of the system, it needs to be resolved, which increases the execution time of the algorithm. The smaller MR is, the higher the probability of the algorithm finding the optimal solution is, that is, the space of the solution is larger. The smaller the fluctuation is, the higher the reliability of the algorithm is. Figure 2 shows that algorithms have a certain MR, especially the CLPSO task partitioning algorithm is not reliable. When the HAR is more than 80%, the MR of RLDRPSO is 0, and the fluctuation is small. It reflects that the RLDRPSO can effectively expand the space of the candidate partitioning solutions.

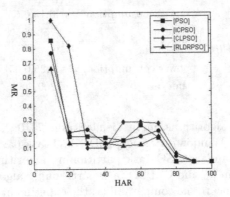

Fig. 2. MR in different HARs

In the next experiment we discuss the influence of HAR on algorithm performance. In order to compare the performance of each algorithm, the fitness value of the optimal solution is normalized to the fitness value of the general processor. From Fig. 3, in the conditions of presence of a certain MR, the performance improvement of all algorithms is almost same. When the HAR is more than 70%, the performance of the RLDRPSO algorithm is still growing compared to other algorithms. Therefore, RLDRPSO task partitioning algorithm has a significant effect on the improvement of the system performance under large HAR.

Figure 4 is the relation of the fitness value with the iteration number, reflecting the partitioning process of algorithms. It can be seen from the figure that PSO, ICPSO and CLPSO algorithm have converged in the initial stage of the algorithm, falling into the local extremum. While RLDRPSO algorithm with reverse learning mechanism can jump out of the local extremum, converging toward the global optimal solution. In the figure, the steep part in RLDRPSO algorithm curve indicates the reverse learning process. Each time the reverse learning mechanism is triggered, the partitioning process has a significant improvement effect. In the case that the number of tasks is 500, RLDRPSO

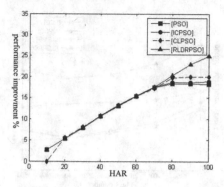

Fig. 3. Performance in different HARs

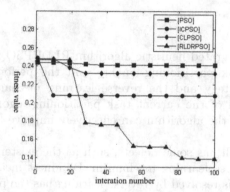

Fig. 4. Iterative process of different algorithms

improves the partitioning quality of 45 % compared to the PSO task partitioning algorithm and 39 % compared to the ICPSO task partitioning algorithm and 20 % compared to the CLPSO task partitioning algorithm. The reverse learning mechanism can effectively solve the local extremum and RLDRPSO algorithm enhance the accuracy of the solution. Finally, RLDRPSO task partitioning algorithm can improve the partitioning quality. As a result, the system performance is improved.

Figure 5 shows the effect of proposed algorithm in different number of tasks. RLDRPSO task partitioning algorithm improved the performance of the system significantly. Compared to PSO task partitioning algorithm, the average performance of the system is improved by 7 %. Compared to the ICPSO task partitioning algorithm, the average performance of the system is improved by 6.3 %. Compared to the CLPSO task partitioning algorithm, the average performance of the system is improved by 4.9 %.

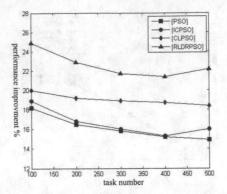

Fig. 5. Performance in different task numbers

5   Conclusions

In this paper, an integrated heuristic algorithm RLDRPSO is proposed, which can improve the task partitioning quality and the performance of system. Dynamic radius strategy and the reverse learning mechanism are proposed to solve the problem of the current task partitioning algorithm. Experimental results show that the algorithm can effectively improve the performance of the system.

The algorithm still has some defects, such as the existence of MR and the blindness of the reverse learning mechanism. Blindness means that the global optimal value which is resolved by reverse learning has the probability of being worse than the former global optimal value. Next research will conduct the discrimination and retention mechanisms to overcome these defects.

Finally, tasks can be executed simultaneously in different processing cores in heterogeneous system. Emerging reconfigurable system changes the existing system model. There is another problem of task scheduling. The combination of partitioning and scheduling will be the trend of future research.

References

1. Pu, W.: Efficient heuristic and tabu search for hardware/software partitioning. J. Supercomput. **66**(1), 118–134 (2013)
2. Mann, Z., Orb, A.: Optimization problems in system-level synthesis. In: Proceedings of the 3rd Hungarian-Japanese Symposium on Discrete Mathematics and Its Applications (2003)
3. Ma, Y., Liu, J., Zhang, C.: HW/SW partitioning for region-based dynamic partial reconfigurable FPGAs. In: 2014 32nd IEEE International Conference on Computer Design (ICCD), pp. 470–476. IEEE (2014)
4. Jemai, M., Ouni, B.: Hardware software partitioning of control data flow graph on system on programmable chip. Microprocess. Microsyst. **39**(4), 259–270 (2015)
5. Ernst, R., Henkel, J., Benner, T.: Hardware-software cosynthesis for microcontrollers. IEEE Des. Test Comput. **4**, 64–75 (1993)

6. Liang, H., Sinha, S., Warrier, R., et al.: Static hardware task placement on multi-context FPGA using hybrid genetic algorithm. In: International Conference on Field Programmable Logic and Applications. IEEE (2015)
7. Liang, Z., Cheng, X., Zheng, T., et al.: Hardware/software partitioning based on greedy algorithm and simulated annealing algorithm. J. Comput. Appl. **7**, 030 (2013)
8. Wang, D., Li, S., Dou, Y.: Collaborative hardware/software partition of coarse-grained reconfigurable system using evolutionary ant colony optimization. In: Asia and South Pacific Design Automation Conference, pp. 679–684. IEEE Computer Society Press (2008)
9. Bhattacharya, A., Konar, A., Das, S., et al.: Hardware software partitioning problem in embedded system design using particle swarm optimization algorithm. In: International Conference on Complex, Intelligent and Software Intensive Systems, pp. 171–176. IEEE Computer Society (2008)
10. Yang, D.: Research on SoC Hardware/Software Partitioning Methodology Based on Particle Swarm Algorithm. Xidian University (2014)
11. Luo, L., He, H., Liao, C., et al.: Hardware/Software partitioning for heterogeneous multicore SOC using particle swarm optimization and immune clone (PSO-IC) algorithm. In: 2010 IEEE International Conference on Information and Automation (ICIA), pp. 490–494. IEEE (2010)
12. Hu, D.: The Research of Hardware/Software Partitioning Based on Partical Swarm Optimazation and Simulated Annesling and Clustering Algorithm. East China Normal University (2014)
13. Sha, E., Wang, L., Zhuge, Q., et al.: Power efficiency for hardware/software parti tioning with time and area constraints on MPSoC. Int. J. Parallel Program. **43**(3), 1–22 (2013)
14. Anantathanvit, M., Munlin, M.A.: Radius particle swarm optimization for resource constrained project scheduling problem. In: 2013 16th International Conference on Computer and Information Technology (ICCIT), pp. 24–29. IEEE (2014)
15. Dick, R., Rhodes, D., Wolf, W.: TGFF: task graphs for free. In: International Workshop on Hardware/software Codesign, pp. 97–101. IEEE (1998)

A Fine-Granular Programming Scheme
for Irregular Scientific Applications

Haowei Huang[1]($\boxtimes$), Liehui Jiang[2], Weiyu Dong[1], Rui Chang[1], Yifan Hou[1],
and Michael Gerndt[3]

[1] State Key Laboratory of Mathematical Engineering and Advanced Computing,
Zhengzhou 450000, Henan, China
haowei.huang@yahoo.com
[2] China National Digital Switching System Engineering and Technological
Research Center, Zhengzhou 450000, Henan, China
[3] Fakultaet Fuer Informatik, Technische Universitaet Muenchen,
85748 Garching Bei Muenchen, Germany

Abstract. HPC systems are widely used for accelerating calculation-intensive irregular applications, e.g., molecular dynamics (MD) simulations, astrophysics applications, and irregular grid applications. As the scalability and complexity of current HPC systems keeps growing, it is difficult to parallelize these applications in an efficient fashion due to irregular communication patterns, load imbalance issues, dynamic characteristics, and many more. This paper presents a fine granular programming scheme, on which programmers are able to implement parallel scientific applications in a fine granular and SPMD (single program multiple data) fashion. Different from current programming models starting from the global data structure, this programming scheme provides a high-level and object-oriented programming interface that supports writing applications by focusing on the finest granular elements and their interactions. Its implementation framework takes care of the implementation details e.g., the data partition, automatic EP aggregation, memory management, and data communication. The experimental results on SuperMUC show that the OOP implementations of multi-body and irregular applications have little overhead compared to the manual implementations using C++ with OpenMP or MPI. However, it improves the programming productivity in terms of the source code size, the coding method, and the implementation difficulty.

1 Introduction

HPC is currently experiencing very strong growth in all computing sectors. Many HPC systems are used for accelerating different kinds of calculation-intensive applications including quantum physics, weather forecasting, climate research, oil and gas exploration, molecular dynamics, and so on [1–4]. The major programming interfaces are OpenMP [5,6], MPI [7–9], and CUDA [10,11]. In addition, a large number of high-level programming models have been developed to improve the programming productivity and implementation efficiency

© Springer Science+Business Media Singapore 2016
J. Wu and L. Li (Eds.): ACA 2016, CCIS 626, pp. 130–141, 2016.
DOI: 10.1007/978-981-10-2209-8_12

as well, e.g., High Performance Fortran (HPF) [12,13], Charm++ [14–16], and Threading Building Blocks (TBB) [17,18]. All these high-level programming approaches are designed to obtain better programming productivity using higher level abstraction or automatic parallelization. However, it is still complicated for programmers to manage irregular scientific applications in an efficient and scalable fashion in terms of decomposing the computational domain, managing irregular communication patterns among processes, and manipulating data migration among processes, maintaining computational load balance, and so on. For example, a molecular dynamics (MD) simulation [19] is a form of N-body [20] computer simulation in which molecules interact with other molecules within a certain domain for a period of time. The molecules may move in the domain according to the interactions with others, which changes their storage layout and communication pattern during execution. In order to improve the performance of such irregular applications, researchers apply linked cells algorithms and bi-section decomposition method which needs runtime re-distribution.

Different from current programming models starting from the global data structure, we present a fine granular programming scheme for irregular scientific applications. It provides a programming interface that supports writing applications by focusing on the finest granular elements and their interactions. They are organized as an *Ensemble*, which manages the elements, topologies, and high-level operations. By using the high-level operations explicitly, developers can control the actions of the elements including communication, synchronization, and parallel operations. In this paper, we introduce an abstract machine model, programming interface, and implementation framework ported on different types of systems on SuperMUC [21].

2   Abstract Machine Model

As can be seen from Fig. 1, the machine model is an abstract architecture composed of a Control Processor (CP) and a large number of distributed Fine Granular Processors (FGPs). The major interactions between the CP and FGPs are described as follows:

1. *Explicit communication among FGPs*: It is triggered by the CP explicitly. Point-to-Point communication between FGPs is not supported due to low efficicency.
2. *Parallel computations of FGPs*: It starts the computation of FGPs in the form of parallel operations.
3. *Collective operations among FGP*: The CP is able to trigger collective operations on a set of FGPs. All the participating FGPs start the operations cooperatively to get collective results.
4. *Collective operations between CP and FGPs*: The CP can access the local memory of FGPs in the machine by explicit collective operations.

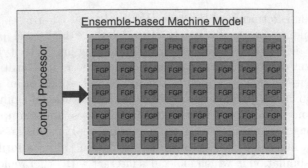

Fig. 1. Abstract machine model

3   Programming Interface

An object-oriented(OO) programming interface is designed on top of the abstract machine model. It consists of a template hierarchy starting from three top-level base templates *ElementaryPoint*, *Ensemble*, and *Topology*. These base templates have derived templates called application-specific templates, which support multi-body, irregular grid, and regular grid applications respectively. User-defined entities with local properties and operations can be defined as C++ classes derived from the application-specific templates. The organization is shown in Fig. 2.

Definition 1. *An ElementaryPoint(EP) is a software entity that represents the finest granular computational object in the domain of an application. The ensemble is a software container that stores a set of EPs and manages their local information, communication patterns, and computation. A topology defines a communication pattern resulting from the need for the information of a set of EPs in the ensemble. The EPs can exchange their status based on certain topologies.*

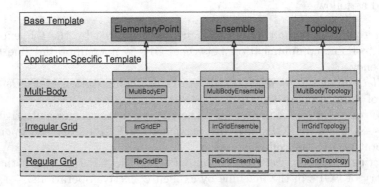

Fig. 2. Organization of the template hierarchy

The base templates for creating elementary points are *ElementaryPoint* and its derived templates *MultiBodyEP*, *IrrGridEP*, and *ReGridEP*. *Ensemble* and its derived templates are used to create the ensemble of an application. The major high-level operations in *Ensemble* are described as follows:

1. *SC-update*: It supports exchanging the complete information as well as partial information of EPs in the ensemble based on a certain topology.
2. *parallel*: It triggers member functions of EPs to execute in parallel. The template parameter is a function object adapted from a member function of *ElementaryPoint*.
3. *collective*: The *collective* operation currently consists of *allReduceOp* and *reduceOp*. *allReduceOp* provides collective reduction operations that return the result in all the involved EPs.
4. *getNghbList*: This operation is called by an individual EP in order to get a list of its neighboring EPs from the ensemble based on a topology. After it is accomplished, the EP can access data in the neighbor list for local computations.

Topology is used to create topologies, which keep the communication patterns of EPs. The major operations of *Topology* are shown as follows:

1. *initialization*: It initialize the internal data structures of *Topology*.
2. *createNeighborList*: If the topology is the root topology, it creates the neighbor EP list for the EPs.
3. *updateTopology*: It rebuilds a new topology according to the runtime information or the information specified by the users.

4 Implementation Framework

The implementation framework consists of machine-specific libraries including a sequential library, an OpenMP-based library, and an MPI-based library ported on SuperMUC. It is currently designed for multi-body and irregular grid applications. A single ensemble-based program can be compiled and linked to different executables by these libraries.

4.1 OpenMP-Based Library

It aggregates the computation of a group of EPs and binds it to a single thread. On NUMAs, all the EPs are initially stored in the physical memory of the socket running the master thread. It is not efficient that the threads residing on other sockets have to access the EPs by non-local memory accesses. Therefore, we apply a reallocation and re-indexing strategy to distribute EPs across different physical memory of the sockets.

Reallocation and Re-Indexing to Manage EPs and Their Shadow Copies. The OpenMP-based library integrates METIS [22] library to distribute the EPs across physically distributed memory. The *indirection* array is generated from the output of METIS. It gives the information of the thread affinity of all the EPs. The size of the array is the size of *EP_Set* called *numEP*. The *numEP/numSocket* elements of the *indirection* array keeps the identifiers of EPs stored in the physically memory of the sockets sequentially. The *indirection* array is organized in such a way. The the first *numEP/numSocket* elements of the *indirection* array (indices from 0 to *numEP/numSocket* − 1) stores the identifiers of EPs stored in the physically memory of socket#0. The second *numEP/numSocket* elements (indices from *numEP/numSocket* to 2 ∗ *numEP/numSocket* − 1) stores the identifiers of EPs stored in the physical memory of socket#1, and so on and so forth. The pseudo code of the EP reallocation is shown in Algorithm 1.

Algorithm 1. The EP reallocation

```
void reallocation (){
    EP *EP_Set = (EP*) malloc(numOfEPs * sizeof(EP));
#pragma omp parallel for
    for ( i =0;i<numOfEPs; i++)
        EP_Set[i] = Buf_EP[indirection[i]];
    free(Buf_EP);
}
```

In order to avoid frequent accesses to the *indirection* array, we create *indexOrigin2New* and *indexNew2Origin* arrays to manage the re-indexing translation. The *indexOrigin2New* array is used for the translation from orignial indices to new indices, while *indexNew2Origin* is used for the translation from the new indices back to orignial indices. Both *indexOrigin2New* and *indexNew2Origin* are organized in such a way. The *indexNew2Origin* array and the *indirection* array described above have the same organization. The *indexOrigin2New* array is generated from *indexNew2Origin* according to the rule:

$$indexOrigin2New[indexNew2Origin[i]] = i;$$

For example, 8 EPs are resided on socket#0 and socket#1, the partitioning result generated from METIS is $[0, 1, 0, 1, 1, 0, 0, 1]$, then the *indirection* is $[0, 2, 5, 6, 1, 3, 4, 7]$, the *indexNew2Origin* array is: $[0, 2, 5, 6, 1, 3, 4, 7]$, while the *indexOrigin2New* array is $[0, 4, 1, 5, 6, 2, 3, 7]$.

4.2 MPI-based Library

The MPI-based library implements the programming interface in C++ with MPI. It employs both the domain decomposition and efficient graph partitioning algorithms to achieve optimal EP distribution and communication.

Storage of EPs and their Shadow Copies. Each process keeps different subsets of the EPs in the ensemble according to an EP distribution, which is determined by the root topology and an optimal EP distribution generated from METIS.

Ensemble Management. As the machine model is mapped on a distributed memory machine, the master thread is duplicated and resided across all the processes. Each process keeps an ensemble, which stores a subset of the EPs, their shadow copies, and references to topologies. The implementation of the *Ensemble* operations are described below:

1. *SC-Update*: It triggers communication among processes according to a topology specified in the operation and EP distribution algorithms.
2. *getNghbList*: It is a local operation implemented on each process. It only references local EPs stored in *loc_SC_Set* according to the topology specified in the operation.
3. *parallel*: Multiple processes executing EPs' member functions in parallel.
4. *collective*: A collective operation of EPs is translated into local collective operations and collective operations among MPI processes.

Topology Management. The topology is managed in a distributed fashion. Each process keeps the root topology, which maintains the neighbor EP list for the local EPs.

MultiBodyTopology. Each process keeps the root *MultiBodyTopology* topology, which maintains the neighbor EP list for all the local EPs. The generation of the neighbor EP list in the multi-body topology is based on the parallel Linked Cells algorithm, which is presented in Algorithm 2.

Algorithm 2. Creation of neighbor EP list

---
1. Forall *ep* in local process
   1) Get cell id *localidCell* of *ep*
   2) Get *ids* of neighbor cell *localidCell*
   3) Get neighbor cells local *NghbCells*
   4) Get *EPs* in the local *nghbCells* and determine whether the distance between the EPs in local *localidCell* and *ep* is smaller than the cut-off radius
   5) If yes, put the address of *EP*
   6) Create neighbor *EPs* for *ep*
  End for
2. *updateTopology()* and go to Step 1

IrrGridTopology. Similar to the multi-body topology, each process keeps the root irregular grid topology, which maintains the neighbor EP list for the EPs in *loc_EP_Set* according to the id-based graph and EP distribution as well. The memory organization of local EPs and their SCs in a single process is shown in Fig. 3. The organization integrates the PARTI/CHAOS library [23]. The shadow copies of local EPs are allocated in the memory as an array, the SCs of remote EPs are stored after the local shadow copies with the indices from n to $n + m$.

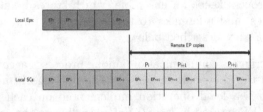

Fig. 3. Local EPs and SC organization

Communication Optimizations. Different communication optimizations are applied in the implementation of the MPI-based library.

1. *Aggregated send receive buffer management*: Each process keeps an aggregated send and receive buffer. The EPs in *loc_EP_Set* are copied into the aggregated send buffer, while EPs received from remote processes are stored in the aggregated receive buffer.
2. *Communication reduction*: It guarantees that an EP is only sent once while a group of remote EPs usually require the it for local computation. It can reduce the communication volume significantly.
3. *Communication coalescing*: A process collects many EPs destined for the same process into a single message, which is stored in the aggregated send buffer. The objective of communication coalescing is to reduce the number of message startups to avoid the "too many short messages" problem.
4. *Automatic adjustment of communication patterns according to the update of topologies*: For multi-body and irregular grid applications, the communication pattern is usually irregular and adaptive. The MPI-based library update the communication pattern accordingly based on runtime information.

5   Experimental Results

5.1   Overview

This section presents the experimental results of multi-body and irregular applications implemented by a manual program and an ensemble-based program. The manual program is implemented in C++, and parallelized with OpenMP and MPI, while the ensemble-based program is implemented by linking the libraries of the implementation framework.

5.2   Experiment Platform

The experimental platform is a number of fat nodes on SuperMUC. A fat node is based on the Intel Westmere-EX processor. It is a shared memory NUMA machine with four sockets, each of which has one Intel Xeon Processor E7-4870 processor and 64 GB of memory. The processor has 10 cores running at the frequency 2.4 GHz with a peak performance of 9.6 GFlops.

5.3   Irregular Grid Applications

Overview. The computational kernel is a simplified version from FIRE [24]. The maximum number of the iterations N is set to 128. The grid size is $128 \times 128 \times 128$, each has 26 nearest neighbors based on the Moore neighborhood. The local values of a point at a time step are determined by the values of its neighbor points at its previous time step according to the arithmetical operations:

$$value^{N+1} = \frac{1}{numOfNeighbors+1}(\sum_{i=1}^{i=numOfNeighbors} Neighbor[i].value^N + value^N)$$

OpenMP Comparison. The execution time of the program on Grid128 using 2, 4, 8, 16, 32 threads is shown Fig. 4. Neither of the programs scale well when the number of threads is increased to 32. The main reason is that non-continuous memory accesses cause a large number of L2 and L3 cache misses. Therefore, we applies the re-indexing and data reallocation strategy to improve the performance on large irregular grids. We can see that the ensemble-based program implemented by the OpenMP-based library with the re-indexing and reallocation strategy scales well up to 32 threads and achieves much better performance than the ensemble-based implementation without re-indexing.

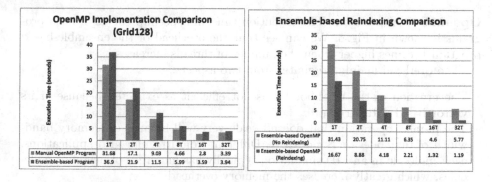

Fig. 4. Execution time of OpenMP programs (Color figure online)

MPI Comparison. The execution time and speedup curves comparison of both programs are shown in Fig. 5. It tells that the MPI-based library can get good performance while the number of processes increases with around 20 %

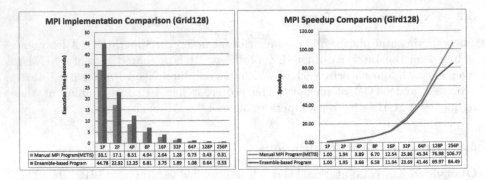

Fig. 5. Execution time comparison with MPI (Color figure online)

overhead compared to the manual MPI program. The ensemble-based program obtains comparative performance and its overhead is stable while scaling up to 256 processes. The execution time and speedup curves are shown in Fig. 5.

5.4   Molecular Dynamics Simulation

Overview. The computational kernel of the MD programs is based on the truncated Lennard-Jones(L-J) potential formula, and the simulation domain is a 3D cubic domain. Each molecule in the domain keeps a randomly generated position and interacts with its neighbor molecules located within the cut-off radius region. The positions of all the molecules are updated according to the molecule-to-molecule interactions and the equations of motion. In the experiments, the number of the molecules is set to 128K (131,072), the number of iteration steps is 8. The cut-off radius is set to 1, the size of the cubic simulation domain is 8.

OpenMP Comparison. The execution time and speedup curves of both programs is shown in Fig. 6. We can see that the overhead of the ensemble-based program becomes higher when the number of threads increases.

The overhead mainly originates from two aspects:

- The creation of the neighbor list is not efficient as expected because of its vector-based data structure.
- The parallel operation that doesn't scale very well because of memory bandwidth of the nodes on SuperMUC. Different from irregular grid applications, each molecule in an MD simulation typically has hundreds of neighbor molecules, which greatly increases the memory overhead.

MPI Comparison. In order to balance the computational load, the manual program uses METIS to decompose the molecules according to the linked cells, while the ensemble-based program links to the MPI-based library. The execution time and speedup curves of both programs is shown in Fig. 7.

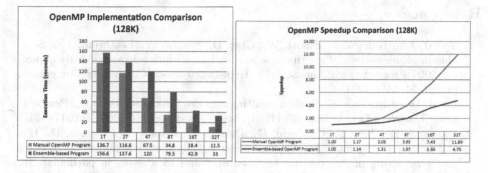

Fig. 6. Execution time and speedup curves of OpenMP MD programs (Color figure online)

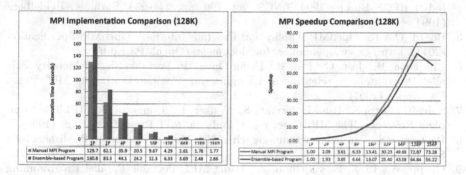

Fig. 7. Execution time and speedup curves of MPI MD programs (Color figure online)

The experimental results show that the ensemble-based implementations of multi-body and irregular applications are a bit slower than the manual implementations using C++ with OpenMP or MPI because of the internal function overheads. However, it improves the programming productivity in terms of the source code size, the coding method, and the implementation difficulty. For irregular grid applications, it saves around 80 % lines of code, while for multi-body applications, the percentage is more than 95 %.

6 Conclusion and Future Work

The fine granular programming scheme is applied to implement irregular scientific applications in a fine granular and SPMD fashion. The experimental results show that with acceptable and reasonable overhead, the ensemble-based programming improve the programming productivity and make parallel programming easier and more straightforward. In the future, we mainly focus on the support for more application areas, e.g., adaptive grid applications. In addition, the implementation for CPU+GPU hybrid architectures can also be exploited in the future in order to take advantages of hybrid programming.

References

1. Board, J.A., Hakura, Z., Elliott, W., Gray, D., Blanke, W., Leathrum, J.F.: Scalable implementations of multipole-accelerated algorithms for molecular dynamics. In: 1994 Proceedings of the Scalable High-Performance Computing Conference, pp. 87–94, May 1994
2. Boyd, D., Milosevich, S.: Supercomputing and drug discovery research. Perspect. Drug Discovery Des. 1, 345–358 (1993). http://dx.doi.org/10.1007/BF02174534
3. Clementi, E., Chin, S., Corongiu, G., Detrich, J., Dupuis, M., Folsom, D., Lie, G., Logan, D., Sonnad, V.: Supercomputing and super computers: for science and engineering in general and for chemistry and biosciences in particular. In: Theophanides, T. (ed.) Spectroscopy of Inorganic Bioactivators. NATO ASI Series, vol. 280, pp. 1–112. Springer, Netherlands (1989)
4. Kremer, K.: Supercomputing in polymer research. In: Gentzsch, W., Harms, U. (eds.) HPCN-Europe 1994. LNCS, vol. 796, pp. 244–253. Springer, Heidelberg (1994)
5. Board, O.A.R.: OpenMP Application Program Interface. OpenMP, Specification (2011). http://www.openmp.org/mpdocuments/OpenMP3.1.pdf
6. Chapman, B., Jost, G., Pas, R.: Using OpenMP: Portable Shared Memory Parallel Programming (Scientific and Engineering Computation). The MIT Press, Cambridge (2007)
7. Snir, M., Otto, S., Huss-Lederman, S., Walker, D., Dongarra, J.: MPI-The Complete Reference. The MPI Core, vol. 1, 2nd edn. MIT Press, Cambridge (1998)
8. Pacheco, P.S.: Parallel programming with MPI. Morgan Kaufmann Publishers Inc., San Francisco (1996)
9. Gropp, W., Lusk, E., Skjellum, A.: Using MPI: Portable Parallel Programming with the Message-Passing Interface. MIT Press, Cambridge (1994)
10. NVIDIA Corporation: NVIDIA CUDA Compute Unified Device Architecture - Programming Guide (2007)
11. Nickolls, J., Buck, I., Garland, M., Skadron, K.: Scalable parallel programming with CUDA. Queue 6(2), 40–53 (2008). http://doi.acm.org/10.1145/1365490.1365500
12. Schreiber, R.: An introduction to HPF. In: Perrin, G.-R., Darte, A. (eds.) The Data Parallel Programming Model. LNCS, vol. 1132, pp. 27–44. Springer, Heidelberg (1996)
13. Kennedy, K., Koelbel, C.: High performance fortran 2.0. In: Pande, S., Agrawal, D.P. (eds.) Compiler Optimizations for Scalable Parallel Systems. LNCS, vol. 1808, pp. 3–43. Springer, Heidelberg (2001)
14. Kale, L.V., Krishnan, S.: Charm++: a portable concurrent object oriented system based on C++. SIGPLAN Not. 28(10), 91–108 (1993). http://doi.acm.org/10.1145/167962.165874
15. Kale, L.V., Ramkumar, B., Sinha, A.B., Gursoy, A.: The CHARM parallel programming language, system: Part I - Description of language features. Parallel Program. Lab. Tech. Rep. #95-02 1, 1–15 (1994)
16. Kale, L.V., Ramkumar, B., Sinha, A.B., Saletore, V.A.: The CHARM parallel programming language, system: Part II - The runtime system. Parallel Program. Lab. Tech. Rep. #95-03 1, 1–14 (1994)
17. Intel: TBB (Intel Threading Building Blocks). In: Padua, D. (ed.) Encyclopedia of Parallel Computing, p. 2029. Springer, Heidelberg (2011)

18. Russell, G., Keir, P., Donaldson, A.F., Dolinsky, U., Richards, A., Riley, C.: Programming heterogeneous multicore systems using threading building blocks. In: Guarracino, M.R., et al. (eds.) Euro-Par-Workshop 2010. LNCS, vol. 6586, pp. 117–125. Springer, Heidelberg (2011)
19. Molner, S.P.: The art of molecular dynamics simulation (Rapaport, D. C.). J. Chem. Educ. **76**(2), 171 (1999). http://pubs.acs.org/doi/abs/10.1021/ed076p171
20. Aarseth, S.J.: Gravitational N-Body Simulations. Cambridge University Press, Cambridge (2003). http://dx.doi.org/10.1017/CBO9780511535246
21. LRZ: SuperMuc petascale system (2012). https://www.lrz.de/services/compute/supermuc/systemdescription/
22. Karypis, G., Kumar, V., MeTis: Unstrctured Graph Partitioning and Sparse Matrix Ordering System, Version 2.0 (1995). http://citeseerx.ist.psu.edu/viewdoc/summary?doi=10.1.1.38.376
23. Das, R., shin Hwang, Y., Uysal, M., Saltz, J., Sussman, A.: Applying the CHPAOS/PARTI library to irregular problems in computational chemistry and computational aerodynamics, in Mississippi State University, Starkville, MS, pp. 45–56. IEEE Computer Society Press (1993)
24. Bericht, I., Gerndt, M.: Parallelization of the AVL FIRE benchmark with SVM-Fortran (1995)

Programmable Two-Particle Bosonic-Fermionic Quantum Simulation System

Yang Wang, Junjie Wu[✉], Yuhua Tang, Huiquan Wang, and Dongyang Wang

State Key Laboratory of High Performance Computing, College of Computer,
National University of Defense Technology, Changsha, China
junjiewu@nudt.edu.cn

Abstract. Quantum computing promises to outperform its classical counterpart substantially. In the past decades, there has been tremendous progress. However, few previous researches have involved programmable systems. Quantum computing is mainly implemented in physics laboratories. This paper proposes a programmable structure. Using the entangled states of photon pairs, we have constructed the whole programmable system including a classical host, constructed with computer and circuits, and a quantum "coprocessor", used for two-particle quantum simulations. A quantum "program" with both classical statements and quantum statements is executed for a certain computation task. The experiment shows high similarity of 95.2 % to theoretical result in boson simulation and 97.1 % in fermion simulation, which demonstrates the feasibility of our programmable system.

Keywords: Quantum computing · Quantum simulation · Programmable · Entanglement · Quantum coprocessor · Quantum program

1 Introduction

Quantum computing is one of the most fascinating technology in the Post-Moore era [31]. It studies computation techniques based on quantum mechanics which promises to outperform its classical counterpart fundamentally. This field was initiated and developed by Paul Benioff in 1980 [3], Richard Feyman in 1982 [11] and David Deutsch in 1985 [8]. In 1994, Peter Shor developed a quantum algorithm solving the integer factorization problem in polynomial time, whereas the well-known classical algorithm takes exponential time [24]. Since the integer factorization forms the base of RSA scheme, a widely used public-key cryptography scheme, quantum computing came to attract more attentions.

There are various technologies [16], such as photons [1,2,22], trapped atoms [21,26], quantum dots [14], superconductors [6], nuclear magnetic resonance (NMR) [25], that can be used for the implementation of quantum computing. On the one hand, researchers have been studying how to reduce decoherence that hinders the scalability of quantum systems. On the other hand, a lot of efforts have been made to construct small-scale quantum devices to demonstrate quantum algorithms. In 2001, Shor's algorithm was demonstrated on a 7-qubit NMR

© Springer Science+Business Media Singapore 2016
J. Wu and L. Li (Eds.): ACA 2016, CCIS 626, pp. 142–156, 2016.
DOI: 10.1007/978-981-10-2209-8_13

computer to factor 15 [28]; in 2012, an all-bulk optics system was constructed at the University of Bristol to factor 21 [20]; in 2013, a quantum boson sampling machine is devised using photons [4,12,27]. Besides, D-Wave systems, although doubted about its quantum speedup, has been built based on Ising model and superconductor technology [9,10,13,17].

Most of these work implemented quantum algorithm [19] only with quantum hardware [5,13,18,20,30], just like classical Application Specific Integrated Circuits (ASIC). They did not run programs as a classical computer. Here, we focus on the programmability of a quantum system, and have implemented a demo system based on photons. The main contributions are listed in the following:

– We propose a programmable structure for two-particle bosonic and fermionic quantum simulation, which completes a certain task controlled by a program. Such a program consists some classical statements and some quantum ones. These quantum statements are executed on the corresponding quantum computation units.
– We have implemented our programmable structure based on entangled photons. To the best of our knowledge, this is one of rare programmable quantum computation systems. Previous work, except D-Wave systems, did not involve any concept of programming.

In the rest of this paper, we first introduce some preliminary knowledge for our simulation system, then report on the structure and implementation of a programmable two-particle bosonic-fermionic quantum simulation system, and finally present the test and evaluation of our system.

2 Preliminary

Quantum State and Entanglement. Quantum state is used to describe the state of a quantum system. It is denoted by a vector in Hilbert space, $|\psi\rangle$. In quantum mechanics, a special quantum state, denoted by $\alpha|\psi_1\rangle + \beta|\psi_2\rangle$, is called a superposition of $|\psi_1\rangle$ and $|\psi_2\rangle$, if $|\psi_1\rangle$ and $|\psi_2\rangle$ are both quantum states where the system stays. The coefficients satisfy $|\alpha|^2 + |\beta|^2 = 1$. However, if we measure[1] the quantum system at $\alpha|\psi_1\rangle + \beta|\psi_2\rangle$, the state collapses to $|\psi_1\rangle$ or $|\psi_2\rangle$ with the probability information. The probability of the possible result $|\psi_1\rangle$ ($|\psi_2\rangle$) is $|\alpha|^2$ ($|\beta|^2$).

A photon can be horizontal polarized or vertical polarized. The polarization state means the oscillating direction of the electrical field of a photon. We can use $|H\rangle$ to express a horizontal polarized state and $|V\rangle$ a vertical one. A photon at the superposition state of $\frac{1}{\sqrt{2}}(|H\rangle + |V\rangle)$ corresponds to the polarization of $45°$, as shown in Fig. 1.

As for a quantum system with more than one photon, with 2 photons for example, the system at the state with two horizontal polarized photons is denoted by $|HH\rangle$. The system with two vertical polarized photons is denoted by $|VV\rangle$.

---

[1] Strictly, the measurement is done in the base of $|\psi_1\rangle$ and $|\psi_2\rangle$.

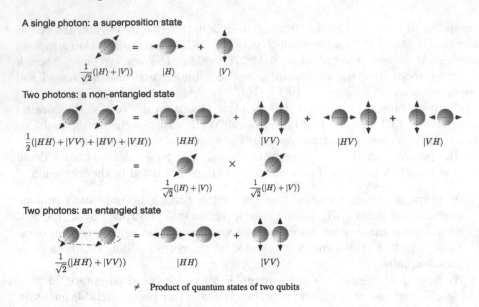

Fig. 1. Superposition and entanglement

It also can be at a superposition state, $\frac{1}{\sqrt{2}}(|HH\rangle + |VV\rangle)$, which is a special state in quantum physics, called *entanglement*. As is shown in Fig. 1, it cannot be written as a tensor product of two quantum states, while a non-entangled state can be written as a tensor product. The second photon must be in $|H\rangle$ ($|V\rangle$) no matter how far it is from the first one, if we detect the first photon at the state $|H\rangle$ ($|V\rangle$). The special phenomenon is often portrayed as quantum non-locality. There are other types of entangled states in two-photon system, such as $\frac{1}{\sqrt{2}}(|HH\rangle - |VV\rangle)$, $\frac{1}{\sqrt{2}}(|HV\rangle + |VH\rangle)$ and $\frac{1}{\sqrt{2}}(|HV\rangle - |VH\rangle)$. The latter two are used in our simulation system.

Bosons and Fermions. In quantum mechanics, there are two kinds of identical particles: bosons (photons, alpha particles, etc.) and fermions (electrons, protons, neutrons, etc.). Identical particles are particles that cannot be distinguished from each other substantially. Suppose the two particles in Fig. 2 have the same internal properties, such as the spin, the frequency. In classical physics, the situation in which the first particle stays at r_1 and the second particle at r_2 is different from the situation in which the first particle stays at r_2 and the second one at r_1. The former situation is described in $|r_1(1)r_2(2)\rangle$, and the latter in $|r_1(2)r_2(1)\rangle$. $r_a(b)$ indicates the particle b stays at r_a. However, it is impossible to distinguish the first particle from the second one. In this case, the system goes into a superposition of $|r_1(1)r_2(2)\rangle$ and $|r_1(2)r_2(1)\rangle$. If the particles are bosons with property of exchange symmetry, the superposition state will be $\frac{1}{\sqrt{2}}(|r_1(1)r_2(2)\rangle + |r_1(2)r_2(1)\rangle)$. If the particles are fermions with exchange antisymmetry, the superposition state will be $\frac{1}{\sqrt{2}}(|r_1(1)r_2(2)\rangle - |r_1(2)r_2(1)\rangle)$.

Classical:
Two particles are distinguished from each other. Exchanging them leads to two different states.

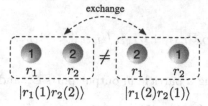

Quantum:
Two identical particles cannot be distinguished from each other, leading to a superposition state.

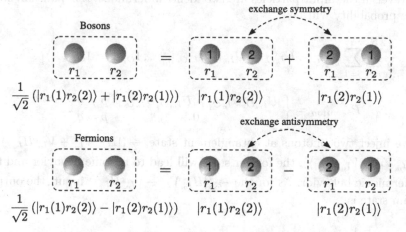

Fig. 2. Quantum identical particles: bosons and fermions

Simulating Two Bosons (Fermions) with Polarization-Entangled Photon Pairs. Photons are bosons as stated in the preceding paragraph. However, the symmetric and antisymmetric entangled photon pairs can mimic two non-interacting bosonic and fermionic particles respectively. The brief principle is derived as follows.

Suppose the quantum simulation network is denoted by a unitary matrix U. If the network has N input ports and N output ports, U will be an $N \times N$ matrix. With two identical particles injected into the input port I_m and I_n (m and n indicate the port number), the system evolves to the quantum state:

$$\sum_{i=1}^{N}\sum_{j=1}^{N} U_{I_m O_i} U_{I_n O_j} |\ldots, 1_{O_i}, \ldots, 1_{O_j}, \ldots\rangle,$$

where $U_{I_m O_i}$ is the element of U in row I_m and column O_i. $|\ldots, 1_{O_i}, \ldots, 1_{O_j}, \ldots\rangle$ denotes that there are a particle in output port O_i and a particle in output port O_j, with no particles in other ports.

If the input particles are two identical bosons, the quantum state will be written as

$$\frac{1}{2}\sum_{i=1}^{N}\sum_{j=1}^{N}\left[(U_{I_mO_i}U_{I_nO_j}+U_{I_mO_j}U_{I_nO_i}]|\ldots,1_{O_i},\ldots,1_{O_j},\ldots\rangle\right].$$

The probability of finding a particle in output ports O_p and O_q respectively is

$$P_{boson}=\begin{cases}|U_{I_mO_i}U_{I_nO_j}+U_{I_mO_j}U_{I_nO_i}|^2 & p\neq q\\ \frac{1}{2}|U_{I_mO_i}U_{I_nO_j}+U_{I_mO_j}U_{I_nO_i}|^2 & p=q\end{cases}.$$

However, if the input particles are two identical fermions, the quantum state and the probability will be

$$\frac{1}{2}\sum_{i=1}^{N}\sum_{j=1}^{N}\left[(U_{I_mO_i}U_{I_nO_j}-U_{I_mO_j}U_{I_nO_i}]|\ldots,1_{O_i},\ldots,1_{O_j},\ldots\rangle\right],$$

$$P_{fermion}=\begin{cases}|U_{I_mO_i}U_{I_nO_j}-U_{I_mO_j}U_{I_nO_i}|^2 & p\neq q\\ 0 & p=q\end{cases}.$$

If we inject two photons at entanglement state $\frac{1}{\sqrt{2}}(|H_{I_m}V_{I_n}+V_{I_m}H_{I_n}\rangle)$ or $\frac{1}{\sqrt{2}}(|H_{I_m}V_{I_n}-V_{I_m}H_{I_n}\rangle)$, the former state will lead to bosonic behavior and the latter fermionic behavior. As for the $\frac{1}{\sqrt{2}}(|H_{I_m}V_{I_n}-V_{I_m}H_{I_n}\rangle)$ input, the output quantum state is

$$\frac{1}{\sqrt{2}}\sum_{i=1}^{N}\sum_{j=1}^{N}\left[(U_{I_mO_i}U_{I_nO_j}-U_{I_mO_j}U_{I_nO_i})|H_{O_i}V_{O_j}\rangle\right].$$

The probability of detecting one photon in O_p and one in O_q is

$$P=\begin{cases}|U_{I_mO_i}U_{I_nO_j}-U_{I_mO_j}U_{I_nO_i}|^2 & p\neq q\\ \frac{1}{2}|U_{I_mO_i}U_{I_nO_j}-U_{I_mO_j}U_{I_nO_i}|^2 & p=q\end{cases}.$$

It is obvious that the probability of detecting two photons in two distinct output ports is the same as that of two fermions. Therefore, we can use a polarization-entangled photon pair at $\frac{1}{\sqrt{2}}(|H_{I_m}V_{I_n}-V_{I_m}H_{I_n}\rangle)$ to simulate the behavior of two fermions.

3   Structure

As is shown in Fig. 3, we design a structure that adopts a quantum "coprocessor" for two-particle bosonic-fermionic quantum simulation. Unlike most previous quantum experiments with only quantum devices, our structure consists of a computer, home-made circuits and quantum elements used for quantum experiments. A user-designed "program" with both classical statements and quantum

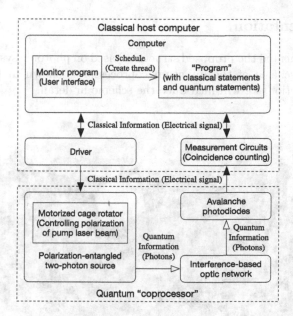

Fig. 3. Structure of the system

statements is executed by the monitor program on computers. When quantum statements are executed, the host will schedule the quantum coprocessor through the controlling driver or the measurement circuits. The driver is applied to receive commands to adjust the entangled states. The measurement circuits are applied to transfer the measured data from quantum parts to the computer.

The quantum coprocessor is constructed with a polarization-entangled two-photon source, an interference-based optic network and several avalanche photodiodes (APDs). The two-photon source produces photon pairs in a certain entangled state controlled by commands. The adjustment is accomplished by a motorized cage rotator, on which a half-wave plate is mounted. The produced photon pairs are send to the interference-based optic network to carry out the simulation. The APDs output electrical signals once they detect photons from optical network. The measurement circuits complete the coincidence counting which is a typical task in photonic experiments.

In this structure, quantum information, carried by photons, only exists in the quantum "coprocessor"; i.e., quantum state like entanglement only occurs in the quantum part. When simulating two bosons, the quantum part employs the entanglement of $\frac{1}{\sqrt{2}}(|HV\rangle + |VH\rangle)$. When simulating two fermions, it employs the entanglement of $\frac{1}{\sqrt{2}}(|HV\rangle + |VH\rangle)$. Besides, two anyons can also be simulated by other entangled states.

4   Implementation

We have implemented the proposed structure based on photonic system as shown in Fig. 4. The scheme of the quantum coprocessor is shown in Fig. 5. In the following subsection, we will introduce the scheme in detail.

Fig. 4. System implementation

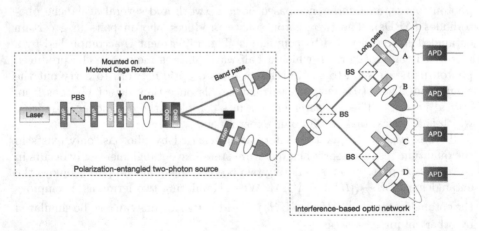

Fig. 5. Scheme of quantum coprocessor for two-particle bosonic-fermionic quantum simulation

4.1   Polarization-Entangled Two-Photon Source

We implement the two-photon source using spontaneous parametric down-conversion (SPDC) [15]. In SPDC, a high-frequency photon can split into a pair of low-frequency photons in accordance with the law of conservation of energy and law of conservation of momentum when it enters a nonlinear crystal. The process of SPDC happens randomly with extremely low probability, which makes the experiment challenging.

A two-crystal geometry is used to construct the polarization-entangled two-photon source. When a vertically polarized photon enters the specially-designed nonlinear crystals, down-conversion will only occur in the first crystal. The emitted light cones will be horizontally polarized, due to the type-I coupling. Similarly, with a horizontally polarized pump injected, down-conversion will only occur in the second crystal, producing otherwise identical cones of vertically polarized photon pairs. A 45°-polarized pump photon will lead to the same probability of down-conversions in either crystal (neglecting losses from passing through the first crystal). The possible down-conversion processes in the two adjacent nonlinear crystals are coherent with one another, as long as the emitted spatial modes for a given pair of photon are indistinguishable for the two crystals. Consequently, the photons in the state $\frac{1}{\sqrt{2}}(|HH\rangle + e^{i\phi}|VV\rangle)$ will automatically be created. ϕ is determined by the details of the phase matching and the crystals thickness, and in our experiment we adjust the wave plate group to set different ϕ for different simulation.

Figure 5 shows the experimental setup used to produce and characterize the entangled photons. The pump beam at 405 nm is directed to the two crystals after passing through: a half-wave plate (HWP) and a polarizing beam splitter (PBS) to adjust the power ($|H\rangle$); a rotatable HWP to adjust the polarization ($\frac{1}{\sqrt{2}}(|H\rangle + |V\rangle)$); and a wave plate group to set ϕ in the final output state ($\frac{1}{\sqrt{2}}(|H\rangle + e^{\phi_p}|V\rangle))^2$. The nonlinear crystals are β-barium borate (BBO). The optic axis of each BBO is cut at 33.9°. For this cut the degenerate-frequency photons($\frac{1}{\sqrt{2}}(|HH\rangle + e^{i\phi}|VV\rangle)$) at 810 nm are emitted into a cone of half-opening angle 3°. An HWP is added to one down-conversion path to get the state of $\frac{1}{\sqrt{2}}(|HV\rangle + e^{i\phi}|VH\rangle)$. Interference filters (IFs) centered at 810 nm with full width at half maximum (FWHM) of 5 nm are placed to reduce the background noise and select only these (nearly) degenerate photons.

4.2   Interference-Based Optic Network

The interference-based optic network in Fig. 5 completes the quantum simulation task of the system. Beam splitters (BSs) with transmittance rate of 50 % transmit a particle with 50 % probability and reflect it with 50 % probability [23]. If we send a classical particle into any input port of the network, each output port will emit the particle with a probability of 0.25. If we send two classical particles into

---

[2] The phase ϕ in down-converted photons is determined by ϕ_p in the pump beam and accumulated phase of photons in the optic path.

Table 1. Probabilities of output particles in different ports of the network

Port No.	Classical particles				Bosons				Fermions			
	A	B	C	D	A	B	C	D	A	B	C	D
A	0.0625	0.0625	0.0625	0.0625	0.125	0.25	0	0	0	0	0.25	0.25
B	0.0625	0.0625	0.0625	0.0625	0.25	0.125	0	0	0	0	0.25	0.25
C	0.0625	0.0625	0.0625	0.0625	0	0	0.125	0.25	0.25	0.25	0	0
D	0.0625	0.0625	0.0625	0.0625	0	0	0.25	0.125	0.25	0.25	0	0

it, the probability of detecting one particle in port i and one in port j will be 0.0625 (0.25×0.25). i and j are A, B, C or D. The probabilities of all cases are listed in Table 1. However, if we send two bosons into the network, it is impossible to detect bosons from A and C simultaneously because of the interference in the first BS; i.e., the two bosons will either be reflected or transmitted by the first BS. This phenomenon is called photon-bunching in physics. If two fermions are input into the network, they will exhibit antibunching behaviour. Table 1 shows all probabilities in classical, bosonic and fermionic situations. Note that two classical particles are distinguished from each other as discussed in the preceding section. The situation that port A output the first particle and B the second one is different from the situation that A output the second particle and B the first one. We will always get the probability of 1 when summarizing all probabilities of these 16 situations ($0.0625 \times 16 = 1$). As for the quantum particles, the two identical particles cannot be distinguished from each other. Therefore, there is no difference between AC and CA in Table 1. In addition, it is impossible for the measurement circuits to distinguish coincidence AC from CA in the experiments.

The key of the experiment is to realize identical, which requires the minimum distance difference between entangled photons arriving at the first BS. If the distance difference is greater than 40 μm, the coherent length of down-converted pump, the two particles will be distinguishable.

4.3   Interface Between Classical Host and Quantum Coprocessor

There is a two-way information flow between classical host and quantum coprocessor. The information flow from quantum coprocessor to classical host relies on the measurement circuits, while the information flow from classical host to quantum coprocessor relies on the driver.

From Quantum Coprocessor to Classical Host. APD will output an electrical pulse in the width of 8 ns once it detects a photon. The pulses from different APDs are sent into a coincidence counting circuits to count the coincident events in a duration time. A coincident event is defined as two pulses arising in a coincidence window. In our experiment, the coincidence window is set to 10 ns. As is discussed above, the coincidence count between A and B is apparently more than that between A and C in a two-boson quantum simulation, which is in contrast to the situation for fermions. We have implemented the circuits on a Xilinx FPGA development board.

From Classical Host to Quantum Coprocessor. The information sent from classical host to quantum coprocessor is to adjust ϕ in the entangled state of $\frac{1}{\sqrt{2}}(|HV\rangle + e^{i\phi}|VH\rangle)$. This task is completed by rotating an HWP on a motorized cage rotator. Once the rotator driver receives commands from the host, it will drive the rotator to the target position. The overall function of the wave plate group can be expressed as the product of Jones matrices in Eq. (1).

$$\frac{1}{\sqrt{2}}\begin{pmatrix} 1 & -i \\ -i & 1 \end{pmatrix}\begin{pmatrix} cos2\theta & sin2\theta \\ sin2\theta & -cos2\theta \end{pmatrix}\frac{1}{\sqrt{2}}\begin{pmatrix} 1 & -i \\ -i & 1 \end{pmatrix} = e^{-i2\theta}\begin{pmatrix} 1 & 0 \\ 0 & e^{i(\pi+4\theta)} \end{pmatrix} \quad (1)$$

The fast axis of each QWP is set at 45° with respect to the horizontal axis. When the state of the input pump laser beam is $\frac{1}{\sqrt{2}}(|H\rangle + |V\rangle)$, the output state will be $\frac{e^{-i2\theta}}{\sqrt{2}}(|H\rangle + e^{i(\pi+4\theta)}|V\rangle)$. We can adjust ϕ in the final entanglement state by rotating the HWP in the wave plate group. The phase prefactor cannot be detected in our system.

4.4 Quantum "Program"

We use Python to implement the monitor program executing a quantum "program". As is shown in Fig. 6, the monitor program communicates with quantum coprocessor and schedule a quantum program. Figure 6 gives an example of a quantum program to simulate fermionic behavior. The statements began with QUANTUM_ are quantum statements used to interact with quantum hardware.

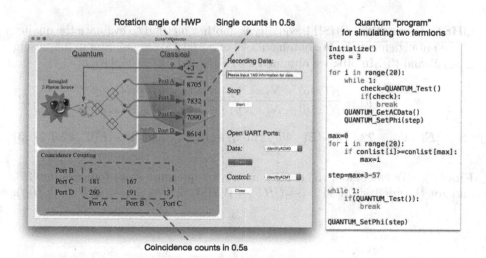

Fig. 6. Moniter program and an instance of quantum "program"

They are encapsulated into python functions. The sample code gets the coincidence counts and controls the entangled state according to the comparison of the counts. It will find a position with the maximum coincidence count between port A and C, which exhibits the fermionic behavior.

5   Evaluation and Analysis

The performance of the system strongly depends on the quality of polarization-entangled two-photon source. Therefore, we first evaluated the polarization-entangled state and then evaluated the final state.

5.1   Polarization-Entangled Two-Photon Source

There are several typical methods to evaluate the quality of an entangled-photon source. We have measured the polarization correlations, the CHSH inequality[3] and the fidelity. The measurement was performed with the pump laser of 63 mW, coincidence window of 10 ns and counting duration of 0.5 s.

Polarization Correlations. The polarization correlations were measured with adjustable polarization analyzers, consisting of a polarizer in front of each coupler. The polarizer in one path was fixed at $0°$ or $45°$, while the polarizer in the other path was rotated. The coincidence rate displayed sinusoidal fringes with nearly perfect visibility. As is shown in Fig. 7, the visibilities are 98.28 % ($\frac{1}{\sqrt{2}}(|HV\rangle + |VH\rangle)$) and 99.65 % ($\frac{1}{\sqrt{2}}(|HV\rangle + |VH\rangle)$) respectively, with a polarizer fixed at $45°$. With a polarizer fixed at $45°$, the visibilities are 98.55 % ($\frac{1}{\sqrt{2}}(|HV\rangle + |VH\rangle)$) and 97.48 % ($\frac{1}{\sqrt{2}}(|HV\rangle + |VH\rangle)$) respectively.

CHSH Inequality. CHSH inequality is another method to evaluate the quality of the entanglement [7]. We obtained 2.72 of S and $15 - \sigma$ violation in 0.5 s using Eqs. (2) and (3). In 50 s, we obtained 2.41 of S and $94 - \sigma$ violation.

$$E(x,y) = \frac{N(x,y) + N(x_\perp, y_\perp) - N(x_\perp, y) - N(x, y_\perp)}{N(x,y) + N(x_\perp, y_\perp) + N(x_\perp, y) + N(x, y_\perp)} \qquad (2)$$

$$S = |E(-45°, -22.5°)| + |E(-45°, 22.5°)| + |E(0°, -22.5°)| + |E(0°, 22.5°)| \quad (3)$$

Fidelity. We calculated the density matrix by quantum state tomography [29], and got the fidelities of 94 % ($\frac{1}{\sqrt{2}}(|HV\rangle + |VH\rangle)$) and 92 % ($\frac{1}{\sqrt{2}}(|HV\rangle - |VH\rangle)$).

---

[3] CHSH stands for John Clauser, Michael Horne, Abner Shimony, and Richard Holt, who derived the inequality.

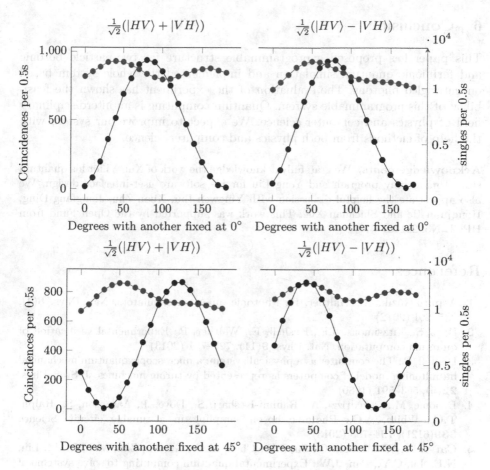

Fig. 7. Correlation of two photons in polarization.

5.2 Two-Particle Bosonic-Fermionic Simulation

The control program adjusted the simulation system to the target states automatically. The similarity(S) of fermionic simulation can be calculated as Eq. (4).

$$S = \frac{\left(\Sigma_{i,j}\sqrt{P_{ij}D_{ij}}\right)^2}{\Sigma_{i,j}P_{ij}\Sigma_{i,j}D_{ij}} \tag{4}$$

P_{ij} is the ideal probability of coincidence between port i and port j given in Table 1. D_{ij} is the experimental coincidence count between port i and port j.

We have tried several quantum programs with different algorithms to test the system. The similarity for bosonic simulation is 95.2 % and for fermionic simulation 97.1 %. There are several factors accounting for the experimental error. First, the dither of the system, including source and detector, influences the count rates, which are the essential input of the script. Second, the quantum programs still have potential to be optimized.

6   Conclusion

This paper has proposed a programmable structure for two-particle bosonic and fermionic quantum simulation and implemented the whole system based on entangled photons. The evaluation of the experiment has shown the feasibility of this programmable system. Quantum computing is an interdisciplinary field of physics and computer science. We expect to improve our system with the help of methods from both physics and computer science.

Acknowledgements. We gratefully acknowledge the work of Xun Yi for his quantum state tomography program and Yong Liu for his software user-interface design. We also appreciate the helpful discussion with Yingwen Liu, Xuan Zhu, Jiangfang Ding, Hongjuan He and Shichuan Xue. This work was supported by the Open Fund from HPCL No. 201401-01.

References

1. Aspuru-Guzik, A., Walther, P.: Photonic quantum simulators. Nat. Phys. **8**(4), 285–291 (2012)
2. Barz, S., Fitzsimons, J.F., Kashefi, E., Walther, P.: Experimental verification of quantum computation. Nat. Phys. **9**(11), 727–731 (2013)
3. Benioff, P.: The computer as a physical system: a microscopic quantum mechanical hamiltonian model of computers as represented by turing machines. J. Stat. Phys. **22**(5), 563–591 (1980)
4. Broome, M.A., Fedrizzi, A., Rahimi-Keshari, S., Dove, J., Aaronson, S., Ralph, T.C., White, A.G.: Photonic boson sampling in a tunable circuit. Science **339**(6121), 794–798 (2013)
5. Cai, X.D., Weedbrook, C., Su, Z.E., Chen, M.C., Gu, M., Zhu, M.J., Li, L., Liu, N.L., Lu, C.Y., Pan, J.W.: Experimental quantum computing to solve systems of linear equations. Phys. Rev. Lett. **110**, 230501 (2013)
6. Clarke, J., Wilhelm, F.K.: Superconducting quantum bits. Nature **453**(7198), 1031–1042 (2008)
7. Clauser, J.F., Horne, M.A., Shimony, A., Holt, R.A.: Proposed experiment to test local hidden-variable theories. Phys. Rev. Lett. **23**, 880–884 (1969)
8. Deutsch, D.: Quantum theory, the church-turing principle and the universal quantum computer. Proc. R. Soc. A Math. Phys. Eng. Sci. **400**(1818), 97–117 (1985)
9. Dickson, N.G., Amin, M.H.: Algorithmic approach to adiabatic quantum optimization. Phys. Rev. A **85**, 032303 (2012)
10. Douglass, A., King, A.D., Raymond, J.: Constructing SAT filters with a quantum annealer. In: Heule, M., Weaver, S. (eds.) SAT 2015. LNCS, vol. 9340, pp. 104–120. Springer, Heidelberg (2015). doi:10.1007/978-3-319-24318-4_9
11. Feynman, R.P.: Simulating physics with computers. Int. J. Theor. Phys. **21**(6), 467–488 (1982)
12. Franson, J.D.: Beating classical computing without a quantum computer. Science **339**(6121), 767–768 (2013)

13. Johnson, M.W., Amin, M.H.S., Gildert, S., Lanting, T., Hamze, F., Dickson, N., Harris, R., Berkley, A.J., Johansson, J., Bunyk, P., Chapple, E.M., Enderud, C., Hilton, J.P., Karimi, K., Ladizinsky, E., Ladizinsky, N., Oh, T., Perminov, I., Rich, C., Thom, M.C., Tolkacheva, E., Truncik, C.J.S., Uchaikin, S., Wang, J., Wilson, B., Rose, G.: Quantum annealing with manufactured spins. Nature **473**(7346), 194–198 (2011)

14. Kane, B.E.: A silicon-based nuclear spin quantum computer. Nature **393**(6681), 133–137 (1998)

15. Kwiat, P.G., Waks, E., White, A.G., Appelbaum, I., Eberhard, P.H.: Ultrabright source of polarization-entangled photons. Phys. Rev. A **60**, R773–R776 (1999)

16. Ladd, T.D., Jelezko, F., Laflamme, R., Nakamura, Y., Monroe, C., O'Brien, J.L.: Quantum computers. Nature **464**(7285), 45–53 (2010)

17. Lanting, T., Przybysz, A.J., Smirnov, A.Y., Spedalieri, F.M., Amin, M.H., Berkley, A.J., Harris, R., Altomare, F., Boixo, S., Bunyk, P., Dickson, N., Enderud, C., Hilton, J.P., Hoskinson, E., Johnson, M.W., Ladizinsky, E., Ladizinsky, N., Neufeld, R., Oh, T., Perminov, I., Rich, C., Thom, M.C., Tolkacheva, E., Uchaikin, S., Wilson, A.B., Rose, G.: Entanglement in a quantum annealing processor. Phys. Rev. X **4**, 021041 (2014)

18. Lu, C.Y., Browne, D.E., Yang, T., Pan, J.W.: Demonstration of a compiled version of Shor's quantum factoring algorithm using photonic qubits. Phys. Rev. Lett. **99**, 250504 (2007)

19. Lu, K., Zhang, Y., Xu, K., Gao, Y.: Approximate maximum common sub-graph isomorphism based on discrete-time quantum walk. In: International Conference on Pattern Recognition, pp. 1413–1418 (2014)

20. Martin-Lopez, E., Laing, A., Lawson, T., Alvarez, R., Zhou, X.Q., O'Brien, J.L.: Experimental realization of Shor's quantum factoring algorithm using qubit recycling. Nat. Photonics **6**(11), 773–776 (2012)

21. Monroe, C.: Quantum information processing with atoms and photons. Nature **416**(6877), 238–246 (2002)

22. O'Brien, J.L.: Optical quantum computing. Science **318**(5856), 1567–1570 (2007)

23. Sansoni, L., Sciarrino, F., Vallone, G., Mataloni, P., Crespi, A., Ramponi, R., Osellame, R.: Two-particle bosonic-fermionic quantum walk via integrated photonics. Phys. Rev. Lett. **108**(1), 140–144 (2012)

24. Shor, P.W.: Algorithms for quantum computation: discrete log and factoring (extended abstract). Proc. Annu. Symp. Found. Comput. Sci. IEEE Comput. Soc. 124–134 (1994)

25. Somaroo, S., Tseng, C.H., Havel, T.F., Laflamme, R., Cory, D.G.: Quantum simulations on a quantum computer. Phys. Rev. Lett. **82**, 5381–5384 (1999)

26. Sørensen, J.J.W.H., Pedersen, M.K., Munch, M., Haikka, P., Jensen, J.H., Planke, T., Andreasen, M.G., Gajdacz, M., Mølmer, K., Lieberoth, A., Sherson, J.F.: Exploring the quantum speed limit with computer games. Nature **532**(7598), 210–213 (2016)

27. Spring, J.B., Metcalf, B.J., Humphreys, P.C., Kolthammer, W.S., Jin, X.M., Barbieri, M., Datta, A., Thomas-Peter, N., Langford, N.K., Kundys, D., Gates, J.C., Smith, B.J., Smith, P.G.R., Walmsley, I.A.: Boson sampling on a photonic chip. Science **339**(6121), 798–801 (2013)

28. Steffen, M., Vandersypen, L., Breyta, G., Yannoni, C., Sherwood, M., Chuang, I.: Experimental realization of Shor's quantum factoring algorithm. Am. Phys. Soc. **414**(6866), 883–887 (2002)

29. Thew, R.T., Nemoto, K., White, A.G., Munro, W.J.: Qudit quantum-state tomography. Phys. Rev. A **66**, 012303 (2002)
30. Walther, P., Resch, K.J., Rudolph, T., Schenck, E., Weinfurter, H., Vedral, V., Aspelmeyer, M., Zeilinger, A.: Experimental one-way quantum computing. Nature **434**(7030), 169–176 (2005)
31. Yang, X.J., Dou, Y., Hu, Q.F.: Progress and challenges in high performance computer technology. J. Comput. Sci. Technol. **21**(5), 674–681 (2006)

An Introduction to All-Optical Quantum Controlled-NOT Gates

Hongjuan He, Junjie Wu[✉], and Xuan Zhu

State Key Laboratory of High Performance Computing,
National University of Defense Technology, Changsha, China
junjiewu@nudt.edu.cn

Abstract. Quantum computer promises to outperform classical computer fundamentally, due to its quantum superposition. Any operations to N qubits can be decomposed into several single-qubit operations and two-qubit controlled-NOT (CNOT) operations in theory. Linear optical quantum computing (LOQC) is one of the most prominent physical quantum systems, which has the advantage of long coherent time and convenience in implementing single qubit operations. However, the realization of two-qubit CNOT gate is the greatest challenge for LOQC, because two photons cannot directly interact with each other by nature. KLM protocol proves the feasibility of LOQC and spurs quantity of research on schematic design and experimental demonstration of CNOT gates by using linear quantum optics system. These researches are very important and nontrivial for LOQC, and this paper gives an overview of different schemes of the proposed CNOT gates and the experimental demonstration.

Keywords: Quantum computing · LOQC · Quantum circuit · CNOT gate

1 Introduction

Quantum computer promises to outperform classical computer fundamentally, due to its quantum superposition [26]. N qubits in a special superposition quantum state can represent 2^N numbers, while N classical bits only represent one of them. Thus, a quantum operation to these N qubits operates all 2^N numbers simultaneously. According to this quantum feature, a lot of quantum algorithms have been developed which achieves a speedup, in complexity theory, of classical best algorithms.

Any operations to N qubits can be decomposed into several single-qubit operations and two-qubit CNOT operations in theory. Therefore, how to implement them is crucial to realizing quantum computing for all kinds of physical systems, including photons [16], trapped ions [3], quantum dots [27,28], superconductors [12] and so on. These systems have their own advantages and disadvantages. Take photon system for example, it has longer coherence time than most other

© Springer Science+Business Media Singapore 2016
J. Wu and L. Li (Eds.): ACA 2016, CCIS 626, pp. 157–173, 2016.
DOI: 10.1007/978-981-10-2209-8_14

systems. Besides, single-qubit optical gates are easy to implemented using linear optical elements including beam splitters, wave plates, phase shifters, mirrors, etc. [8,10,11,18]. Thus, quantum computation using photons is called LOQC.

However, the realization of two-qubit CNOT gate is the most challenge in LOQC, because two photons cannot directly interact with each other by nature. It was believed that optical nonlinearities, stronger than those available in conventional non-linear media, are essential for LOQC. In 2001, Knill, Laflamme and Milburn proved that it is possible to realize quantum computing by using linear optics, single photons (ancilla), and single photon detectors (also called post-selection), which has been famous as the KLM protocol [8]. The protocol proves the feasibility of LOQC and spurs quantity of research on schematic design and experimental demonstration of CNOT gates by using linear quantum optics system [4,7,13,20–24]. These researches are very important and nontrivial for LOQC.

2   LOQC

2.1   Qubits

A qubit is an elementary unit in quantum computer, which plays the similar role as classical bit. In LOQC, a qubit is usually a single photon with two modes on one certain degree of freedom such as spatial modes and polarization modes [10].

A photon encoded in spatial modes is called a spatial qubit or a dual-rail qubit. The spatial qubit has a choice of two different modes $|0\rangle_L = |1, 0\rangle$ and $|1\rangle_L = |0, 1\rangle$. If a single photon occupies path 0 and a vacuum state in path 1, it is the logical $|0\rangle_L$. Vice versa, logical $|1\rangle_L$. Different spatial modes mean different paths.

When the photons internal polarization degree of freedom is used to be the two modes, we call the photon a polarization qubit. In general, a photon horizontally (H-) polarized represents the logical 0, and a photon vertically (V-) polarized represents the logical 1. A polarization qubit and a spatial qubit can interconvert into each other. In quantum computing, a photon can live in the superposition state, so a qubit contains information of both logical 0 and logical 1. While in classical computing, one bit can only be either 0 or 1.

2.2   Optical Components

There are fundamental building blocks in LOQC, such as half-wave plates (HWPs), quarter-wave plates (QWPs), several different beam splitters and so on.

Wave Plates. HWPs and QWPs are common wave plates that can manipulate the polarization encoded photons, and they are made of birefringent crystals that induce a relative phase shift. Its needed that the incident light should be perpendicular to the plain of HWPs and QWPs. The effect of the two wave plates is characterized by the angle θ rotating from the optical axis to horizontal

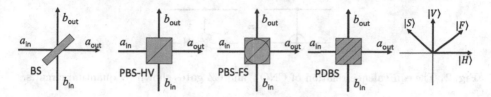

Fig. 1. Schematic diagrams of several BSs and orientations of the HV and FS bases.

polarization, which decides how the polarization amplitudes are split. Usually, we mark the HWP with rotating angle θ as HWP(θ). An arbitrary unitary operation U on a single qubit can realized by three wave plates: QWP(α), HWP(β) and QWP(γ).

Beam Splitters. A Beam Splitter (BS) is a significant component to operate spatial qubits in LOQC [10]. It is a device that can redistribute the amplitudes of two spatial inputs, which is decided by the reflection probability R. In addition, transmission probability T can be deduced by R, since $R + T = 1$. The most common one is 1/2BS, which represents $R = 1/2$. A matrix describing its effect is U_{BS} as follows:

where a_i and b_j can be comprehended as the amplitude of the input or output in port a_i and b_j respectively, as shown in Fig. 1.

A BS designed to configure parameters with respect to the polarization of the input qubits, called polarizing beam splitter (PBS). It means that PBS can deal with both spatial and polarized information of input photons. The most common PBS transmits H-polarized photons and reflects V-polarized photons totally. Through rotation, PBS can be in different bases, such as HV and FS bases shown in Fig. 1 [23]. In this paper, we mark them as PBS-HV (or PBS) and PBS-FS respectively shown in Fig. 1.

Another important subclass of PBS is the polarization dependent beam splitter (PDBS) [7]. A PDBS is characterized by two parameters, transmission probability for horizontal polarization, t_H, and for vertical polarization, t_V, in both output modes. A PDBS used latter with parameters of $t_H = 1$ and $t_V = 1/3$, transmits H-polarized photons totally and V-polarized photon with probability 1/3, while reflects V-polarized photons with probability 2/3.

2.3   Quantum Circuit Model

Analogous to an electrical circuit of a classical computer, a quantum circuit builds a quantum computer, containing wires and several elementary quantum gates [17]. Wires are used to transfer information and quantum gates manipulate it. Classical gates cannot be used to quantum computing, since they cannot deal with the quantum superposition.

Quantum gates in circuit model can be divided into the single and the multiple qubit gates [14]. A single qubit gate is to convert a single qubit from one

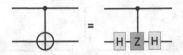

Fig. 2. The equivalence relation of CNOT and CZ gates shown by quantum circuits.

form to another. The commons are quantum NOT gate, X gate and Z gate. NOT gates effect is exchanging the state of 0 and 1, and the Z gate is to add negative sign to logical 1.

CNOT gate is an important multiple qubit quantum gate. It contains the control qubit and the target qubit. The goal of CNOT gate is to flip the logical state of the target photon if the control photon is logical 1, while do nothing if logical 0. The control qubit remains unchanged. Another multiple qubit gate is the controlled phase gate (CZ gate). The operation of CZ gate is that if the control and target qubits are both logical 1, π phase shift is induced. The CNOT gate can be realized by the CZ gate with two Hadamard gates on input and output of target qubit, as Fig. 2 shown.

3   Schemes of CNOT Gates and Experimental Demonstrations

Since the CNOT gate is universal and important, researchers propose a lot of schemes to implement it. Those schemes all require post-selection based on KLM protocol that leads to nonlinearity required by the CNOT gate operation. In this review, we divide those schemes into four classes, that is, the CNOT gate based on bases transformation, the CNOT gate based on path interference, the CNOT gate based on interference of polarized photons and the simplified CNOT gate particular for special cases.

3.1   CNOT Gates Based on Bases Transformation

This subsection introduces one fundamental CNOT gate [22,23] and two improved CNOT gates based on the fundamental one [4,21,24]. They all use polarization encoded qubits and the photon horizontally polarized represents the logical 0, and the photon vertically polarized represents the logical 1.

A Fundamental CNOT Gate. The fundamental CNOT gate is demonstrated by T.B. Pittman et al. Fig. 3(a) shows its schematic graph and two detecting bases. The flip of target qubit is caused by bases transformation on PBS-FS that reflects S-polarized photons and transmits F-polarized photons totally.

In the device, two single photons are incident on a PBS-FS, respectively formed as control and target input qubits. A polarization-sensitive detector including two single photon detectors and a PBS in path 2 completes the post-selection operation.

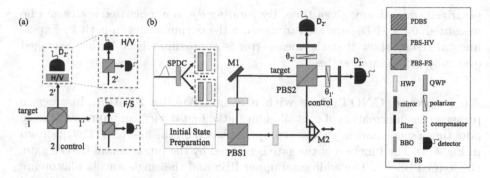

Fig. 3. The CNOT gate based on bases transformation (a) Schematic graph and two detecting bases [23] (b) experimental setup of the CNOT gate [22]

Considering the case that the target photon is an arbitrary polarization state, $|in\rangle_1 = \alpha H_1 + \beta V_1$, and the control photon is V-polarized, $|in\rangle_2 = V_2$, the total initial state can be written in FS bases:

$$\Psi_{in} = |in\rangle_1 \otimes |in\rangle_2 = [\frac{\alpha}{\sqrt{2}}(F_1 - S_1) + \frac{\beta}{\sqrt{2}}(F_1 + S_1)] \otimes \frac{1}{\sqrt{2}}(F_2 + S_2)$$

The PBS-FS transforms it into:

$$\Psi_{2'1'} = \frac{1}{2}[\alpha(F_{2'}F_{1'} - S_{2'}S_{1'}) + \beta(F_{2'}F_{1'} + S_{2'}S_{1'})] + \frac{1}{\sqrt{2}}\Psi_{II}$$

Where II includes the amplitudes of the unsuccessful cases that D2 doesn't receive one or only one photon. Rewriting the amplitudes in mode 2 back in HV bases:

$$\Psi_{2'1'} = \frac{1}{2}[H_d(\alpha V_{1'} + \beta H_{1'}) + V_d(\alpha H_{1'} + \beta V_{1'})] + \frac{1}{\sqrt{2}}\Psi_{II}$$

If we accept the outputs of first term, D_2 detects only one H-polarized photon, the output collapses to the state $\alpha V_1 + \beta H_1$. This is a flip of the input state when the control state is V-polarized.

The case that control photon state is H-polarized keeps the output of target state unchanged, by using the same device and post-selection operation as above case.

In summary, when the detector receives only one H-polarized photon, the CNOT gate succeeds with a probability of 0.25, which can be increased to 0.5 by using feed-forward control techniques [24].

Figure 3(b) shows experimental setup according to Fig. 3(a), and graphic representation of all components which are used for all following figures. All process be-fore PBS2 are to generate arbitrary input state of control and target qubits. PBS2 realized the PBS-FS in Fig. 3(a). Rather than rotating the PBS through 45°, it is more convenient to rotate the photons polarization and the detector bases by HWPs. Polarization-sensitive detector is realized by a rotatable polarization analyzer $\theta_{2'}$ and a single photon detector, which can only detect one polarized state at any given time. By rotating $\theta_{2'}$, any polarized states can be measured. $\theta_{1'}$ and $D_{1'}$ are used to measure the output states in path 1'. Experimental results show that the mean error is approximately 8 % when averaged over all possible input states.

An Improved CNOT Gate with a Single Ancilla Photon. In order to preserve the information of control qubit in the first device, an improved scheme adopting a single ancilla photon is proposed based on the first CNOT [21], shown in Fig. 4(a). The function of the gate is realized by the fundamental CNOT gate, the lower PBS-FS. The additional upper PBS and the single ancilla photon are used to copy the control photon state, which is called quantum encoder, and output into two ports. One is acted as the output of the control qubit, and the other is to interact with the target qubit to implement CNOT operation. Therefore, a CNOT gate with both target and control output is implemented. When a coincidence of three detectors happens and detector DA receives only one H-polarized photon, the gate succeeds with probability of 1/8, which can be increased to 1/4 by using feed-forward control techniques.

In detail, the single ancilla photon is generated in state $(H_a+V_a)/\sqrt{2}$, and the control qubit is arbitrary state $\alpha H + \beta V$. When the ancilla photon and control photon are mixed on the upper PBS, the output state is $\alpha H_a H + \beta H_a V + \alpha V_a H + \beta V_a V$. Through post-selection that one and only one photon is detected in both output ports, the state $\alpha H_a H + \beta V_a V$ is chosen, which copies the control state.

The experimental setup is shown Fig. 4(b). The block of initial state preparation is to prepare three photons with required polarized states. Then three photons are incident into A, C and T port, respectively acting as the ancilla, control and target qubits. The lower PBS in Fig. 4(a) rotated 45° with respect to the upper one is accomplished by a fpc (calibrated fiber polarization controller) between the two PBS. Post-selection and qubit analysis are realized by polarizers and single-photon detectors $D_{A,C,T}$.

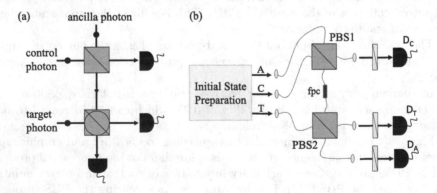

Fig. 4. The CNOT gate with single ancilla photon [21]. (a) Schematic graph (b) experimental setup.

An Improved CNOT Gate with Entangled Ancilla Photon Pair.
Another improved CNOT gate proposed by Pittman et al. [23] is demonstrated
by Gasparoni et al. [4]. The scheme requires an entangled ancillary pair photon and two simpler gates, as Fig. 5(a) shown. The lower fundamental CNOT
gate and the upper quantum encoder have been analyzed above. The encoder
together with the maximally entangled Bell state copies the control qubit into
ports b_1 and a_4. Port b_1 is the output of control qubit, and the photon from a_4 is
to interact with the target qubit on PBS2 to implement the function of CNOT
gate. When detector D_3 receive F-polarized state and D_4 detects H-polarized
state simultaneously, the CNOT gate succeeds with probability 1/16, which can
be increased to 1/4 by using feed-forward control techniques.

The experimental setup is shown in Fig. 5(b). Pump laser passes through
BBO twice and generates two pairs of entangled photons. One pair entangled
photon pair acts as the entangled Bell state, and the other pair is disentangled
into two single photons by passing through appropriate polarizers. Two single
photons are transformed into any initial state by HWPs, and act as the control
and target photons respectively. Photons in path a_2 and a_4 interfere on PBS2,
and photons in a_1 and a_3 interact on PBS1. Finally, the CNOT gate is realized
by post-selection, with the fidelity of about 80 %.

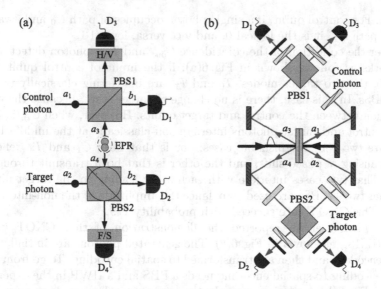

Fig. 5. The CNOT gate with entangled ancilla photon pair [4] (a) schematic graph (b)
experimental setup.

3.2   A CNOT Gate with Path Interferences

This subsection recommends the fourth CNOT gate, a gate with path interferences [6,25]. The control and the target qubits of this gate are both spatial

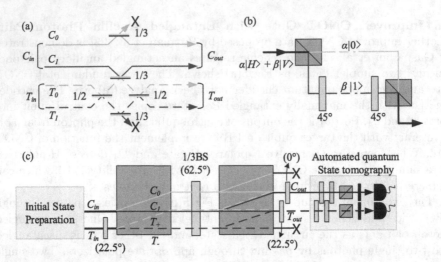

Fig. 6. A CNOT gate with path interference [18]. (a) Schematic graph. (b) A polarization qubit and a spatial qubit converted into each other. (c) The schematic experimental realization.

encoded. For control qubit, if a single photon occupies of path C_0 and a vacuum state in path C_1, it is the logical 0, and vice versa, logical 1.

Under the condition of the coincidence C_{out} and T_{out} photon detection, the gate works as follows shown in Fig. 6(a): if the input of control qubit C_{in} is logical 0, the two target modes, T_0 and T_1, are interfering classically twice on two 1/2BSs. In this case, there is no change of target state, because there is no interaction between the control and target qubits. However, when C_{in} is logical 1, the control and target photons interfere non-classically at the middle 1/3BS. There are two indistinguishable cases: one is that both C_1 and T_+ reflect on 1/3BS causing π phase shift, and the other is that both transmit through the 1/3BS. That two cases interfere with each other leading to the target flipping. The other two 1/3BSs are used to balance the amplitude of the non-interference output. This CNOT gate succeed with probability 1/9.

J.L. O'Brien et al. reported the demonstration of that CNOT gate in NATURE [18], as shown in Fig. 6(c). The generated photons are initially polarization encoded, and then are transformed to spatial encoding. To go from polarization encoding to spatial encoding needs a PBS and a HWP in the experiment shown in Fig. 6(b), and vice versa. In the experimental setup, two input polarized qubits pass through the first PBS and are transformed into spatial encoding. Two HWPs(22.5°) implement two 1/2BSs, where the two classical interferences happen, and the middle HWP(OA = 62.5°) implements the three 1/3BSs. The second PBS translates the polarized information after HWP(62.5°) into spatial modes to complete post-selection. Experimental fidelity is 84%.

3.3 A CNOT Gate with Polarized Photons Interference

This is a CNOT gate with polarized photon interference [7,13,20]. Two input qubits are polarization encoded, and H-polarization is logical 0, V-polarization is 1. Implementation of the CNOT gate is shown in Fig. 7. This gate is realized mainly by three PDBSs. PDBS0 with parameters of $t_H = 1$ and $t_V = 1/3$, and two PDBSa/b have reverse parameters, $t_H = 1/3$ and $t_V = 1$. Whats more, reflection on PDBS0 once causes a $\pi/2$ phase-shift. The flip of target state when control state is 1, is realized by the process of a π phase shift and two HWPs(22.5°) in input and output of target qubit. The phase shift is caused by interference of two indistinguishable cases when two V-polarized photons are mixed on PDBS0. One case is that both of the two photons transmit with probability 1/3, and the other case is that both of them reflect with probability 2/3 leading to a phase shift totally. The other two subsequent PDBSs are used to balance the output amplitudes. HWPs, QWPs and PBSs are to analyze the output state and post-selection. The gate succeeds when two detectors obtain a coincidence in the output with probability of 1/9 and experimental fidelity is 81.8 %.

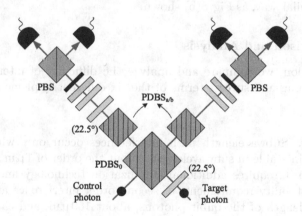

Fig. 7. Implementation of the CNOT gate with polarized photons interference [7].

3.4 A Simplified Version of CNOT Gate with a Particular Target Qubit State

Five schemes of CNOT gate described previously are all for the arbitrary control and target states. However, there are some special applications that the target state is bases logic in quantum circuits, for example, target state is the initial state, logical 0 or 1.

The CNOT gate with target state being logical 0 is easy to be realized by only one PBS and one HWP, as Fig. 8(a) shown [2,15]. The control qubit state is arbitrary, written as $\alpha H + \beta V$, while the target qubit state is H. Target qubit

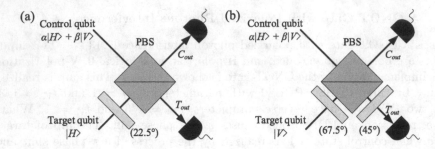

Fig. 8. A simplified version of CNOT gate with bases target qubit state. (a) The input of target qubit is H-polarized state. (b) The input of target qubit is V-polarized state.

state is transformed to be state $(H + V)/\sqrt{2}$ after HWP(22.5°). Thus $(\alpha HH + \beta VH + \alpha HV + \beta VV)/\sqrt{2}$ is the state of whole system. When passing through the PBS-HV, state $(\alpha HH + \beta VV)/\sqrt{2}$ is obtained under the condition of a coincidence of the two outputs, with success probability $1/2$.

We can also realize the special CNOT gate that the target qubit is V-polarized state in the similar way, as Fig. 8(b) shown.

3.5   Comparison and Analysis

In this subsection, we compare and analyze the difficulty of interferences, resources consuming and success terms of the six different implements of CNOT gates above.

Interferences. Subwavelength path interferences occur only when the path lengths maintain stable in subwavelength, about the order of $1\,\mu m$. It is a harsh term in lab, so it requires additional stabilization technology and equipment. However, the stability requirements of second order interference are relaxed to the coherence length of the qubit photons, about $150\,\mu m$, and can be fulfilled easily without any stability methods. Thus the realization of subwavelength path interference is much more difficult than that of second order interference.

Table 1 shows the comparison of the interference in CNOT gates demonstrated. Only the 4th scheme is spatial encoded, and only it contains subwavelength path interferences. We have discussed that the realization of this gate is very difficult, and such difficulty will restrict its application for scalable LOQC. Compared with the 4th CNOT gate, the other CNOT gates just require at most two second order interferences, thus they all can be implemented more easily.

Resources Consuming. We roughly divide resources required into three parts, the number of required qubits, components and detectors. From the Table 2 we can see that, the 3rd and the 2nd CNOT gates need 4 and 3 single photons and the others are all require 2 photons. For required components and detectors, the first and last one require less and the others are almost similar. The terms in

Table 1. Comparison of the interferences in CNOT gates demonstrated

Scheme number	Encoded mode	Subwavelength	Second order
1st	polarization	0	1
2nd	polarization	0	2
3rd	polarization	0	2
4th	path	2	1
5th	polarization	0	1
6th	polarization	0	1

Table 2. Resources requirement of the demonstrated CNOT gates

Scheme number	Qubits number	Component	Detector number
1st	2	PBS*1+polarizer*1(PBS*2)	2(3)
2nd	3	PBS*2+polarizer*1(PBS*3)	2(4)
3rd	4	PBS*2+polarizer*2(PBS*4)	2(4)
4th	2	PBS*2+HWP*4	2
5th	2	PDBS*3+HWP*2	2
6th	2	PBS*1+HWP*1	2

Table 3. Success terms of the CNOT gates

Scheme number	Indication	Probability	Function
1st	state	1/4(1/2)	loss
2nd	state	1/8(1/4)	destructive
3rd	state	1/16(1/4)	non-destructive
4th	coincidence	1/9	destructive
5th	coincidence	1/9	destructive
6th	coincidence	1/2	limited

brackets are all response to the case using feed-forward control techniques to increase success probability in Table 3, which requires more resources and are more complex.

Success Terms. In Table 3, the success indications of the first three CNOT gates are all states. It means that the CNOT gates succeed when detectors receive particular states, which needs one more polarizer or PBS (with one additional detector). While the success indication of the last three is a coincidence detection of two output photons. The success probability indicates that the last scheme provides the highest probability. The 1st one can also reach highest using feed-forward control techniques, while requires more resources and are more complex.

The first scheme realizes a CNOT gate that losses the information of the control qubit, and the last one is limited to the cases that target qubit is logical 0 or 1. The destructive CNOT gates work only when all output ports each detect one photon simultaneously. Without reliable quantum nondestructive measurement (QNM) [9], the detection of the post-selection will destruct the output photons of control and target, so the gates are called destructive gates. Although those CNOT gates preserve the information of control qubit, its destructive property make it difficult to apply to scalable quantum computing. The only one nondestructive CNOT gate is the 3rd one, since its two outputs are not needed to detect by post-selection operation. As Fig. 5 shown, if D3 and D4 detect one particular photon simultaneously, the CNOT gate is successful.

Summary. Generally, the more powerful the CNOT gate is, the more resources it requires. The nondestructive gate is very useful in scalable quantum computing that contains multiple CNOT gates, but it costs more resources than the others. The fifth CNOT gate maybe a promising candidate to implement the scalable quantum computing together with QNM, since it is not resource-consuming and easier to be realized than the others that implement the same function. And from the view of the optical experimental setups, the 5th are simpler.

It may be more efficient to adopt different scheme of CNOT gate according to practical requirements. For example, if the target qubit state is logical 0 or 1, we use the sixth CNOT gate. For the CNOT gate in the middle of circuits, we could adopt the third scheme. Therefore, we combine several schemes to realize a quantum circuit in order to maximize resource efficiency. Until now, the scale of quantum circuits is so small that the scheme of quantum gate is chosen manually. However, in the future, when the scale of quantum circuits grows larger and larger, the choice would have to be made automatically which is similar to the function of compilers in classical computer.

4   Implementation of Quantum Algorithms in the Quantum Circuit Model

The above sections introduce the all-optical quantum CNOT gates, and analyze their properties. This section introduces the application of the CNOT schemes to several important quantum algorithms.

Before describing details, we give an overview of the development of linear optical quantum computer, compared with the classical computers [29,30]. As shown in Fig. 9, the hierarchical structure of classical computer is mainly divided into three levels, software, architecture and hardware. Those three phases would be passed through to implement an algorithm on classical computer. While for quantum computers, there are no software and architecture till now. Thus, a quantum algorithm is directly implemented by the quantum circuits and optical components, just like achieving an algorithm on FPGA.

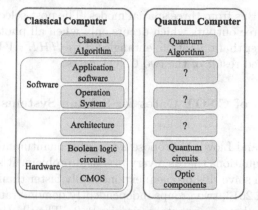

Fig. 9. Hierarchical structure of quantum computer and classical computer.

4.1 Application of CNOT Gates for Shors Quantum Factoring Algorithm

Shors algorithm [26] is the most famous and prominent quantum algorithm. It can factor large numbers in polynomial time on a quantum computer, while the best classical method need exponential time. ChaoYang Lu et al. report an all-optical demonstration of a compiled version of the algorithm [15]. They choose to factorize 15, the simplest instance. This experiment proof-of-principle proves that Shors algorithm can be realized by using photonic qubits.

The simplified quantum circuit of Shors algorithm and experimental setup are shown in Fig. 10(a) and (b). Two consecutive CNOT gates are the kernel of the circuit. Considering the target qubits of both CNOTs are logical 0, the 6th CNOT scheme is adopted. Two target qubits are both transformed from H to $(H \pm V)/\sqrt{2}$ by HWPs(22.5°). In Fig. 10(c), three $H \pm V$ polarized photons are

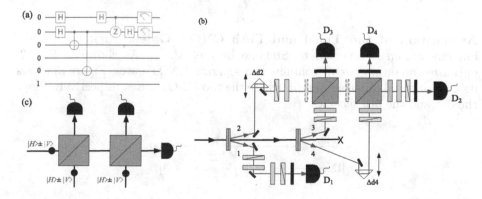

Fig. 10. Shors algorithm [15]. (a) The quantum circuit for $N = 15$. (b) Experimental setup. (c) Two consecutive 6th CNOT gate.

incident into two PBSs from three spatial modes. The post-selection operation is a coincidence of three outputs which occurs only when all photons are reflected or transmitted. After that operation, entangled state $HHH \pm VVV$ is outputted, which is the required result of the two CNOT gates.

4.2   Application of CNOT Gates for Solving Systems of Linear Equations

Harrow, Hassidim and Lloyd [5] propose a powerful quantum algorithm to solve systems of linear equations that is a very practical problem. It shows that quantum computers can solve this problem exponentially faster than classical ones in some situations. In 2013, two groups independently demonstrated the algorithm based on different photonic quantum circuits [1,2]. They both realize the simplest instance of the algorithm for solving 2×2 linear equations on a quantum computer for various input vectors, demonstrating the working principle of the quantum algorithm.

Application of the Simplified CNOT Gate. The simplified quantum circuit designed by X.-D. Cai et al. is shown in Fig. 11 [2]. It uses four qubits. Two CNOTs are contained in the circuit. Because the target qubits of both CNOTs are H-polarized, the 6th scheme is adopted to implement the two consecutive CNOT as 4.1 does.

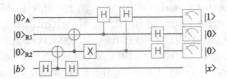

Fig. 11. The 1st optimized quantum circuit for solving systems of linear equations.

Application of the Third and Fifth CNOT Gates. Another different implementation is reported by Stefanie Barz et al. [1]. As shown in Fig. 12, optimized quantum circuit contains two separate CNOT gates. Figure 13 shows its experimental implementation, where the two CNOT gates respectively adopt the 3rd and the 5th schemes.

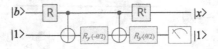

Fig. 12. The 2nd optimized quantum circuit for solving system of linear equations.

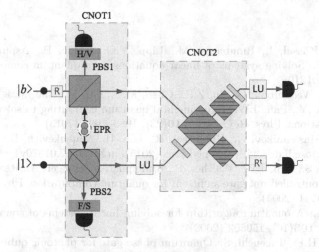

Fig. 13. Experimental implementation of the optimized circuit.

As previous discussion of the 3rd scheme, the valid outputs of CNOT1 are passed to CNOT2 without measurement. This non-destructive CNOT gate cannot be replaced by destructive one, except that the destructive CNOT gates are combined with QNM. CNOT2 is realized by the 5th scheme and succeeds when the coincidence of two final detectors occurs. They choose this scheme because it is more stable and efficient.

In the scalable quantum computing, the output of the former gate usually pass to the next one. Destructive CNOT gates without QNM are less useful, since they have to measure outputs to judge if it succeeds, leading to destruction. In fact, we have to measure the output of each destructive CNOT gates one by one.

Summary. Comparing the two demonstrations, we observe that the same quantum algorithm can be compiled into different circuits, leading to different realization and resources consuming. The simpler quantum circuits optimize to be, the less resources will consume to implement them. Therefore, optimizing circuits is very important and necessary.

5   Discussion

Despite of great progress made in all-optical CNOT gates, there are still some problems to be solved, such as low success probability and low efficiency [19]. In addition to the technology of controlling photons, the technologies of generating and detecting photons in lab are also significant to optical quantum computing. LOQC based on photonic qubits requires large number of indistinguishable single photons that depend on the generation technology of photon sources. Post-selection is to realize two-qubit quantum gates, therefore, the efficiency and accuracy of single photon detectors is crucial for LOQC.

References

1. Barz, S., Kassal, I., Ringbauer, M., Lipp, Y.O., Dakic, B., Aspuruguzik, A., Walther, P.: Solving systems of linear equations on a quantum computer (2013). arXiv:1302.1210v1
2. Cai, X.D., Weedbrook, C., Su, Z.E., Chen, M.C., Gu, M., Zhu, M.J., Li, L., Liu, N.L., Lu, C.Y., Pan, J.W.: Experimental quantum computing to solve systems of linear equations. Phys. Rev. Lett. **110**(23), 1983–1988 (2013)
3. Ding, S., Maslennikov, G., Hablutzel, R., Loh, H., Matsukevich, D.: A quantum parametric oscillator with trapped ions (2015). arXiv:1512.01670v1
4. Gasparoni, S., Pan, J.W., Walther, P., Rudolph, T., Zeilinger, A.: Realization of a photonic controlled-not gate sufficient for quantum computation. Phys. Rev. Lett. **93**(2), 020504 (2004)
5. Harrow, A.: A quantum algorithm for solving linear systems of equations. Phys. Rev. Lett. **103**(10), 150502 (2008)
6. Hofmann, H.F., Takeuchi, S.: Quantum phase gate for photonic qubits using only beam splitters and postselection. Phys. Rev. A **66**(2), 207–212 (2001)
7. Kiesel, N., Schmid, C., Weber, U., Ursin, R., Weinfurter, H.: Linear optics controlled-phase gate made simple. Phys. Rev. Lett. **95**(21), 210505 (2005)
8. Knill, E., Laflamme, R., Milburn, G.J.: A scheme for efficient quantum computation with linear optics. Nature **409**(6816), 46–52 (2001)
9. Kok, P., Lee, H., Dowling, J.P.: Single-photon quantum nondemolition detectors constructed with linear optics and projective measurements. Phys. Rev. A **66**(6), 317–322 (2002)
10. Kok, P., Munro, W.J., Nemoto, K., Ralph, T.C., Dowling, J.P., Milburn, G.J.: Linear optical quantum computing with photonic qubits. Rev. Mod. Phys. **79**(1), 135–174 (2007)
11. Ladd, T.D., Jelezko, F., Laflamme, R., Nakamura, Y., Monroe, C., O'Brien, J.L.: Quantum computers. Nature **464**(7285), 45–53 (2010)
12. Lahaye, M.D., Rouxinol, F., Hao, Y., Shim, S.B., Irish, E.K.: Superconducting circuitry for quantum electromechanical systems. In: Proceedings of SPIE - The International Society for Optical Engineering, vol. 9500 (2015)
13. Langford, N.K., Weinhold, T.J., Prevedel, R., Resch, K.J., Gilchrist, A., O'Brien, J.L., Pryde, G.J., White, A.G.: Demonstration of a simple entangling optical gate and its use in bell-state analysis. Phys. Rev. Lett. **95**(21), 210504 (2005)
14. Lipp, Y.O.: Experimental realization of an interferometric quantum circuit to increase the computational depth. Ph.D. thesis, University of Vienna, Vienna (2011)
15. Lu, C.Y., Browne, D.E., Yang, T., Pan, J.W.: Demonstration of a compiled version of shor's quantum factoring algorithm using photonic qubits. Phys. Rev. Lett. **99**(25), 250504 (2007)
16. Murray, E., Ellis, D.P., Meany, T., Floether, F.F., Lee, J.P., Griffiths, J., Jones, G.A.C., Farrer, I., Ritchie, D.A., Bennett, A.J., et al.: Quantum photonics hybrid integration platform. Appl. Phys. Lett. **107**(17), 171108 (2015)
17. Nielsen, M.A., Chuang, I.L., Grover, L.K.: Quantum computation and quantum information. Am. J. Phys. **70**(5), 558–559 (2012)
18. O'Brien, J.L., Pryde, G.J., White, A.G., Ralph, T.C., Branning, D.: Demonstration of an all-optical quantum controlled-NOT gate. Nature **426**(6964), 26–47 (2003)
19. O'Brien, J.L.: Optical quantum computing. Science **318**(5856), 67–70 (2008)

20. Okamoto, R., Hofmann, H.F., Takeuchi, S., Sasaki, K.: Demonstration of an optical quantum controlled-NOT gate without path interference. Phys. Rev. Lett. **95**(21), 210506 (2005)
21. Pittman, T.B., Fitch, M.J., Jacobs, B.C., Franson, J.D.: Experimental controlled-NOT logic gate for single photons in the coincidence basis. Phys. Rev. A **68**(3), 032316 (2003)
22. Pittman, T.B., Jacobs, B.C., Franson, J.D.: Demonstration of non-deterministic quantum logic operations using linear optical elements. Physics **88**(25 Pt. 1), 222–223 (2001)
23. Pittman, T.B., Jacobs, B.C., Franson, J.D.: Probabilistic quantum logic operations using polarizing beam splitters. Phys. Rev. A **64**(6), 656–656 (2001)
24. Pittman, T.B., Jacobs, B.C., Franson, J.D.: Demonstration of feed-forward control for linear optics quantum computation. Phys. Rev. A **66**(5), 357–364 (2002)
25. Ralph, T.C., Langford, N.K., Bell, T.B., White, A.G.: Linear optical controlled-NOT gate in the coincidence basis. Phys. Rev. A **65**(6), 440–444 (2002)
26. Shor, P.W.: Polynomial-time algorithms for prime factorization and discrete logarithms on a quantum computer. SIAM J. Comput. **26**(5), 1484–1509 (1997)
27. Singh, M., Pacheco, J.L., Perry, D., Garratt, E., Eyck, G.T., Bishop, N.C., Wendt, J.R., Manginell, R.P., Dominguez, J., Pluym, T.: Electrostatically defined silicon quantum dots with counted antimony donor implants. Appl. Phys. Lett. **108**(6), 133–137 (2016)
28. Taylor, R.L., Bentley, C.D.B., Pedernales, J.S., Lamata, L., Solano, E., Carvalho, A.R.R., Hope, J.J.: Fast gates allow large-scale quantum simulation with trapped ions (2016). arXiv:1601.00359v1
29. Yang, X.J., Dou, Y., Hu, Q.F.: Progress and challenges in high performance computer technology. J. Comput. Sci. Technol. **21**(5), 674–681 (2006)
30. Yang, X., Liao, X., Xu, W., Song, J., Hu, Q., Su, J., Xiao, L., Lu, K., Dou, Q., Jiang, J.: Th-1: Chinas first petaflop supercomputer. Front. Comput. Sci. China **4**(4), 445–455 (2010)

Performance Analysis of Sliding Window Network Coding in MANET

Baolin Sun[1(✉)], Chao Gui[1], Ying Song[1], Hua Chen[2(✉)], and Xiaoyan Zhu[3]

[1] School of Information and Engineering, Hubei University of Economics, Wuhan 430205, China
{blsun,prisong}@163.com, gui_chao@126.com
[2] Department of Public Basic Course, Wuhan Technology and Business University,
Wuhan 430065, China
qiuchen_1022@163.com
[3] School of Mathematics and Computer Science, Jianghan University, Wuhan 430056, China
zhuxy@jhun.edu.cn

Abstract. Network coding (NC) enables us to mix two or more packets into a single coded packet at relay nodes and improve performances in mobile ad hoc networks (MANETs). Sliding window network coding is a variation of NC that is an addition to data packet streaming and improves the data delay on MANETs. In this paper, we propose a Sliding Window Network Coding in MANETs (SWNCM). SWNCM preserves the degree distribution of the encoded data packets through the recombination at the nodes. SWNCM enables to control the decoding complexity of each sliding window independently from the data packets received and recover the original data. The performance of the SWNCM is studied using NS2 and evaluated in terms of the network throughput, encoding overhead, decoding delay, packet transmission rate when data packet is transmitted. The simulations result shows that the SWNCM with our proposition can significantly improve the network throughput and achieves higher diversity order.

Keywords: MANET · Sliding window · Network coding · Performance analysis

1 Introduction

With the wide application of wireless communication technology, the traditional local area network couldn't satisfy people's needs, so the Mobile Ad Hoc Networks (MANET) appeared and developed rapidly [1–5]. Recently, wide attention has focused on a transmission mode called data packet transmission to maximize the link utilization of a given wireless channel.

The advantages of network coding (NC) come however at the price of additional computational complexity, mainly due to the packet encoding and decoding process. Random linear network coding is a feasible encoding tool for network coding, especially for the non-coherent network, and its performance is important in theory and application. In [3], Guang *et al.* study the performance of random linear network coding for the well-known butterfly network by analyzing some failure probabilities. In multi-user cooperative networks, network coding in higher Galois Field has been proved with solid

J. Wu and L. Li (Eds.): ACA 2016, CCIS 626, pp. 174–183, 2016.
DOI: 10.1007/978-981-10-2209-8_15

performance improvement over binary codes. Xiao et al. [4] proposed the use of diversity network codes (DNCs) over finite fields so as that the destination is able to rebuild the user information from a minimum possible set of the coded packets. The network encoder is on the top of channel encoder, and the network decoder is combined with channel decoder leveraging the tentative decisions from channel decoder.

This paper proposes a Sliding Window Network Coding in MANETs (SWNCM). We apply network coding over $GF(2^q)$ on symbols rather than on packets to fully exploit the advantages of network coding including sliding window, increase traffic and robustness. The performance of the SWNCM is studied using NS2 and experimentation to assess the encoding efficiency, the decoding complexity of SWNCM enabled mobile node. The SWNCM is shown to achieve significant performance gain.

The rest of the paper is organized as follows. Section 2 discusses the some related work. Section 3 describes models of sliding encoding window model in MANETs. Some simulating results are provided in Sect. 4. Finally, the paper concludes in Sect. 5.

2 Related Works

In [5], Chen et al. considered the transmission scenario of network coding in which the cluster head node sends encoded signals to sink node over a lossy and noisy wireless channels. The application of compressed sensing conception was explored to break the limitations and improve the performance of network coding when the mutual correlations of information are existent. Qin et al. [6] proposed an energy-saving scheme for wireless sensor networks based on network coding and duty-cycle (NCDES). The scheme determines the node's status based on the ID information which embedded in data information. When combining network coding and duty-cycle in wireless sensor networks, it will reduce transmission coding coefficients and retransmissions. Jiang et al. [7] proposes an energy-efficient multicast routing approach to achieve the data forwarding in the multi-hop wireless network. Analysis of the multi-hop networks energy metric and energy efficiency metric. Then the corresponding models are given network coding is used to improve network throughput. Antonopoulos et al. [8] proposed a network coding-based cooperative ARQ (NCCARQ) scheme for wireless networks. Compared to simple cooperative ARQ protocols, the proposed solution improves up to 80 % the energy efficiency of the system without compromising the offered QoS in terms of throughput and delay.

Considering the feature of strong node mobility in mobile ad hoc networks, Wang et al. [9] proposed a hop-by-hop network coding algorithm based on ad hoc networks. In [10], Halloush et al. develop Multi-Generation Mixing (MGM), which is a generalized approach for generation based network coding. The proposed MGM framework allows the encoding among generations for the purpose of enhancing NC decodability. Guo et al. [11] questioned whether these requirements are enough when there are various intersecting nodes along a path, and they proposed a new coding-aware routing metric, Free-Ride-Oriented Routing Metric (FORM), able to exploit a larger number of coding opportunities, regardless of the number of flows and intersecting nodes. Kiss et al. [12] proposes a scalable approach for increasing transmission reliability in wireless sensor networks, based on a cooperative scheme that uses Reed–Solomon codes as network code.

Vazintari *et al.* [13] proposes an effective NC scheme intended for sparse DTNs comprising nodes of limited storage capacity. They aim at demonstrating the drastic overhead reduction accomplished when the application of NC reinforced by the optimal MMA proposed is combined with either the Epidemic or the PRoPHET protocol. In [14], Ploumidisa *et al.* explores the throughput and delay that can be achieved by various forwarding schemes, employing multiple paths and different degrees of redundancy, focusing on linear network coding. The analytical framework is generalized for an arbitrary number of paths and hops per path. In [15], Chen *et al.* explores a multipath transmission scheme employing network coding for providing better rate-delay trade-offs, being also adjustable according to QoS constraints. In [16], Zhang *et al.* investigate the impact of imperfect CSI on the performance of analog network coding (ANC) for a two-way relaying system based on opportunistic relay selection (ORS). An exact and generalized closed-form expression for system outage probability is presented in a Rayleigh flat-fading environment. Liu *et al.* [17] describes the model for the dynamic decode-and-forward (DDF) protocol and network coding (NC) (DDF-NC) cooperative communications system. Shen *et al.* [18] propose a novel routing protocol named Location-Aware Routing Protocol (LARP) for UWSNs, where the location information of nodes is used to help the transmission of the message.

Although some network coding algorithms are proposed to improve network performance, most of these approaches do not consider mobile data packet streaming scenario. In our work, we target mobile multimedia streaming networking problem in wireless networks. By constructing the appropriate network coding structure, we can achieve the higher free viewpoint multimedia streaming.

3 Sliding Encoding Window Model

We now focus to the sliding window and the random network coding approaches. When using this approach, not all data packets need to be coded together in a generation, just the ones in the same window. This simplifies the solving of the Gaussian-elimination on the receiver side, but requires constant feedback between the nodes to determine which packets have been seen at the receiver and thus remove them from the sender's linear combinations.

3.1 Network Model

The network model is a generalization of the insertion-only data packet model in which we seek to compute function f over only the most recent elements of the data packet.

The network model is represented as $G = (V, E)$ where V represents the set of nodes in the network and E denotes the set of directed edges. Each link $(i, j) \in E$ means that node i can transmit to node j. We assume links are symmetric that if $(i, j) \in E$; $(j, i) \in E$ as well. Whether two links interfere with each other depends on the interference model adopted.

In the present paper, as both the probabilistic selection of the coding coefficients and the number of packets to be stored are independently decided at each MANET node, the proposed scheme, data packet flows from a single source node to a single destination node. This scheme, when data packet is need to transfer, the source node to encode data packet operation, the destination nodes are allowed to decode the received coded packets whereas intermediate nodes can only forward randomly created linear combinations of incoming packets. The destination nodes would have to wait until reception of all the packets of a generation. Figure 1 visualizes the network model in MANETs.

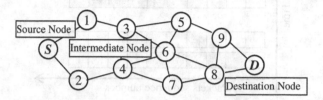

Fig. 1. Network Network model in MANETs.

The random linear network coding (RLNC) scheme [17] adopts a block transmission strategy which can approach the capacity with less feedback overhead. Because this RLNC scheme can provide near-capacity performance and it becomes more attractive in several industrial standards recently. In addition, it works over non-binary Galois Field and can seamlessly combine with network coding. The proposed scheme is illustrated in Fig. 2, in which we use network codes over finite fields, on top of channel coding, to encode relayed and local messages. The network coding scheme is time-invariant in each relay node. The information messages D_1 and D_2 of node 1 and node 2, respectively, are realized over GF(2^q). Network coding is also in GF(2^q). All transmission blocks are subject to independent fading.

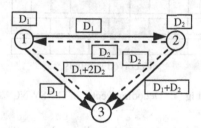

Fig. 2. Two-node cooperative networks with proposed designed network codes over finite fields.

3.2 Sliding Encoding Window Construction

SWNCM adopts the encoding strategy similar to RLNC [3], but the block of packets to be encoded in each slot is sliding forward at a constant speed V. For each packet P to transmit, the source selects the blocks $(x_0, x_1, \ldots, x_{N-1})$ and coding coefficients $(c_0, c_1, \ldots, c_{N-1})$ to combine with in a sliding encoding window of size $1 \leq W \leq N$, If the coefficient is chosen from $F(2^q)$, number of choices of coding vectors would be (2^q-1). Obviously, the all zero vector has to be avoided. The size of the sliding window $W = e - f + 1$, for N elements, there are $N - W + 1$ possible sliding windows of size W. A sliding encoding window of size W is a sequence of blocks $(x_f, ..., x_e)$ where $0 \leq f, e \leq N - 1$ and $f \leq 1$ and $e - f + 1 = W$. We define f_i and e_i the leading edge and the trailing edge of the i-th sliding encoding window. Figure 3 shows the encoding vector for sliding encoding windows.

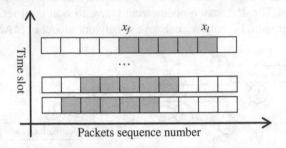

Fig. 3. Encoding vector of CC-SWNC.

After overhearing the coded symbols from the source, the destination node attempts to decode the original packets through Gauss elimination approach. A typical example of the decoding process is shown in Fig. 4, in which the Gauss-Jordan Elimination can be performed progressively as the coded packet arrives and finally the original packets can be retrieved when the reduced matrix has full rank.

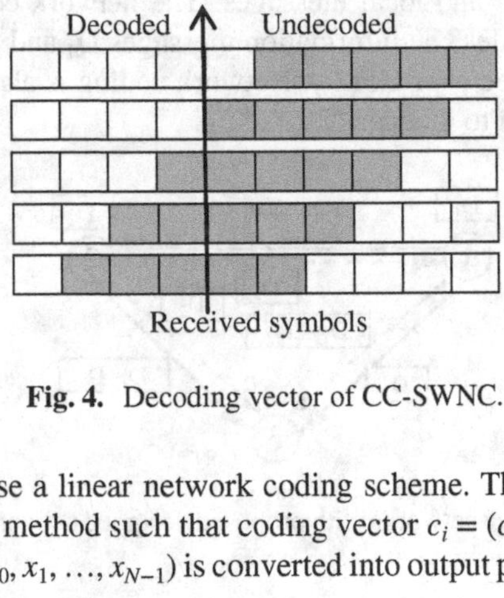

Fig. 4. Decoding vector of CC-SWNC.

In this paper, we use a linear network coding scheme. The linear network coding scheme is an encoding method such that coding vector $c_i = (c_{i0}, c_{i1}, ..., c_{iN-1})$ is given, and input packet $X = (x_0, x_1, ..., x_{N-1})$ is converted into output packet P_i by the following expression.

$$P_i = \sum_{j=0}^{N-1} c_{ij} x_j \tag{1}$$

Then, the elements c_i of the encoding vector g are set to one with probability $p = 0.5$ for $i \in [f, e]$, with probability $p = 0$ otherwise. The destination node can decode input packets because the coding vector $c_i = (c_{i0}, c_{i1}, \ldots, c_{iN-1})$ and output packet data $P = (P_0, P_1, \ldots, P_{N-1})$ are obtained from the received packets, and an inverse matrix exists in G.

3.3 Network Coding Over Data Packet Streams

Network coding has been shown to dramatically improve network performance; however, implementing it can be a challenge. In order to develop practical coding techniques, random linear network coding (RLNC) [3] has been used by a large number of coding schemes because of its simplicity and effectiveness in most network scenarios. Each node selects coefficients over the Galois field randomly and independently. Therefore computational complexity of this scheme is significantly lower than its centralized counterpart. The coefficients are uniformly distributed, the probability of being able to randomly find an admissible network code is a function of the field size, the number of receivers, and also of the number of links involved in the graph G. Assume that we want to send a file consisting of data packets p_i, $i \in P$, where P is the set of data packet indexes. Within these data packet streams, RLNC can be used to add redundancy by treating each p_i as a vector in some finite field $F(2^q)$. Random coefficients $\alpha_{ij} \in F(2^q)$ are chosen, and linear combinations of the form $c_i = \sum_{j \in P} \alpha_{ij} p_j$ are generated. These coded packets are then inserted at strategic locations to help overcome packet losses in loss networks.

Management of the coding windows for these data packets network coding schemes generally fall within the following sliding window based scheme. In sliding window scheme, data packets are dynamically included or excluded from linear combinations based on various performance requirements.

In addition, the code window is greater, its decoding complexity and communication overhead is greater, also. Algorithm describes the policy for the sliding-window coding scheme shown in Fig. 3.

4 Simulation Experiments

In this section, simulation results are presented and discussed concerning the performance of the enhanced by the innovative SWNCM scheme proposed. We use the NS-2 simulator [19] to evaluate the Cooperative Communication with Sliding Window Network Coding in wireless networks (SWNCM).

4.1 Simulation Scenario

We evaluate SWNCM in a data packet streaming scenario where one source distributes a data packet sequence to multiple cooperating receiver nodes.

MANET nodes follow the Random Waypoint (RWP) Mobility Model. To study how the proposed scheme is affected by the nodes mobility, the node speed ranges have been in [0, 20] m/s speed. Nodes are randomly and uniformly located over a 1000 m × 1000 m area, with a node transmission range of 250 m [20]. The network sparseness may be quantified by the mean node degree, i.e. the average number of neighbors in the network,

$\rho = \pi \cdot d \cdot r^2$, where d and r are the node density and the transmission range, respectively. The results of the simulation are positive with respect to performance.

We analyze the performance of SWNCM from the point of view of the encoding efficiency. The encoding efficiency of SWNCM depends on the generation size N and on the sliding encoding window size W (W = 100). The SWNCM algorithm was compared with NCCARQ algorithm [8] and PRoPHET [13] in MANETs environment. The corresponding simulation parameters are summarized in Table 1.

Table 1. Simulation parameters

Number of nodes	100
Network area	1000 m × 1000 m
Transmission range	250 m
Simulation time	600 s
Transmission range	250 m
Node density (d)	4
Sliding encoding window size	$W = 100$
Communication model	Constant Bit Rate (CBR)
Message size (b_{msg})	512 bytes/packet
Examined algorithm	NCCARQ [8], PRoPHET [13]

4.2 Simulation Results

The results shown in Fig. 5, the packet throughput of SWNCM is always higher than that of NCCARQ and PRoPHET that with the network size increasing. Therefore we can conclude that, with sliding window network coding in wireless links, SWNCM can complete data packet transmission faster and perform better than NCCARQ and PRoPHET in MANETs. SWNCM is effective in improving the network throughput.

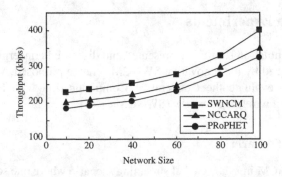

Fig. 5. Network throughput vs. Network size.

Figure 6 show that, the encoding overhead of SWNCM is smaller than that of NCCARQ and PRoPHET, which means that SWNCM can transmit data packet faster than NCCARQ and PRoPHET. SWNCM reduces the encoding overhead the better.

Figure 5 shows the encoding overhead of SWNCM, NCCARQ and PRoPHET, which use the sliding window network coding that minimize the encoding overhead.

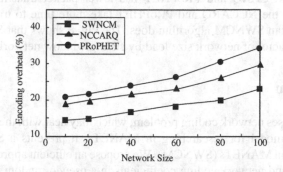

Fig. 6. Network throughput vs. Network size.

In Fig. 7, we test the SWNCM performance in decoding delay. It can be seen from Fig. 7 that, using sliding window network coding, decoding delay is reduced. We can also observe that the sliding window network coding more gracefully than other algorithm when network size increases. It demonstrates that SWNCM scheme is more suitable as the variation of the network size increases.

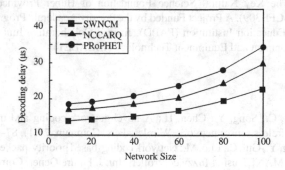

Fig. 7. Decoding delay with different network size.

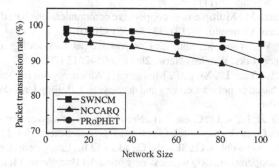

Fig. 8. Packet transmission rate with different network size.

The results shown in Fig. 8 reveal that, the packet transmission rate of SWNCM is always higher than that of NCCARQ and PRoPHET. The main reason is that the data packets by the NCCARQ and PRoPHET has lower packet transmission rate than SWNCM has, so the NCCARQ and PRoPHET take more time to transmit the same amount of data than SWNCM algorithm does. The Fig. 8 shows that SWNCM enable to increase by a factor of network size load by sliding window network coding.

5   Conclusion

This paper discusses network coding problem, which may deal with the sliding window network coding model for researching in MANETs. It presents a Sliding Window Network Coding in MANETs (SWNCM). We propose an efficient approach to construct sliding window and network coding coefficients in a pseudo-random manner on each node. We provide a thorough description of sliding window and network coding in MANETs (SWNCM), a novel class of network codes. The performance of the SWNCM is studied using NS2 and experimentation to assess the network throughput, encoding overhead, decoding delay, packet transmission rate of SWNCM enabled mobile node. The SWNCM is shown to achieve significant performance gain.

Acknowledgment. This work is supported by The National Natural Science Foundation of China (No. 61572012), The Key Natural Science Foundation of Hubei Province of China (No. 2014CFA055, 2013CFB309). A Project Funded by the Priority Academic Program Development of Jiangsu Higher Education Institution (PAPD). Jiangsu Collaborative Innovation Center on Atmospheric Environment and Equipment Technology (CICAEET).

References

1. Sun, B.L., Gui, C., Song, Y., Chen, H.: A novel network coding and multi-path routing approach for wireless sensor network. Wireless Pers. Commun. **77**(1), 87–99 (2014)
2. Sun, B.L., Song, Y., Gui, C., Luo, M.: Network coding-based priority-packet scheduler multi-path routing in MANET using fuzzy controllers. Int. J. Future Gener. Commun. Netw. **7**(2), 137–147 (2014)
3. Guang, X., Fu, F.W.: On random linear network coding for butterfly network. Chin. J. Electron. **20**(2), 283–286 (2011)
4. Xiao, M., Skoglund, M.: Multiple-user cooperative communications based on linear network coding. IEEE Trans. Commun. **58**(12), 3345–3351 (2010)
5. Chen, S., Meng, W., Wang, K., Sun, Z.: Compressive network coding for error control in wireless sensor networks. Wireless Netw. **20**(8), 2605–2615 (2014)
6. Qin, T.F., Li, L.L., Yan, L., Xing, J., Meng, Y.F.: An energy-saving scheme for wireless sensor networks based on network coding and duty-cycle. J. Beijing Univ. Posts Telecommun. **37**(4), 83–87 (2014)
7. Jiang, D.D., Xu, Z.Z., Li, W.O., Chen, Z.H.: Network coding-based energy-efficient multicast routing algorithm for multi-hop wireless networks. J. Syst. Softw. **104**, 152–165 (2015)
8. Antonopoulos, A., Verikoukis, C., Skianis, C., Akan, O.B.: Energy efficient network coding-based MAC for cooperative ARQ wireless networks. Ad Hoc Netw. **11**(1), 190–200 (2013)

9. Wang, Y., Xu, H., Jia, P.F.: Design and analysis of a network coding algorithm for ad hoc networks. J. Central South Univ. **22**(4), 1358–1365 (2015)
10. Halloush, M., Radha, H.: Network coding with multi-generation mixing: a generation framework for practical network coding. IEEE Trans. Wireless Commun. **10**(2), 466–473 (2011)
11. Guo, B., Li, H., Zhou, C., Cheng, Y.: Analysis of general network coding conditions and design of a free-ride-oriented routing metric. IEEE Trans. Veh. Technol. **60**(4), 1714–1727 (2011)
12. Kiss, Z.I., Polgar, Z.A., Stef, M.P., Bota, V.: Improving transmission reliability in wireless sensor networks using network coding. Telecommun. Syst. **59**(4), 509–521 (2015)
13. Vazintari, A., Vlachou, C., Cottis, P.G.: Network coding for overhead reduction in delay tolerant networks. Wireless Pers. Commun. **72**(4), 2653–2671 (2013)
14. Ploumidisa, M., Pappasb, N., Sirisc, V.A., Traganitis, A.: On the performance of network coding and forwarding schemes with different degrees of redundancy for wireless mesh networks. Comput. Commun. **72**, 49–62 (2015). doi:10.1016/j.comcom.2015.05.001
15. Chen, P.-Y., Ao, W.-C., Chen, K.-C.: Rate-delay enhanced multipath transmission scheme via network coding in multihop networks. IEEE Commun. Lett. **16**(3), 281–283 (2012)
16. Zhang, C.S., Ge, J.H., Li, J.: Performance analysis and enhancement for opportunistic analog network coding with imperfect CSI. Wireless Pers. Commun. **72**(4), 2945–2956 (2013)
17. Liu, W.-C., Shih, C.-H.: The Performance of systems featuring dynamic decode-and-forward and network coding. Wireless Pers. Commun. **80**(2), 521–541 (2014)
18. Shen, J., Tan, H.W., Wang, J., Wang, J.W., Lee, S.Y.: A novel routing protocol providing good transmission reliability in underwater sensor networks. J. Internet Technol. **16**(1), 171–178 (2015)
19. The Network Simulator - NS-2. http://www.isi.edu/nsnam/ns/
20. Waxman, B.: Routing of multipoint connections. IEEE J. Sel. Areas Commun. **6**(9), 1617–1622 (1988)

A Model for Evaluating and Comparing Moving Target Defense Techniques Based on Generalized Stochastic Petri Net

Guilin Cai[✉], Baosheng Wang, Yuebin Luo, and Wei Hu

College of Computer, National University of Defense Technology, Changsha, China
cc_cai@163.com, wangbaosheng@126.com, luoyuebin@nudt.edu.cn,
huwei@nscc-tj.gov.cn

Abstract. Moving Target Defense has been proposed as a way to alter the asymmetric situation of attacks and defenses, and there has been given a great number of related works. Currently, the performance evaluation of these works has largely been empirical, but lacks the application of theoretical models. Further, the evaluation is usually for a specific approach or a category of MTD approaches, and few work has been taken to compare different MTD techniques. In this paper, we consider a Web server as a deployment scenario for the three typical kinds of MTD techniques, and develop a generalized abstract performance evaluation and comparison model for existing MTDs through using generalized stochastic Petri Net (GSPN). We also take a case study to describe the usage of the model. The model enables us to analyze and understand the benefits and costs of an MTD approach, and can be viewed as an attempt to fill the gap of MTD comparison.

Keywords: Moving target defense · Generalized stochastic petri net · Evaluation model

1 Introduction

With the rapid growth of information technologies, Internet has become a national key infrastructure. However, cyber-attacks (such as IP prefix hijacking [1], botnet [2], DDoS attack [3]) can still be found everywhere, and major security incidents have been frequently reported in recent years (such as the PRISM [4], the Heartbleed Bug [5], eBay data leakage). Such security disasters are repeatedly showing that, the security of the Internet is always facing severe challenges. One of the major reasons of the severe Internet security situation is that the network configurations nowadays are typically deterministic, static, and homogeneous [6,7]. These features reduce the difficulties for cyber attackers scanning the network to identify specific targets and gather essential information, which gives the attackers the advantages of building up, launching and spreading attacks. Therefore, in the struggle between cyber network attack and defense, the attackers typically have asymmetric advantages and the defenders are always disadvantaged by being passive.

© Springer Science+Business Media Singapore 2016
J. Wu and L. Li (Eds.): ACA 2016, CCIS 626, pp. 184–197, 2016.
DOI: 10.1007/978-981-10-2209-8_16

To alter the asymmetric situation between attacks and defenses, Moving Target Defense (MTD) is proposed as one of the "game-changing" themes in cyber-security [6,8], which attempts to create, evaluate, and deploy mechanisms and strategies which are diverse, continually shift and change over time to increase complexity and costs for attackers, limit the exposure of vulnerabilities and opportunities for attack, and increase system resiliency [6]. Currently, there has been proposed a multitude of MTD approaches. The performance evaluation for these MTD approaches is usually empirical, but lacks the application of theoretical models. Until now, only three related works introduced existing urn models to the MTD area, and use them to evaluate the performance of Network Address Shuffling [9], Port Hopping [10], and combination of deception defense and movement (actually, Network Address Shuffling) [11], respectively. Furthermore, there lacks the comparison between different MTD techniques except the work of Jun Xu [12]. Petri Net (PN) is created as a mathematical tool to describe and model the information system, and system performance evaluation is one of its most successful applications [13]. In this paper, we attempt to introduce Petri Net theory into MTD area for evaluating and comparing different MTD techniques.

To build the generalized abstract evaluation model for MTD system, we choose a Web server as the deployment platform. There are two reasons to consider this scenario. The one is that Web server is an very important target in network, which is worth deploying MTD to increase its security and resiliency. The other is that the three main typical MTD techniques (Software Transformations (ST), Dynamic Platform Techniques (DPT), and Network Address Shuffling (NAS) [14]) can be deployed on a Web server alone or simultaneously. Specifically, an MTD approach based on ST can be used on server application to improve its capacity against attacks from network. The DPT can be used on the running platform of the Web server to complicate the attacks. Meanwhile the NAS approaches can also be applied to server's network address to confuse attacker.

In our prior research, we have analyzed the running patterns of MTD techniques that provide proper defense [14]. In this paper, we will extend classic process of Web service, describe a complete process of service and defense of a Web server which can deploy the three typical MTD techniques, and develop a generalized abstract performance evaluation model for existing MTD approaches through using generalized stochastic Petri Net (GSPN). Then we take an MTD approach in NAS category as a use case to describe the usage of the proposed model. For simplicity, we have only modeled the situation that MTD is performed when the system is serving in this paper. Modeling and discussing a more realistic service and defense process is our future work.

2   Problem Formulation

2.1   Petri Net

A basic Petri Net (PN) [13] can be viewed as a directed graph, in which the nodes are Places and Transitions, and the edges are Arcs. It is usually described as a 3 tuple, i.e., $PN = (S, T; F)$.

- S: S represents the set of places, which describes the local state of system. A place is usually represented as a circle graphically.
- T: T represents the set of transitions, which describes the event or the actions that induces state change. A transition is usually denoted as a rectangle or a line graphically.
- F: F represents the set of arcs. Arcs connect the Place and Transaction to describe the relationship between the local states and events. An arc is usually denoted as an directed arc graphically.

The three basic elements of a basic Petri Net has the following four properties. The first one is $S \cup T \neq \varnothing$. The second one is $S \cap T = \varnothing$. The third one is $F \subseteq (S \times T) \cup (T \times S)$. The forth one is $dom(F) \cup cod(F) = S \cup T$, and in which $dom(F) = \{x | \exists y : (x, y) \in F\}$, $cod(F) = \{x | \exists y : (y, x) \in F\}$.

A place from which an arc originates is considered to be an input place of a transition in which the arc terminates. A place in which an arc terminates is considered to be an output place of a transition from which the arc originates. Token, is another important sign in Petri Nets. It is usually denoted as solid dot and contained in places to represent the state of the Petri Net, i.e., its dynamic change in the place is used to represent the different state of the system. One specific distribution of tokens over a Petri Net can be used to represent a specific state of described system and called marking.

The dynamic behavior of a PN is managed and controlled by its firing rule. If all the input places of a transition contain at least one token, the transition is enabled and it can be fired to cause the state change of the system. If a transition is fired, all of its input places would remove a token, and all of its output places would add a token.

2.2   SPN and GSPN

The concept of time is not introduced into basic PN. If there is a random delay between a transition's enabling and firing, in other words, each transition is associated with a fire rate, the PN is extended to become a Stochastic Petri Net (SPN) [13].

Generalized Stochastic Petri Net (GSPN) [13] is an extension of SPN. There are two main differences between GSPN and SPN. The one is that the transitions in GSPN can be divided into two sub-types, immediate transitions and timed transitions. The other is there exists inhibitor arcs in GSPN. A Generalized Stochastic Petri Net model is usually described as a 6 tuple, i.e., $GSPN = (S, T; F, W, M_0, \lambda)$.

- S: the definition is same to the basic PN.
- T: In GSPN, transitions can be divided into two category, Immediate Transitions and Timed Transitions. $T = T_1 \cup T_2$, $T_1 = \{t_1, t_2, ..., t_m\}$ denotes the timed transitions and each of which is associated with a random delay time between enabling and firing, and they are usually represented as empty rectangles graphically. Meanwhile $T_2 = \{t_{m+1}, t_{m+2}, ..., t_n\}$ denotes the immediate

transitions which can be fired randomly and the delay is zero, and they are usually represented as solid rectangles or lines.
- F: In GSPN, there exists inhibitor arcs, which can only form places to transitions, and make the enabled conditions to be disenabled.
- W: W is the weight function for the arcs, and it satisfies $F \to N^+$.
- M_0: M_0 is the initial marking, and it satisfies that, $\forall s \in S : M_0(s) \le K(s)$, in which $K : S \to N^+ \cup \{\infty\}$ is the place capacity function.
- λ: $\lambda = \{\lambda_1, \lambda_2, ..., \lambda_m\}$, and it is set of the firing rates corresponding to the timed transitions. Each rate is the average firing times of transition in unit time.

3   A GSPN Model for Evaluating MTD Techniques

In this paper, we choose a Web server that deploys MTD techniques as an evaluation scenario. We firstly describe the process of Web service and defense of the example evaluation scenario. We assume that only in the process of serving, there may occur the event of timer expiring which according the periodic or unfixed attack surface shifting, or a security alert.

(1) The Web server system is ready to provide service after completing its functionality and defense configuration.
(2) User send the synchronize request to acquire the current network address of server. If the server deploys one or more of the approaches based on Software Transformations, Dynamic Platform Techniques, and the Network Address Shuffling approach in mutation pattern, the synchronization is usually achieved by routing update and DNS request/respond. If the server deploys the NAS in hopping pattern, the synchronization is usually achieved by time synchronization scheme, or exchanging the hopping pattern information, or pre-setting the same function and initial value [15].
(3) After obtaining the service address, user can establish connection with the server. And then user would send its service request and wait for the service.
(4) During the process of service, the deployed MTD approach would shift the attack surface of the Web system according to the pre-setting scheme (the timer expires) or an anomalous event.
    If there deploys ST or DPT, it needs to preserve or migrate the current service state (such as connections, data) for the new variant or platform to pursue the task of the previous variant or platform.
    If NAS is deployed, there are two cases.

A. If there is aid mechanism to ensure that the ongoing connections would not be broken down (such as MT6D [16], RHM [17], spatio-temporal address mutation [18]), the system would continue to provide service.
B. Otherwise, we would consider the two sub-cases.
    a. If the NAS is in hopping pattern, the two sides are fully aware of the hopping pattern information (including the hopping sequence and hopping timeless) of both, or one side (e.g. the clients) is fully aware of the

hopping pattern information of the other side (e.g. the server). Then the user can get the service address timely, and it can directly establish the connection with server.

b. If the NAS is in mutation pattern, the user do not know the shuffling information of the server, thus it has to send the synchronization request and wait for connection.

Next, we model the process of service and defense using GSPN as Fig. 1. In most of existing MTD approaches, it usually shifts to a new variant/platform/address after a time interval controlled by a timer. What's more, some of them would shift according to a security alert, such as ChameleonSoft [19], TALENT [20], and MAS [21]. The shifting based on fixed or adjustable time interval can be described as time transition, while the shifting driven by the security alert can be described as immediate transition. Therefore, we choose GSPN as the modeling tool. The places correspond to the system state in the process of service and defense, and the transitions correspond to the actions in the process of service and defense.

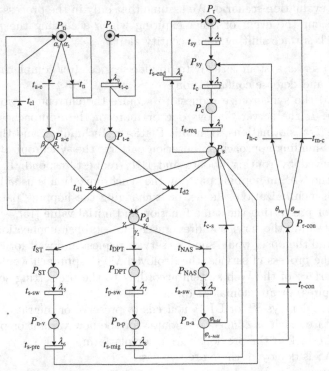

Fig. 1. The GSPN model for the Web server deployed typical MTD Technology.

The signification of the places and transitions in Fig. 1 are described as follows (seen in Tables 1 and 2).

In Table 2, in addition to the signification of transitions, we also describe the types of each transition. What's more, we take Timed as the abbreviation of timed transition, and Immed as the abbreviation of immediate transition.

Table 1. Signification of the places.

Places	Signification
P_r	System is ready to provide service
P_t	The timer is counting
P_n	There is no security alert
P_{t-e}	The timer expired
P_{a-e}	There is an anomalous event
P_{sy}	System is in the state of synchronization
P_c	System is in the state of establishing connection
P_s	System is serving
P_d	System is in the state of defense
P_{ST}	System is changing its software variant to provide service
P_{n-v}	System is using a new variant to serve
P_{DPT}	System is changing the properties of its platform
P_{n-p}	System is with new properties of its platform
P_{NAS}	System is changing its network address
P_{n-a}	System is with the new address
P_{r-con}	User re-connects with the server

In this model, we use an inhibitor arc from P_{t-e} to t_{d1}, which means that when there are tokens in place P_{a-e}, P_{t-e}, and P_s, only the transition t_{d2} can be fired, and the transition t_{d1} is disenabled. In real system, when the system is serving, and if the timer expires or there is a security alert, the system would respond to the two events to defense. What's more, the alternative actions for responding to the two events (i.e., t_{d1} and t_{d2}) belonged to the same set of actions which consists of the three actions named software transformations, changing the properties of running platform, and shuffling the system's network address, respectively. As a result, when the system is serving, and the timer expires meanwhile there is a security alert, the system just needs to respond to one event. The corresponding representation in the GSPN model is that only one transition, t_{d1} or t_{d2}, needs to be fired. Here we assume that transition t_{d2} can be fired, and the transition t_{d1} is disenabled.

In this model, we define five random switches.

The first one is for the immediate transitions t_n and t_{a-e}. We define that the probability that the transition t_{a-e} fires is α_1, and the probability that the transition t_n fires is α_2 (i.e., $p(t_{a-e}) = \alpha_1$, and $p(t_n) = \alpha_2$), which describes the probability that there is a security alert, or not, respectively. Their values satisfy that

Table 2. Signification of the transitions.

Transitions	Type	Signification
t_{t-e}	Timed	Timer expires during the process of service
t_{a-e}	Immed	Security alert occurs during the process of service
t_n	Immed	There is no security alert occurs
t_{sy}	Timed	Send synchronization request to get service address
t_c	Timed	Establish connection with server
t_{s-req}	Timed	Send service request
t_{s-end}	Timed	User obtains the required service, and the service terminates normally
t_{d1}	Immed	System cleans the alert and responds to the security alert
t_{cl}	Immed	Clean the alert
t_{d2}	Immed	System responds to the event of timer expiring
t_{ST}	Immed	System chooses the defense approach based on Software Transformations
t_{s-sw}	Timed	Switching the software variant
t_{s-pre}	Timed	Preserving the service state
t_{DPT}	Immed	System chooses the defense approach belonging to Dynamic PlatformTechniqu
t_{p-sw}	Timed	Switching the properties of running platform
t_{s-mig}	Timed	Migrating the service state
t_{NAS}	Immed	System chooses the defense approach belonging to Network Address Shuffling
t_{a-sw}	Timed	Switching the server's network address
t_{c-s}	Immed	Server continues the service
t_{r-con}	Immed	User starts to re-connect with the server
t_{h-c}	Immed	User initiate the re-connection in hopping pattern
t_{m-c}	Immed	User initiate the re-connection in mutation pattern

$$\alpha_1 + \alpha_2 = 1, \alpha_1, \alpha_2 \in \{0, 1\}$$

The second one is for the immediate transitions t_{cl} and t_{d1}. we define the random switch is that, under the condition $M(P_s) = 1$,

$$\begin{cases} p(t_{cl}) = \beta_1 = \dfrac{M(P_{t-e})}{M(P_{a-e}) + M(P_{t-e})}, \\ p(t_{d1}) = \beta_2 = \dfrac{M(P_{a-e})}{M(P_{a-e}) + M(P_{t-e})}, \end{cases} \quad if\, M(P_{t-e}) \neq 1\, or\, M(P_{a-e}) \neq 1;$$

$$\begin{cases} p(t_{cl}) = \beta_1 = 1, \\ p(t_{d1}) = \beta_2 = 0, \end{cases} \quad if\, M(P_{t-e}) = M(P_{a-e}) = 1.$$

The third one is for the immediate transitions t_{ST}, t_{DPT}, and t_{NAS}. We define that $P(t_{ST}) = \gamma_1$, $P(t_{DPT}) = \gamma_2$, and $P(t_{NAS}) = \gamma_3$. In other words, γ_1, γ_2, and γ_3 represent the probability of that the system would deploy the defense approach based on Software Transformations, or deploying the defense approach belonging to Dynamic Platform Techniques, or deploying the defense approach belonging to Network Address Shuffling, respectively. Their values satisfy that

$$\gamma_1 + \gamma_2 + \gamma_3 = 1, 0 \leq \gamma_1, \gamma_2, \gamma_3 \leq 1$$

In addition, we call one attack surface shifting a round. We assume that in each round, the values of γ_1, γ_2, and γ_3 satisfy that $\gamma_1, \gamma_2, \gamma_3 \in \{0, 1\}$. It means that different types of MTD approaches can be chosen in different rounds, but only one type of MTD techniques can be used in each round.

The forth one is for the immediate transitions t_{c-s} and t_{r-con}. We define that $p(t_{c-s}) = \varphi_{hold}$ and $p(t_{r-con}) = \varphi_{n-hold}$. φ_{hold} and φ_{n-hold} represent the probability whether the defense approach is equipped with the aid mechanism to keep the ongoing connections active, or not, respectively. The values of φ_{hold} and φ_{n-hold} are determined by the designer, and they satisfy that

$$\varphi_{hold} + \varphi_{n-hold} = 1, \varphi_{hold}, \varphi_{n-hold} \in \{0, 1\}$$

The fifth one is for the immediate transitions t_{h-c} and t_{m-c}. We define that $p(t_{h-c}) = \theta_{hop}$ and $p(t_{m-c}) = \theta_{mut}$. θ_{hop} and θ_{mut} represent the probability of using the NAS approach in hopping pattern or NAS approach in mutation pattern, respectively. The values of θ_{hop} and θ_{mut} relate to the defense policy selected by defender, and they satisfy that

$$\theta_{hop} + \theta_{mut} = 1, \theta_{hop}, \theta_{mut} \in \{0, 1\}$$

4   A Case Study

We have modeled the process of service and defense of a Web server that deploys typical MTD techniques through using GSPN in Sect. 3. Now we will present a case study to describe the usage of our model.

We choose the RHM [17] as a case study. Firstly we obtain the GSPN model for RHM form the generalized model shown in Fig. 1.

In RHM, each host is associated with an unused address range (i.e., the set of virtual IPs). RHM uses a two-phase mutation approach which consists of LFM (Low Frequency mutation) and HFM (High Frequency mutation) to assign vIP. A LFM interval contains multiple HFM intervals. In each LFM interval, a random network address range denoted as VAR (virtual address range) is selected for each MT (Moving Target) host using SMT (Satisfiability Modulo Theories). Then in each HFM interval, a random vIP within the VAR assigned during last LFM is selected for the MT host. Comparing to the operational cost in each HFM interval, the operational cost in each LFM interval can be ignored. More importantly, for the users, only the HFM interval associates with them and may influence them. Therefore, we should only consider the timer for HFM. In addition, RHM is designed to only respond to the event of timer expiring.

The RHM is an approach in the category of NAS, and thus $\gamma_1 = 0$, $\gamma_2 = 0$, $\gamma_3 = 1$. In addition, as described previously, RHM has the aid mechanism to ensure that ongoing connections would not be broken down during the shifting. Therefore, $\varphi_{hold} = 1$ and $\varphi_{n-hold} = 0$.

Because of these properties of RHM, the GSPN model for RHM can be simplified as shown in Fig. 2 form Fig. 1. what's more, in Fig. 2, the transitions t_{d2} and t_{NAS} are immediate transitions, thus the two transitions can merge, and the place P_d can be removed. The transition t_{c-s} is also an immediate transition, and thus the place P_{n-a} can be removed. Therefore, we can get the final GSPN model for RHM as shown in Fig. 3.

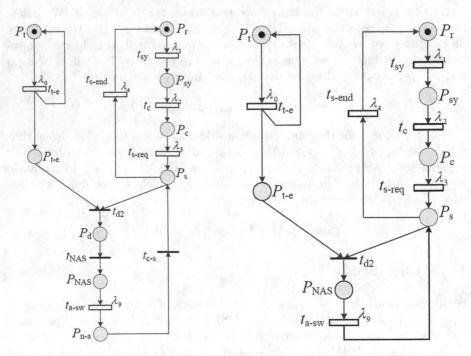

Fig. 2. The GSPN model for RHM.   **Fig. 3.** The final GSPN model for RHM.

Then, we can use PIPE2 (Platform-Independent Petri Net Editor 2) [22,23] to analyze the performance of RHM. PIPE2 is an open-source tool for the performance evaluation of GSPN models. With its easy-to-use graphical user interface, user can easily construct and analyze a GSPN model, obtain the set of tangible states and the basic performance parameters (such as the steady state distribution of tangible states, throughput of timed transitions, the staying time of tangible states, and so on).

We firstly draw the model in Fig. 3 in PIPE, as shown in Fig. 4.

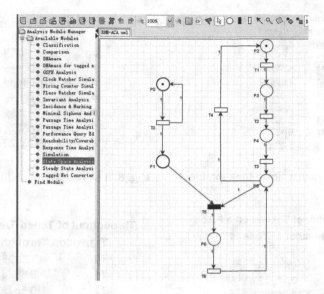

Fig. 4. The GSPN model for RHM in PIPE.

To ensure the boundness and safeness of this model, we set $K(P_0) = 1$ and $K(P_1) = 1$, i.e., the capacities of place P_0 and P_1 are both set to 1 in Fig. 4. Then we set the firing rates as follows: $\lambda_0 = 1.2$ for the transition T_0, $\lambda_1 = 36$ for the transition T_1, $\lambda_2 = 72$ for the transition T_2, $\lambda_3 = 180$ for the transition T_3, $\lambda_4 = 1$ for the transition T_4, $\lambda_6 = 4$ for the transition T_6. Thereafter, we take the GSPN analysis to get the set of tangible states (Fig. 5) and the steady state distribution for the tangible states (Fig. 6), and we also can obtain the values of some parameters as shown in Figs. 7, 8, 9, and 10.

Based on above results, we can take some further analysis, such as the average delay of service, average throughput of system, the operational efficiency for each link of system, and so on. Here we take the average delay of service as an

Set of Tangible States

	P0	P1	P2	P3	P4	P5	P6
M0	1	0	1	0	0	0	0
M1	1	0	0	1	0	0	0
M2	1	1	1	0	0	0	0
M3	1	0	0	0	1	0	0
M4	1	1	0	1	0	0	0
M5	1	0	0	0	0	1	0
M6	1	1	0	0	1	0	0
M7	1	0	0	0	0	0	1
M8	1	1	0	0	0	0	1

Steady State Distribution of Tangible States

Marking	Value
M0	0.01848
M1	0.00909
M2	0.00062
M3	0.00361
M4	0.00046
M5	0.68733
M6	0.00021
M7	0.21555
M8	0.06467

Fig. 5. The set of tangible states.

Fig. 6. The steady state distribution of tangible states.

Sojourn times for tangible states	
Marking	Value
M0	0.02688
M1	0.01366
M2	0.02778
M3	0.00552
M4	0.01389
M5	0.45455
M6	0.00556
M7	0.19231
M8	0.25

Fig. 7. The Sojourn times for tangible states.

Token Probability Density		
	μ=0	μ=1
P0	0	1
P1	0.93405	0.06595
P2	0.98091	0.01909
P3	0.99045	0.00955
P4	0.99618	0.00382
P5	0.31267	0.68733
P6	0.71978	0.28022

Fig. 8. The token probability density.

Average Number of Tokens on a Place	
Place	Number of Tokens
P0	1
P1	0.06595
P2	0.01909
P3	0.00955
P4	0.00382
P5	0.68733
P6	0.28022

Fig. 9. The average number of tokens on a place.

Throughput of Timed Transitions	
Transition	Throughput
T0	1.12086
T1	0.68733
T2	0.68733
T3	0.68733
T4	0.68733
T6	1.12086

Fig. 10. The throughput of timed transitions.

example. The computation of the average delay is based on Little's law [24], which is described as

$$N = \lambda T$$

N is the average number of tokens for this system, and it can be calculated as $N = u(P_1) + \sum_{i=3}^{6} u(P_i) = 1.04687$. λ is the token flowing rate of transition, and here it can be calculated as $\lambda = R(T_0, P_1) + R(T_1, P_3) = 1.62742$. Therefore, the average delay of service is $T = N/\lambda = 0.64$ (unit time).

For comparison, each evaluator should design his own rule. In other words, he can assign a weight for each chosen performance parameter according to his specific requirement. For each MTD approach, the evaluator can compute the values of each parameter, and then get a final result based on the values of performance parameters and their associated weight for comparison.

5   Related Work

Petri Net has been proposed by Carl Adam Petri in 1962, and it has many extensions and has been wildly applied in many filed. However, the application of Petri Nets in the MTD area is still few.

Leyi S et al. have used Stochastic Petri Net to evaluate the performance of service hopping system proposed by them [25]. After obtaining the steady-state probabilities of all states in the underlying continuous-time Markov chain, they analyzed the average latency and throughout of the hopping system. Thereafter they also discussed the relationships between the two parameters and the efficiency of synchronization and data swapping.

W C Moody et al. have used Stochastic Petri Nets to model a defensive maneuver cyber platform which utilizes moving target defense and deceptive defense tactics [26]. The use SPN to describe each node comprised the platform and the whole system, and discuss the trade-offs between security and operations in the defensive maneuver cyber platform. Specifically, they enumerated the categorized the state space of the model, and discuss the transition firing rate impact.

Compared with the existing works, there are three main advantages in our work:

The first one is that the model we proposed is a generalized abstract model, and it is suitable for all the three typical categories of MTD technology. The literature [25] has modeled a service hopping system, which can be classified as Network Address Shuffling. The moving target defense technique described in literature [26] is can be classified as dynamic platform techniques. Either the Network Address Shuffling, or the combination of dynamic platform techniques and deceptive defense, is one category of MTD techniques.

The second one is that the model can be used to compare different MTD approaches. Each MTD approach can be represented as a specific GSPN model, and the values of its performance parameters can be obtained. Then, based on the comparison rule designed by the evaluators, the approaches can be compared.

The third one is that the model can not only evaluate an MTD system that only deploys one specific MTD techniques, but also can evaluate an MTD system that deploys more than one kind of MTD techniques. In this case, the corresponding GSPN model is an unfolding form of Fig. 1.

6   Conclusion and Future Works

In this paper, we use a Web server system as the deployment scenario, and introduce GSPN to model existing three main types of MTD techniques. Then we take as a case study to describe the usage of this model, which can help the subsequent researcher. The proposed model is suitable for the three typical MTD techniques or the combination of them. However, it is still not suitable the MTD techniques that incorporate deceptive defense, and which maybe our future direction.

In this paper, we have only modeled the situation that MTD is performed when the system is serving. Actually, a timer can expire or a security alert may occur at any time from sending a synchronization request to ending the service successfully. In other words, MTD can be performed in any state of P_{sy}, P_c and P_s. For simplicity, we only consider the situation that MTD is performed in the state P_s. In the future work, we will take the situation that MTD is performed in the state P_s and P_c into account, model and discuss a more realistic service and defense process.

References

1. Liu, Y., Peng, W., Jinshu, S.: A study of IP prefix hijacking in cloud computing networks. Secur. Commun. Netw. **7**(11), 2201–2210 (2014)
2. Wang, T.-Z., Wang, H.-M., Liu, B., Ding, B., Zhang, J., Shi, P.-C.: Further analyzing the sybil attack in mitigating peer-to-peer botnets. KSII Trans. Internet Inf. Syst. **6**(10), 2731–2749 (2012)
3. Wang, F., Wang, H., Wang, X., Jinshu, S.: A new multistage approach to detect subtle DDoS attacks. Math. Comput. Model. **55**(1), 198–213 (2012)
4. Prism. https://en.wikipedia.org/wiki/PRISM_(surveillance_program). Accessed 18 Nov 2013
5. The heartbleed bug. http://heartbleed.com/. Accessed 1 Oct 2014
6. NITRD, CSIA, and IWG: Cybersecurity game-change research and development recommendations. http://www.nitrd.gov/pubs/CSIA_IWG_NITRD. Accessed 20 Aug 2013
7. CSIA: Trustworthy cyberspace: strategic plan for the federal cybersecurity research and development program. The United States Government. http://www.whitehouse.gov/sites/default/files/microsites/ostp/fed_cybersecurity_rd_strategic_plan_2011.pdf. Accessed 10 Dec 2012
8. Chong, F., Lee, R.B., Acquisti, A., Horne, W., Palmer, C., Ghosh, A.K., Pendarakis, D.: National cyber leap year summit 2009 co-chairs report. NITRD. https://www.nitrd.gov/nitrdgroups/index.php?title=Category:National_Cyber_Leap_Year_Summit_2009. Accessed 1 Jan 2014
9. Carroll, T.E., Crouse, M., Fulp, E.W., Berenhaut, K.S.: Analysis of network address shuffling as a moving target defense. In 2014 IEEE International Conference on Communications (ICC), pp. 701–706, June 2014
10. Luo, Y.B., Wang, B.S., Cai, G.L.: Effectiveness of port hopping as a moving target defense. In: 2014 7th International Conference on Security Technology (SecTech), pp. 7–10, December 2014
11. Crouse, M., Prosser, B., Fulp, E.W.: Probabilistic performance analysis of moving target and deception reconnaissance defenses. In: Proceedings of the Second ACM Workshop on Moving Target Defense, MTD 2015, pp. 21–29. ACM, New York (2015)
12. Xu, J., Guo, P., Zhao, M., Erbacher, R.F., Zhu, M., Liu, P.: Comparing different moving target defense techniques. In: Proceedings of the First ACM Workshop on Moving Target Defense, pp. 97–107. ACM (2014)
13. Lin, C.: Performance Evaluation of Computer Networks and Computer Systems (in Chinese), 1st edn. Tsinghua University Press, Beijing (2001)
14. Cai, G., Wang, B., Luo, Y., Li, S., Wang, X.: Characterizing the running patterns of moving target defense mechanisms. In: 2016 18th International Conference on Advanced Communication Technology (ICACT), pp. 191–196, January 2016
15. Cai, G., Wang, B., Wang, X., Yuan, Y., Li, S.: An introduction to network address shuffling. In: 2016 18th International Conference on Advanced Communication Technology (ICACT), pp. 1–2, January 2016

16. Dunlop, M., Groat, S., Urbanski, W., Marchany, R., Tront, J.: The blind man's bluff approach to security using IPv6. IEEE Secur. Priv. **10**(4), 35–43 (2012)
17. Al-Shaer, E., Duan, Q., Jafarian, J.H.: Random host mutation for moving target defense. In: Pietro, R., Keromytis, A.D. (eds.) SecureComm 2012. LNICST, vol. 106, pp. 310–327. Springer, Heidelberg (2013)
18. Jafarian, J.H.H., Al-Shaer, E., Duan, Q.: Spatio-temporal address mutation for proactive cyber agility against sophisticated attackers. In: Proceedings of the First ACM Workshop on Moving Target Defense, pp. 69–78. ACM (2014)
19. Azab, M., Hassan, R., Eltoweissy, M.: Chameleonsoft.: a moving target defense system. In: 2011 7th International Conference on Collaborative Computing: Networking, Applications and Worksharing (CollaborateCom), pp. 241–250, October 2011
20. Okhravi, H., Comella, A., Robinson, E., Haines, J.: Creating a cyber moving target for critical infrastructure applications using platform diversity. Int. J. Crit. Infrastruct. Prot. **5**(1), 30–39 (2012)
21. Huang, Y., Ghosh, A.K.: Introducing diversity and uncertainty to create moving attack surfaces for web services. In: Jajodia, S., Ghosh, A.K., Swarup, V., Wang, C., Wang, X.S. (eds.) Moving Target Defense. Advances in Information Security, vol. 54, pp. 131–151. Springer, New York (2011)
22. Bonet, P., Lladó, C.M., Puijaner, R., Knottenbelt, W.J.: Pipe v2.5.: a petri net tool for performance modelling. In: Proceedings of the 23rd Latin American Conference on Informatics (CLEI) (2007)
23. Dingle, N.J., Knottenbelt, W.J., Suto, T.: Pipe2: a tool for the performance evaluation of generalised stochastic petri nets. ACM SIGMETRICS Perform. Eval. Rev. **36**(4), 34–39 (2009)
24. Trivedi, K.S.: Probability and Statistics with Reliability, Queuing and Computer Science Applications, 2nd edn. Wiley, Chichester (2002)
25. Shi, L., Jia, C., Lv, S.: Performance evaluation of service hopping system using stochastic petri net. Acta Scientiarum Naturalium Universitatis Nankaiensis **42**(1), 72–75 (2009). (in Chinese)
26. Moody, W., Hongxin, H., Apon, A.: Defensive maneuver cyber platform modeling with stochastic petrinets. In: International Conference on Collaborative Computing: Networking, Applications and Worksharing (CollaborateCom), pp. 531–538. IEEE (2014)

Subway Timetable Adjusting Method Research of Bi-directional Trains Arriving at a Station Asynchronously

Dan Yan[1,2], Jianhua Mao[1], Xuefeng Liu[1], and Minglai Yang[2,3(✉)]

[1] School of Communication and Information Engineering,
Shanghai University, Shanghai, China
15026903162@126.com, {mjh,xf02}@shu.edu.cn
[2] Shanghai Advanced Research Institute,
Chinese Academic of Science, Shanghai 201210, China
yand@sari.ac.cn, yangminglai@sari.ac.cn
[3] Shanghai Institute of Technology, Shanghai 201418, China
yangminglai@163.com

Abstract. Metro transmits, as the backbone of urban public transit, plays an important role in alleviating congested traffic and shaping low-carbon and comfortable trip mode. With the rapid development of urban rail transit, the traffic of the city cannot be separated from the subway; however, large passenger flow triggers heavy traffic accident easily and reduces the degree of comfort greatly, especially when up and down trains arriving at the same station simultaneously. To implement urban railway transit system optimization and to achieve the goal of up and down trains arrive at a station asynchronously, situations of trains arriving at the platform are studied, and a quantitative analysis of different time periods and different types of platforms are completed. The definition of the train conflict time of arriving at a station simultaneously is given. Through the derivation and calculation of the total use of the subway conflict time, to identify the key variables that affect the conflict time, a solution of using greedy algorithm to adjust conflict time is proposed. Simulation through Visual C++ platform demonstrates that the algorithm can provide optimal railway timetables while satisfying operational constraints. Comparative analysis of the results showed that: if passenger flow is considered, departure time, interval time and dwell time are invariant, only adjusting the morning peak-hours is 19.76 % superior than the unadjusted state, while adjusting the morning and evening peak-hours is 34.85 % prior. The models can be further expanded to develop models and algorithms for estimating the conflict time of up and down trains and reduce the conflict time.

Keywords: Metro transit · Train conflict time · Greedy algorithms · Enumeration method · Timetable optimization

1 Introduction

With the quick and continuous development of urban rail transport services, the subway becomes the preferred means of transport and effectively solves the problem of urban traffic congestion, as it's high passenger volume, efficient and convenient,

© Springer Science+Business Media Singapore 2016
J. Wu and L. Li (Eds.): ACA 2016, CCIS 626, pp. 198–210, 2016.
DOI: 10.1007/978-981-10-2209-8_17

punctual, fair and orderly [1]. However, the high-density traffic aggregation leads to metro internal environmental comfort and safety problems. Theoretical research and the actual situation show that when the up and down trains arrive at the station simultaneously, a steady stream of traffic, coupled with the passengers up and down the line to get off the train at the same time, it is likely to cause large-scale traffic congestion once the number of passengers exceeds the station capacity. Therefore, avoiding subway arriving simultaneously at the morning and evening peak-hours is one of the key points to reduce passenger flow density, improve operational efficiency, service quality and keep public safety. The existing schedule formulation models are Periodic Event Scheduling Problem (PESP) model [2, 3], and much subway timetable optimization research is based on this model [4]. There are following schedules optimization methods: reducing costs and passengers waiting time optimization method; section algorithm [5], algorithms based on different period [6], algorithms based on variable operational requirements [7], algorithms based on variable running time [8], algorithms based on security constraints, heuristic algorithm [9], stochastic optimization methods [10–12], the genetic algorithm method, and a method to maximize the use of regenerative braking energy [13–15].

In this paper, combined with the actual situation and needs of Shanghai Metro Line 2, and according to the theoretical derivation of the subway time schedule, the theoretical model of using minimum conflict time to solve the problem of passenger flow congestion is proposed. Through the model, an adjusting timetable for peak-hours is available. This method of optimal adjustment of time schedule has reduced the conflict time, and achieved the goal of up and down trains arriving at the same station in rush hours asynchronously. Compared with the traditional timetable schedule optimization method, this paper has solved the congestion problem in a new dimension, with low computational complexity and easy implementation.

2 Metro Dispatcher Model

To study how to avoid the conflict of bi-directional trains arrive at the subway station simultaneously in peak-hours as far as possible, the definition of up and down trains arriving at the station simultaneously is given. By analyzing the congestion situation, subway dwell time can be divided into two sections: one section is from train arrival time to the train gate closing time (passenger having completed getting on and off the train); another section is from train gate closing to the train departure time. While the main subway conflict time is the former, the definition of conflict time in this paper is that the smallest arrival time difference of up and down lines reaching a station minus the time of first train leaving the station except $\tau.\tau$ is an adjusting parameters, which is currently defined to be the time from closing the door time to departure time of the first departure train. Thus the following studies are carried out.

2.1 The Time-Factor Model

2.1.1 Building Model Analysis

The up and down trains reach the station simultaneously will cause traffic congestion easily when passenger flow is huge, so the research of this paper should take the impact of passenger flow into account. Typically, the greater the traffic is, the greater influence that the up and down trains reaching the platform simultaneously will be, for the platform is more crowding. As the actual situation is that only when the traffic reaches a certain level, the above problems will occur and the research of how to avoid up and down trains arriving simultaneously makes sense. According to Shanghai Metro Line No. 2 Statistics provided by Shanghai Shentong Metro Group Co., Ltd, firstly, the capacities of stations are preliminarily measured. The average capacity of stations is 7318 people per hour and standard deviation is 1701.

2.1.2 Model Assumption

There are four or eight carriages grouping marshalling railway in Shanghai subway. And the area size of each station is different. But before the urban rails' construction, the passenger flow, station sizes and length of which grouping marshalling railways and other factors are considered. So in this paper, we only consider the impact on the number of passengers, exceeding factors such as the sizes of the metro stations and railway length when the passengers number factor model. That is to say that the model assumption is the station capacity of each station is equal.

2.1.3 Time-Factor Model Building

Time and passenger number factor (time-factor) is a variable that reflects the degree of traffic congestion by average number of passengers per hour. The greater the passengers flow is, the greater likelihood of congestion will be, and the higher requirement of reducing the conflict time will be. And during the same amount of conflict time, the impact on passenger congestion is greater, therefore, the time-factor is bigger.

The factor is defined according to following facts: when passenger number is small, the situation that the two trains arrive at a station simultaneously will not cause congestion. And when the passenger number is close to the average number of the station capacity, the number and time factor can be considered as 1. When the number becomes lager, more detail classifications are given because the affection degree is more obvious. And mathematically, it is essential to ensure that the definition of the time-factor is continuous. The relationship between the above parameter and time-factor can be expressed by the following formula:

$$
\text{s.t.} \begin{cases}
0 < = X < \frac{m}{2} & \delta = 0 \\
\frac{m}{2} < = X < m & \delta = 1 \\
m < = X < 2m & \delta = 1 * \frac{X}{m} \\
2m < = X < 3m & \delta = 2 * \frac{X}{m} - 2 \\
3m < = X < 4m & \delta = 3 * \frac{X}{m} - 5 \\
X > = 4m & \delta = 4 * \frac{X}{m} - 9 \\
\delta > = 10 & \delta = 10
\end{cases}
\tag{1}
$$

where

X = the number of passengers,
m = the average number of station capacity,
δ = the time-factor.

As is show in formula (1), time-factor is solved basing on mean and variance.

2.2   Railway Conflict Time Model

2.2.1   Building Model Analysis

Metro up and down trains are likely to arrive at a station simultaneously due to features such as a short station distance, travel speed and high traffic density. What's more, the stranded large passenger flow makes the station passenger congestion. If up and down trains reach the station asynchronously, the peak congestion can be alleviated in a large degree. The time of up and down trains staying at the same station is defined as the Railway conflict time. Thus reducing the conflict can be a solution to the metro staggering problem.

2.2.2   Model Assumptions

In order to establish a reasonable mathematical model, the model presented in this paper relies on several key assumptions:

- Train running time is invariant. In reality, the railway operation speed will be affected by subway traffic, weather and human impact, resulting in running time fluctuations. In this study, we will ignore the impact of fluctuations in the running time of a conflict of time.
- This model only considers single-line subway operation situations but not the complex underground network. In actual situation, the complex subway network is difficult to build a proper model let alone simulation. To simplify the model, combined with the project requirements, this model will be based on Shanghai Metro Line 2 to find a peak-hours adjusting solution.

2.2.3   Model Building

This paper aims to find an optimal schedule to adjust the passenger flow congestion due to the up and down trains arriving at a station simultaneously in order to improve the service quality and safety of metro (Tables 1 and 2).

Model variables are defined as following table:

- Definitions of Collection.
- Parameters

There are n trains leaving from subway station during a period of time t (t is less than the subway running time of a full working day) within, as any train that is operating, the **total conflict time S** can be expressed by the following formulation:

Table 1. Collection table

Number	Set	Meaning
1	I, J	Train collection. i, j represents the trains i, j
2	K	Station collection. k represents *the k-th* site
3	T	Conflict time collection. T_{ij} represents train i and j total time of conflict
4	C	Reaching station time collection. C_{ik} represents the time of train i reach the k station
5	O	Leaving station time collection. O_{ik} represents the time of train i leave the k station
6	R	Railway running time collection. R_k represents the train running time that train moves from k station to $k - 1$ station
7	B	Departure time collection. B_i represents the departure time of train i
8	P	Train travel time. P_{ik} represents dwell time of train i in station k
9	Δt	Train regulation time collection. Δt_{ik} that represents regulation time of train i in station k
10	N	Stations number of trains have travel. N_i represents the total number of stations that train i has arrived

Table 2. Parameter lists

Symbol	S	F	t	n
Meaning	Total conflict time	Conflict time calculation functions, $F(C_{ik}, O_{ik}, C_{jk}, O_{jk})$ represents conflict time function related to the reaching and leaving time	Trains operating time	The number of trains sent from the subway during a period of time

$$S = \sum_{i=0}^{n} \sum_{j=0}^{n} T_{ij} \tag{2}$$

where $T_{ij} = $ *the* total conflict time of train i and train j.

Then the target of the shortest conflict time **Min (S)** can be solved by minimizing the total conflict time:

$$Min(S) = Min\left(\sum_{i=0}^{n} \sum_{j=0}^{n} T_{ij}\right) \tag{3}$$

Next, the representation of T_{ij} is next goal.

Assuming that the train is an up line train and train j is a down line train. The conflict time of trains i and j can be as represented in Fig. 1.

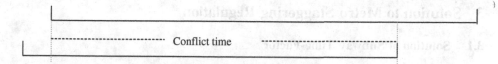

Fig. 1. Single station train collision time map

The train Conflict time calculation can be written as:

$$F\left(C_{ik}, O_{ik}, C_{jk}, O_{jk}\right) = \begin{cases} 0 & C_{ik} > O_{jk} \;||\; C_{jk} > O_{ik} \\ O_{jk} - C_{ik} & C_{ik} > C_{jk} \;\&\&\; O_{jk} < O_{ik} \\ O_{ik} - C_{jk} & C_{ik} < C_{jk} \;\&\&\; O_{jk} > O_{ik} \end{cases} \quad (4)$$

For a train i, departure time from the subway is B_i, *the* running time from station $k-1$ to station k is R_{ik}. The dwell time of the station k is P_{ik}, regulation time of train i is Δt_{ik} at station k. Then the entire operation cycle of train i can be shown in Fig. 2.

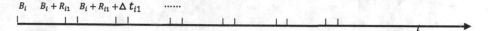

Fig. 2. The train arrival time diagram

Then for station k, its train reaching station time and departure time can be described by Eq. (5a) and (5b):

$$C_{ik} = B_i + (R_{i1} + \ldots + R_{ik}) + (P_{i1} + \ldots + P_{ik-1}) + (\Delta t_{i1} + \ldots + \Delta t_{ik-1}) \quad (5a)$$

$$O_{ik} = B_i + (R_{i1} + \ldots + R_{ik}) + (P_{i1} + \ldots + P_{ik}) + (\Delta t_{i1} + \ldots + \Delta t_{ik}) \quad (5b)$$

The dwell time P_{ik} is constant. In the formula, C_{ik} and O_{ik} are linear functions of the k parameters: $\Delta t_{i1}, \ldots, \Delta t_{ik}$.

In the Eq. (4), $F\left(C_{ik}, O_{ik}, C_{jk}, O_{jk}\right)$ is a linear function with respect to $C_{ik}, O_{ik}, C_{jk}, O_{jk}$, referring to the formula (2), for the trains i, j, the total conflict time of train i and train j can be defined in (6).

$$T_{ij} = \sum_{1}^{N1} \sum_{1}^{N2} F\left(C_{ik}, O_{ik}, C_{jk}, O_{jk}\right) \quad (6)$$

From the above derivation, it is clear that T_{ij} is also a liner function about B_i, $\Delta t_{i1}, \ldots, \Delta t_{ik}$. The total conflict time S is *a* linear function *of* $B_1, \ldots, B_i$, $\Delta t_{i1}, \ldots, \Delta t_{ik}$. It means that S is a multi-parameter linear function [16, 17].

3   Solution to Metro Staggering Regulation

3.1   Solution of Subway Time-Factor

According to the definition of formula (1), the time-factors of Shanghai Metro Line 2 from GLR (Guang Lan Road) station to XJD (Xu Jing Dong) station are calculated.

As is show in Fig. 3, time-factor of each station has high values at morning and evening peak time. The results coincide well with the conclusion that the congestion situation is more serious at morning and evening peak-hours through the investigation and theoretical analysis in Sect. 2.1.

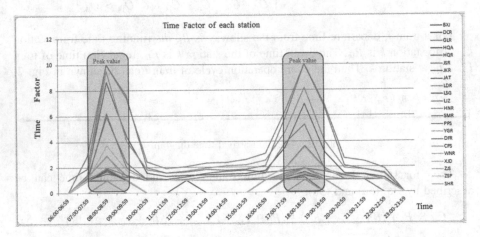

Fig. 3. The time-factor graph

In the processes of building timetable adjustment model, considering the time factor, excludes meaningless calculations in the case of small passenger flow which would not cause large-scale congestion even arrive simultaneously. So the model synthetically studies the impact that different scale of passenger flow makes.

3.2   The Solution to Metro Peak Load Shifting

3.2.1   The Solution to Scheduling Problem Based on Greedy Algorithm

Through the above analysis, we can see that, by the solution of adjusting the train departure time or dwell time, the total subway conflict time is influenced. Thus it plays a regulatory role in up and down trains reaching a station simultaneously.

By formula (6), it is easy to figure out that the problem to be solved is an optimal solution of multi-parameter linear equations. In processes of seeking optimal solutions for multi-parameter linear equations, it's too conflicted to consider the influence of all the parameters, so greedy algorithm is proposed to simplify the multi-parameter problem. A greedy algorithm is an algorithm that follows the problem solving heuristic of making the locally optimal choice at each stage with the hope of finding a global optimum [18–20]. Then, it comes to the specific data and formula analysis. In the formula (5a), (5b), by comparing the relevant parameters of C_{ik}, O_{ik}, mathematically, it's not difficult to figure out:, $C_{i1} \propto B_i$, $O_{i1} \propto (B_i, \Delta t_{i1})$, $C_{i2} \propto (B_i, \Delta t_{i1})$, $O_{i2} \propto (B_i, \Delta t_{i1}, \Delta t_{i2})$.… For each C_{ik} and O_{ik}, B_i will inevitably affect them, and the impact of other parameters is much less. For related variables B_i, $\Delta t_{i1}, \ldots, \Delta t_{ik}$, of C_{ik}, O_{ik}, it's too tough to build a model including all of the adjustment program. According to the greedy algorithm thinking, we only take the main variables into account. Therefore, both C_{ik} and O_{ik} can be approximately regard as a linear function with respect to B_i. Similarly, T_{ij} is deduced to be a linear function with respect to B_i. Finally, the total conflict time S proves to be a linear function respect to B_i. The optimal solution can *be* evaluated by adjusting the subway departure time.

Time is a continuous variable. Nevertheless, in order to simplify the processing, a method of discretization is applied to time. The smallest unit is second in the model. According to needs of project, in terms of subway headway time, the range of adjusting time is 3 min (180 s) or less. Here, the exhaustive method is applied to adjust the conflict time [21]. The basic idea is that making a measurement of the answer according to the available conditions. So in this paper, in order to gain the best load shifting regulation scheme, through enumerating all adjusting time from −180 s to 180 s, total conflict time is calculated.

3.2.2 Algorithm Flowchart

According to the greedy algorithm based on constraints, the proposed algorithm procedure is shown as the following figure. The reference value is the total conflict time before optimization (Fig. 4).

3.2.3 Adjustment Scheme and Research Results

The case of this paper is aimed to reduce the total conflict time of Shanghai Metro Line 2 from East Xujing to Guanglan Road in a normal working day. The main three factors can be found by analyzing the results of this research: whether to consider traffic factors, considering all stations or only consider the transfer station, morning and evening peak adjustment is an adjustment. So there are 9 models to choose. But by comparison, considering the passengers flow, all stations, the morning and evening peak- hours is the optimal scheme. Here are several results of the above schemes are listed in Table 3 and Figs. 5 and 6.

(1) The total time of conflict before adjusting
    Above the foundation in Sect. 2.1, through simulation computation, the total conflict time factor is 63,086 s.
(2) Regardless of morning and evening peak
    It can be obtained from the figure, when adopting the full line of adjustment scheme, 159 s (159 s ahead of the up train departure), minimum conflict time is 44,194 s.
(3) Morning and evening peak
    It can be obtained from the figure, when the morning rush hour adjustment time is 135 s (the first up train departs 135 s early), minimum conflict time is 23,537 s;

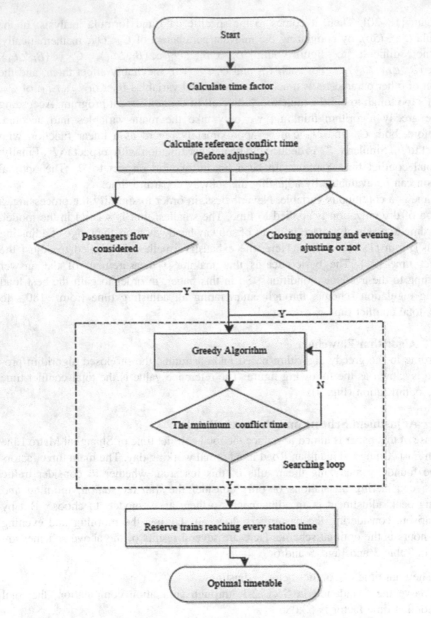

Fig. 4. Algorithm structures diagram

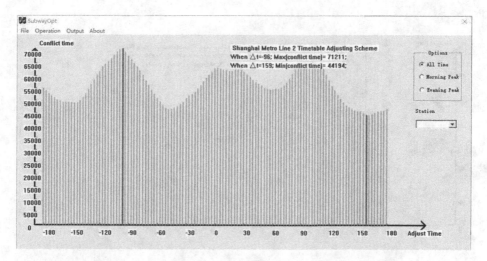

Fig. 5. The conflict time of Shanghai metro Line 2 (Adjusted)

when the evening peak adjustment time is 165 s (the first up train departs 135 s early), minimum conflict time is 17,567 s, the total time of 41,104 s conflict.

Note:

- Passenger: No represents without considering the impact of passenger flow, that is to say time-factor isn't added to the model, not the number of added time factor; yes means considering the time-factor.
- Consider all stations: No means only considering the transfer station, yes means considering all stations on Line 2;
- Morning and evening peak: NO represents the full range of adjustment, the morning and evening peak adjusted separately.
- Adjustment: adjusted here via the above line in advance (deferred downlink) time is positive, 1 refers to the full range of adjustment, by means 2, 3, 4 morning peak and evening peak time are adjusted.

With optimization effects of the various schemes compared, considering the morning and evening peak-hours is prior than only consider the morning peak-hours. The reason is obvious that: the morning adjusting has no effect to the evening adjusting, and the former give an optimization to evening adjusting. Consider the time-factor helps to obtain a scientific more comprehensive, more scientific result. Eventually, under the consideration of passenger flow, the morning and evening peak-hours are considered to adjust respectively. The new conflict time table is calculated and the optimal railway timetable is obtained.

It takes a lot of related work papers to complete this paper successfully. Do preliminary research such as formulating and optimizing metro timetables, and building optimization model; achieve further studies about how to solve the problems and the solution to the model; try to collect actual and helpful data for the model, and make algorithm simulations; analysis above researches and simulation results.

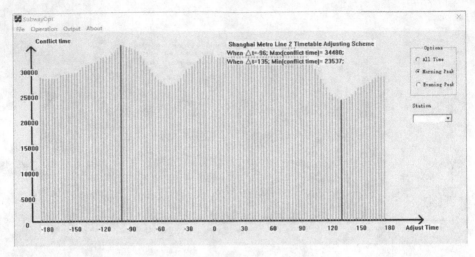

(a) Adjusting the morning peak-hours

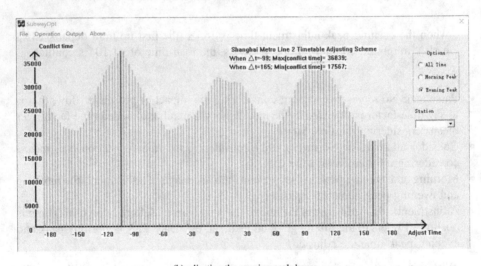

(b) adjusting the evening peak-hours

Fig. 6. The maximum and minimum peak time of conflict of Shanghai metro Line 2 (Adjusted)

4 Conclusion

The primary objective of the study is to build a simulation model for optimizing the timetable to avoid the up and down line trains reach the station simultaneously in peek-hours. In addition, the greedy algorithm theoretically proves to be optimal. Firstly, the problem is analyzed comprehensively. Secondly, a time-factor model is proposed. Then an adjusting model of greedy algorithm is presented to verify the availability for the problem. Finally, based on the operation data from Shanghai Metro Line 2, we have performed numerical examples to prove that the proposed algorithm

Table 3. Various adjustment programs comparison table

Factors No.	Passenger	Consider all stations	Morning and evening peak	Adjustment method (s)	The total conflict time before adjusting (s)	The total conflict time after adjusting (s)	Optimization effect
1	No	No	No	185	5786	4796	17.02 %
2	No	No	Yes	Morning: 180, Evening: 230	5780	4732	18.13 %
3	Yes	No	Yes	Morning: 171, Evening: −177	29973	24049	19.76 %
4	Yes	Yes	Yes	Morning: 135, Evening: 165	63086	41104	34.85 %

can reduce the total conflict time by 19.76 % on average for morning peak-hours adjusting and 34.85 % for morning and evening peak-hours adjusting.

The simulation results show that the optimization algorithm proposed in this paper can effectively reduce the subway conflict time. This model has some reference value in guiding the safety performance improvement and subway train schedule optimization design. In many problems, a greedy strategy does not in general produce an optimal solution, but nonetheless a greedy heuristic may yield locally optimal solutions that approximate a global optimal solution in a reasonable time. There are four usual operation levels in the subway system and the system will automatically adjust its operation level to adjust the arrival time, so the small amplitude fluctuations will not cause too much impact on the application of the method. In addition, the computation time is short enough to apply the algorithm to the onboard control system for a real-time adjustment of the timetable.

References

1. Peng, P., Liu, Y.: The impact of metro development on urban modernization. Urban Insight (2012)
2. Nachtigall, K.: Periodic network optimization with different arc frequencies. Discrete Appl. Math. **69**, 1–17 (1996)
3. Peeters, L.W.P.: Cyclic Railway Timetable Optimization. Erasmus University Rotterdam, Rotterdam (2003)
4. Serafini, P., Ukovich, W.: A mathematical model for periodic scheduling problems. SIAM J. Discrete Math. **2**(4), 550–581 (1989)
5. Odijk, M.A.: A constraint generation algorithm for the construction of periodic railway timetables. Transp. Res. Part B: Methodol. **30**(6), 455–464 (1996)

6. Nachtigall, K.: Periodic network optimization with different arc frequencies. Discrete Appl. Math. **69**(1), 1–17 (1996)
7. Cordone, R., Redaelli, F.: Optimizing the demand captured by a railway system with a regular timetable. Transp. Res. Part B: Methodol. **45**(2), 430–446 (2011)
8. Kroon, L.G., Peeters, L.W.P.: A variable trip time model for cyclic railway timetabling. Transp. Sci. **37**(2), 198–212 (2003)
9. Odijk, M.A., Romeijn, H.E., van Maaren, H.: Generation of classes of robust periodic railway timetables. Comput. Oper. Res. **33**(8), 2283–2299 (2006)
10. Kroon, L., Maróti, G., Helmrich, M.R., et al.: Stochastic improvement of cyclic railway timetables. Transp. Res. Part B Methodol. **42**(6), 553–570 (2008)
11. Khan, M.B., Zhou, X.: Stochastic optimization model and solution algorithm for robust double-track train-timetabling problem. IEEE Trans. Intell. Transp. Syst. **11**(1), 81–89 (2010)
12. Yugang, Z., Baohua, M., Yu, J.: Stick buffer time based on train running time deviation subway train operation diagram. China Railway Sci. **2**(1), 118–121 (2011)
13. Albrecht, T.: Reducing power peaks and energy consumption in rail transit systems by simultaneous train running time control. WIT Trans. Built Environ. **74** (2004)
14. Chen, J.F., Lin, R.L., Liu, Y.C.: Optimization of an MRT train schedule: reducing maximum traction power by using genetic algorithms. IEEE Trans. Power Syst. **20**(3), 1366–1372 (2005)
15. Kim, K.M., Oh, S., Han, M.: A mathematical approach for reducing the maximum traction energy: the case of Korean MRT trains. Power **219**, 15.3 (2010)
16. Wang, S.: Research on randomized greedy algorithm for k-median problem. Comput. Sci. **1**(7), 98–101 (2011)
17. Toint, P.L.: On sparse and symmetric matrix updating subject to a linear equation. Math. Comput. **31**(140), 954 (1977)
18. Abalakin, I.V., Kozubskaya, T.K.: A multi-parameter family of schemes of high accuracy for a linear transport equation. Matematicheskoe Modelirovanie **7**, 55–66 (2007)
19. He, Z., Li, H., Miao, J., et al.: Research on Greedy train rescheduling algorithm (2009)
20. He, Z.: Research on improved greedy algorithm for train rescheduling. In: International Conference on Computational Intelligence and Security, pp. 1197–1200. IEEE (2011)
21. Park, J.K., Lee, K.H., Lee, J.H., et al.: An exhaustive method for characterizing the interconnect capacitance considering the floating dummy-fills by employing an efficient field solving algorithm. In: 2000 International Conference on Simulation of Semiconductor Processes and Devices, SISPAD 2000, pp. 98–101. IEEE (2000)

Author Index

Printed in the United States
By Bookmasters